Praise for *The Daring Life and Dangerous Times of Eve Adams*

"An audacious lesbian pioneer, long hidden from both LGBT and Jewish history, Eve Adams finally gets her due in this wonderful book."

—**Arlene Stein,** author of *Reluctant Witnesses*

"**This is a truth-stranger-than-fiction narrative that is compelling, gripping, and revelatory.** Through imaginative research, Katz has uncovered the story of a Jewish immigrant who was both a political radical and an open lesbian a century ago. He has restored to history a life that we need to know about."

—**John D'Emilio,** author of *Queer Legacies:*
Stories from Chicago's LGBTQ Archives

"Once again, through indefatigable sleuthing informed by historical erudition and political sophistication, Jonathan Ned Katz has uncovered and reconstructed a lost LGBTQ life. And what a life! **Anarchist, lesbian, Jew, writer, anthropologist, and freedom fighter Eve Adams lived her beliefs and her desires boldly and died the victim of small-mindedness and barbarity. A fascinating, groundbreaking book.**"

—**Judith Levine,** journalist and
coauthor of *The Feminist and the Sex Offender*

"**Katz shows us once again how much astonishing LGBTQ history remains out there to be explored and shared.**"

—**Hugh Ryan,** author of *When Brooklyn Was Queer*

"**Bohemian lesbians, radical activism, police entrapment—this first biography of Eve Adams offers an immigrant history unlike any other!**"

—**Elizabeth Heard,** adjunct professor,
Steinhardt School of Culture, Education,
and Human Development, New York University

"**Absolutely wonderful, so timely, so important!** Eve Adams played a courageous pioneering role in lesbian history, fighting US government officials' homophobic, anti-radical, anti-immigrant, anti-Semitic, right-wing acts during the 1920s and 1930s that censored, attacked, and destroyed many lives."

—**Deborah Edel,** cofounder of the Lesbian Herstory Archives

"**Praises for Jonathan Ned Katz, who keeps rescuing from oblivion fascinating twentieth-century LBGTQ pioneers,** including the lesbian bohemian Eve Adams."

—**Alix Kates Shulman,**
author of *Memoirs of an Ex–Prom Queen*
and coeditor of *Women's Liberation!*

"**This book documents an important part of early-twentieth-century LGBT American and European history.** The research is extraordinary and Katz's writing brings Eve Adams to life."

—**Ken Lustbader,** cofounder of NYC LGBT Historic Sites Project

THE DARING LIFE AND DANGEROUS TIMES OF EVE ADAMS

JONATHAN NED KATZ

CHICAGO REVIEW PRESS

Copyright © 2021 by Jonathan Ned Katz
All rights reserved
Published by Chicago Review Press Incorporated
814 North Franklin Street
Chicago, Illinois 60610
ISBN 978-1-64160-516-8

Original edition of *Lesbian Love* "printed for private circulation only"
by Evelyn Addams [Eve Adams] in 1925

Library of Congress Control Number: 2021930292

Typesetting: Nord Compo
For interior photo credits, see p. 199

Printed in the United States of America
5 4 3 2 1

Contents

Introduction

Searching for Eve

I BEGAN TO INVESTIGATE EVE Adams's life on December 1, 2016, the day I read a reference in the *New York Times Book Review* to a "Polish-Jewish immigrant" accused of "'a homosexual advance' toward an undercover cop." I wondered why I didn't recall having heard a thing about the intriguing Eve. My interest increased when I learned that, in 1925, Eve had published a book titled *Lesbian Love*, a book that sounded like no other of its time, a book no researcher had seen.

My ignorance of Eve startled me because forty-five years earlier, in 1971, as a tracer of missing persons, I had begun to seek evidence of a then-invisible US lesbian and gay male history. I would go on to publish four books on sexual and gender history, so I thought I knew the names of the pioneers.

Never wanting to reinvent the wheel, I began to ask, *What's already known about Eve Adams?* I was greatly aided in answering that question by the earlier, extensive research and thesis of Martha Lynn Reis; the detailed investigation and generosity of playwright Barbara Kahn and her co-sleuth, the late librarian and archivist Steven Siegel; and the support of Eran Zahavy, in Israel, whose grandfather was Eve's brother. Eran provided a valuable file of documents and led me to Daniel Olstein in Basel, Switzerland, the nephew of Eve Adams's companion Hella Olstein

Soldner. Daniel Olstein generously shared a file of Hella and Eve's letters, cards, and photos saved by his father, Hella's brother André. Thanks to Nina Alvarez, for the first time I could read, analyze, and present Eve's book, *Lesbian Love*, a copy of which Alvarez found twenty-plus years ago in the lobby of her building in Albany, New York. The one copy held by an archive, Yale's Sterling Library, disappeared mysteriously as of July 3, 1998.

I learned that Eve had immigrated from Poland to the United States in 1912 and joined the political work of anarchist activists Emma Goldman and Alexander Berkman. Eve had also become friends with Goldman's romantic partner, the larger-than-life Ben Lewis Reitman. Eve's association with anarchist leaders, and her work as traveling saleswoman for radical periodicals, resulted in her being spied on by the young J. Edgar Hoover and the agents of the Bureau of Investigation, the forerunner of the FBI.

Claims about Eve Adams's life, some true and many false, now circulate untamed on the Internet. Today, as the mass media daily relay false fact claims to millions, it's important to examine the evidence that documents Eve Adams's poignant, intriguing, disturbing life. Most people don't leave substantial records, but in Eve's case just enough documents exist to provide us with her words, and a sense of her character.

Despite that evidence, information about Eve's life is fragmentary. I have filled in Eve's story with relevant information about her closest friends and lovers, and the social and historical eras she inhabited. But I suspect that Eve's self-described "wanderlust" will always lead her off again just as we're getting to know her better. The surviving evidence about Eve Adams will, I suspect, always leave us wanting more.

As I began to investigate Eve's life (for an article, I first thought), it seemed obvious—it went almost without saying: Eve's history sounded an all-too-pertinent warning. Just a month earlier, Donald J. Trump, scandal sheet playboy, reality show star, real estate mogul, woman groper, and con man, had lost to his opponent by 2.87 million votes and yet been elected US president. His racist, anti-immigrant rhetoric spoke to White voters angered by the failure of their American dreams, a loss blamed not on an unjust system but on Black and Brown people and immigrants.

An active animus directed at immigrants desperate for a better life was once again surfacing in the United States and many other countries. Authoritarian dictators and outright fascist leaders were on the rise again around the world. The servants of surveillance states were once more searching out, jailing, torturing, and sometimes killing critics and organizers—liberals, leftists, socialists, social democrats, communists, anarchists, left libertarians, democracy activists. Anti-homosexual groups were spewing hate, often religiously rationalized, that led sometimes to murder.

Anti-Jewish groups were on the march again, when once we'd thought them vanquished, or at least marginalized. Deep into my research on Eve, an anti-Jewish terrorist invaded the Tree of Life synagogue in Pittsburgh and killed eleven old Jews as a they prayed—one of the deadliest attacks on the Jewish community in US history.

White nationalists and other far-right, racist groups were inciting violence against people of color and their supporters. In Charlottesville, Virginia, at a White nationalist rally joined by Ku Klux Klanners and neo-Nazis, a nationalist plowed his car into counterdemonstrators, injuring many and killing one. There were "very fine people" among the White nationalists and neo-Nazis, declared President Trump.

There's more to be said, of course. But it's best, I think, for us to reconnect after you've met Eve, heard her story, and considered her life and times.

"Eve Zloczower," as Eve Adams spelled her original Polish surname on a passport photo from 1941. The anchor images on Eve's scarf are fitting, since this photo was for an international steamship trip for which Eve was yearning.

1

Eve Speaks

ON OCTOBER 16, 1926, Assistant Secretary of Labor William Walter Husband, the US Department of Labor's expert on immigration, called for hearings so a Polish, Jewish alien could "show cause why she should not be deported." Evidence demonstrated, claimed Husband, that Eve Adams had violated the US Immigration Act of 1917. She'd earlier been found guilty and jailed for publishing an "indecent book," *Lesbian Love*.

On November 30, 1926, at her deportation hearing at the women's penitentiary on Welfare Island (now Roosevelt Island), Eve responded to the indecent book charge:

> I admit having written a book entitled *Lesbian Love*, based on true acts and living characters of today. . . . The object of the book was to show the exact things that are happening from day to day, and every character contained therein is a true character except she is given an assumed name. I had 150 copies of the book published for private circulation only, particularly among artists and poets of Greenwich Village. At the time of my arrest I just had about ten copies of that edition in my possession, and they were all taken by the police authorities.

Playing the "private circulation only" card, Eve argued that because her book had so few readers, it was limited in its ability to "deprave and corrupt" those open to corruption, a requirement of English obscenity law applied then in the United States.

"I believe the book is not in any way immoral, indecent, or vulgar," Eve stressed. "There is not one word in the whole book that is vulgar." She protested:

> I can't see why I should be singled out and sentenced to imprisonment for writing my book which was only meant to show the humorous side of life, the serious side of life and tragedy, all in one.

Eve had also been found guilty of a second charge, "disorderly conduct," for supposedly attempting sex with the undercover policewoman, Margaret Leonard, sent to entrap her. But when the immigration inspector at Eve's deportation hearing asked Eve the details of her alleged conduct, she responded sassily: "I don't know. You will have to ask the policewoman who made the charge."

Asked again to specify the act charged against her, Eve answered that the policewoman said, "I danced with her in a public restaurant on Broadway and Fiftieth Street and that my dance was not to her liking." The two had waltzed. "From this restaurant she accompanied me to my room at 38 Washington Square. . . ."

> INSPECTOR: What transpired in your room between you and this policewoman?
> EVE: Nothing. I went there to write a few letters and she waited for me. . . .

Asked "Did you attempt to make love to her while she was in your bedroom?" Eve denied it.

> INSPECTOR: Did you make any improper advances to her of an immoral nature?
> EVE: No.

Asked how she became acquainted with policewoman Leonard, Eve responded:

> She had come into my tearoom several times and cultivated my acquaintance. She made the acquaintance of an artist there also and went out with him.

Eve's popular tearoom had occupied the basement of 129 Mac-Dougal Street in Greenwich Village. She didn't know the name of the artist, but the inspector next asked if Eve knew Jay Fitzpatrick. Eve did not.

The sworn, written testimony of Fitzpatrick was read aloud. On June 23, 1925, he had taken the ferry back and forth to Ellis Island to leave his testimony with an inspector at the US Immigration Service. Fitzpatrick described himself as an "artist" with a studio at 50A Washington Square, and identified one Mrs. A. Marchesini as Eve's "landlady." He swore that Marchesini "is thoroughly conversant with what goes on upstairs and has furnished Eve Adams with extra keys for the use of girls who patronize her."

That reference to girls who "patronize" Eve in Fitzpatrick's 1925 testimony is the earliest suggestion of a plot by Fitzpatrick and US Immigration Service officials to establish Eve as prostitute, a crime that justified a noncitizen's deportation. Initiating Eve's deportation hearing the following year, William Husband had accused her of "practicing prostitution," "managing a house of prostitution," and entering the United States "for an immoral purpose."

Fitzpatrick swore that he had first seen Eve's "illicit relations with another girl" about a year earlier, in 1924:

> I have seen her take girls into her apartment, serve them drinks, and within a short space of time had the girls stripped and lying on her bed where she practiced her habits as a conenlinguist [*sic*, cunnilinguist].

The reputed expertise of lesbians at oral sex performed on girls and women is a repeated theme of anxious male commentary in the 1920s, as later examples will illustrate.

On "a number of occasions," Fitzpatrick added, he saw Eve approach girls in restaurants and other places throughout Greenwich Village under the pretext of selling copies of the magazine the *Quill*, taking some of them directly to her apartment as stated. I have seen her at this about a dozen times. . . .

"I know personally of decent girls who have been corrupted by this woman," Fitzpatrick claimed, "and to put a stop to it I have taken time to make this report."

Earlier, about April 1925, Fitzpatrick swore, he had reported the acts and "undesirability" of "Eve Zlotchever" under her "alias Eve Adams" to Mrs. Mary Hamilton, Chief of Women Police, New York City. The police had then opened a file on Eve, Fitzpatrick said, but "sufficient action has not as yet been taken." So Fitzpatrick was reporting Eve's behavior to the US Immigration Service "for proper action."

When Eve was asked how Fitzpatrick was "able to testify to the fact that you have been practicing immoral acts on young girls in your room and that you have corrupted decent girls," she responded, "I don't know, I would like to be confronted with him."

That confrontation never happened. Fitzpatrick was never called to testify at Eve's hearing; he never had to explain how he, a man passionately opposed to Eve's alleged sex acts, happened to be in her room watching her have sex.

In his 1925 sworn statement, Fitzpatrick identified Eve's residence as 38 Washington Square West and referred to Eve taking girls "upstairs" to an exactly located apartment: "top floor front, single room." It's vital to note that conclusive evidence proves that Eve lived in a first-floor room, not on the top floor. But at Eve's hearing, neither she nor her new-to-the-job lawyer noticed this glaring discrepancy in a major government witness's sworn statement. Fitzpatrick's testimony was later repeatedly cited by the US officials deciding Eve's fate, and his false assertion, and the absurdity of his sensational claims, were never questioned.

At Eve's hearing, the immigrant inspector asked her, "Had you been in the habit of picking up young girls in the street or elsewhere, taking them to your room and having intimate or immoral relations with them?"

Eve replied, "No," adding:

I often took boys and girls to my room on a Sunday afternoon but I never took them there for an immoral purpose. Let that man confront me in person and make that statement to me.

Asked "Did you ever commit any degenerate acts while you lived in Chicago?" Eve again responded "No." Asked about "degenerate acts" in New York, Eve denied them. She vehemently disputed the prostitution charge:

> There is not a man rich enough in the United States or the whole world who could buy my body, and it is not for sale either. Many a day I starved and [went] without something to eat, but the thoughts never entered my mind to sell my body.

Policewoman Margaret Leonard testified at Eve's deportation hearing, describing Eve's alleged attempted sex. After a complaint made to the police against Eve's tearoom, Leonard swore, she was sent there three times. The first time, Eve told her, said Leonard, "about a little suit she had just altered." (Eve listed "Tailoress" as her occupation on arriving in the United States.)

On Leonard's third visit, on June 11, 1926, the policewoman swore, Eve had asked her what she was doing the next afternoon.

> LEONARD: I said, "Nothing in particular," and she asked if I would call to accompany her to a show and I met her the next afternoon about one o'clock in her apartment and we proceeded from there in a taxi to the Times Square Theatre. . . .

The show they saw on June 12 was *Love 'Em and Leave 'Em.*

Asked "How long were you in the theater with her?" Leonard responded, "About two and a half hours."

> INSPECTOR: Did she try any liberties with you there?
> LEONARD: She kept her arm around my shoulder all through the performance. In the taxicab she put her hand under my coat and had her hand on my bosom. She kissed me profusely.

Policewoman Margaret Leonard.

After the show, said Leonard, Eve "asked me to dinner, she said we would make it an evening, and I suggested a restaurant on Fiftieth Street and Broadway," Joy Young's.

> LEONARD: We had dinner and danced, and during this dinner, Miss Adams made mention of the book. She said if I would accompany her to her room, she would give me a copy of this book she had written and I would learn to know her better and understand her.

The two took the Fifth Avenue bus to Washington Square, to what Leonard described as Eve's "very small room containing a chair, bed, a desk and dresser"—Eve did not live lavishly.

> LEONARD: She bathed her face, told me to make myself comfortable, and I said, "Are you forgetting the book you promised me?" She said, "No," and got this book out of a closet and handed it to me and took it away again on second thought and said she would autograph it. She laid it on the desk at the foot of the bed. She passed me . . . and slid a bolt on the door. Facing me, she slid her hands under my arms and thrust me on my back on the bed. Of course, I warded her off and asked her if she was crazy. She said, "No, I am not crazy,

but I am crazy in one sense and you do not understand me."
I said, "Have you autographed the book,—we will go down
to the tearoom," and she said, "Yes," if I would come back
and stay all night with her. So, with that, she autographed
the book and also wrote a note to a little girl that was in
the show, asking her to come down to the tearoom; she was
there every afternoon herself.

INSPECTOR: Who paid for the expenses of the theater and dinner?

LEONARD: Miss Adams paid all that.

The government's major witness contradicted its attempt to establish
Eve as cash-hungry prostitute. The policewoman's presentation of Eve as
predatory lesbian, trying to buy her way into an innocent young woman's
bed, clashed with the prosecutor's presenting Eve as gold-digging whore.

In fact, when asked if Eve had requested "any money," Leonard
testified to the contrary:

LEONARD: She didn't ask me but was going to give me everything and take me on a vacation to Chicago and to a beauty
parlor where I could have my hair and nails done at her
expense.

Such behavior, Eve's impulse to "lavish presents" on attractive women,
was mentioned in a memoir by her friend Ben Reitman.

INSPECTOR: She didn't take any further liberties with you in her
room?

LEONARD: Well, thrusting me down on the bed was an attempt
at an indecent act.

Questioned by her lawyer, Eve again emphatically denied an
attempted sex act.

EVE: We had one dance, a waltz, in the restaurant. She said, "I
don't care to stay here any longer, let's go." We went back
to the room, because I had to stop there to write a couple of
letters, and I gave her a copy of my book. . . . I deny having

attempted any immoral act on Miss Leonard in my room. I didn't throw her on the bed and I didn't bolt the door except at night when I went to sleep.

LAWYER: Coming down in the taxi, did you place your hands on her person?

EVE: No.

LAWYER: Did you put your arm around Miss Leonard in the show?

EVE: If I did, I probably did it unconsciously.

Eve was asked, "Did you send a note in to one of the pretty girls on the stage that you would like to meet her?" She sometimes sent her tearoom's business cards "to show people," Eve responded, because a "theatrical crowd" gathered at her Greenwich Village establishment.

After Leonard visited her room, Eve recalled that she

came with me and sat down in the tearoom and I got busy. The only reason she has for making this charge against me is that this book deals on this subject and that is why she imagines these things.

2

Departure and Arrival

ON MAY 25, 1912, CHAWA ZLOCZEWER (Polish pronunciation: KHAH-vah zlo-CHE-ver) first walked up the gangplank in Antwerp, Belgium, heading for New York City, a second-class passenger on the Red Star Line's *Vaderland*, one of the twenty-four million or so immigrants who ventured to the United States between 1881 and 1924.

Chawa's second-class ticket cost about $52.50 (about $1,400 today), and her passage was paid for by an uncle, probably her mother's financially successful businessman brother, Alexander Migdall, an earlier immigrant. Asked the name and address of her nearest relative, Chawa listed her father, Josef Zloczewer of Mława, Poland, sixty-five miles north of Warsaw. Her father, mother (Mariem-Ruchla Migdall Zloczewer), and siblings lived at 15 Działdowska Street, where her parents operated a grocery store. The Kingdom of Poland was then part of the Russian Empire, so Chawa's "Nationality" was "Russian."

Chawa's US government immigration document listed her "Race or People" as "Hebrew." A year before her arrival, the US Immigration Commission's *Dictionary of Races or Peoples* explained that among the "race or people" called "Hebrew, Jewish, or Israelite," most spoke Yiddish, derived from German, the language of the people with whom Jews had long been associated. The "'Jewish nose'" and other facial characteristics, the report claimed, "are found well-nigh everywhere throughout the race." Jewish immigration to the United States at that time annually exceeded "any other race with the exception of the Italian." New York City had "the largest Jewish population of any city in the world": an estimated one million, one-fourth of the city's population.

Though Chawa's departure document listed her age as "18," she was actually twenty. The immgration official probably guessed the young-looking passenger's age.

On an 1891 birth certificate, in Russian, Josef Zloczewer, twenty-five, testified that his twenty-four-year-old wife Mariem-Ruchla had given birth to a baby girl, Chawa, on June 15 (according to the Julian calendar then in use in the Russian Empire, thirteen days behind the US Gregorian calendar). In the United States, Chawa later also claimed March 31, 1891, as her birth date—perhaps a date with special meaning, perhaps just a sign of her determined self-making, perhaps a sign of her culture's casual relation to recorded birth dates.

Chawa was "single," her departure document stated, and her "Calling or Occupation" was "Tailoress"—many Jewish women got jobs in New York's busy "rag trade," its bustling garment factories. Chawa's "Final Destination," her "Intended future permanent residence," was "NY."

On Tuesday, June 4, 1912, after a nine-day voyage, Chawa walked down the gangplank in New York City. She'd come a long way (4,203 miles, actually) from Mława, Poland. In New York Harbor, she and other first- and second-class passengers embarked directly to the mainland after being examined aboard ship by public health and immigration inspectors. Third-class and steerage passengers were taken to Ellis Island for examination. Before she even stepped ashore, Chawa had experienced US class distinctions in action.

Chawa's US entry document recorded her arriving with $23 (about $600 today). She swore that she had never been in prison, an almshouse, or insane asylum. She wasn't a "Polygamist" or "Anarchist" (the latter was probably a lie) and her health, mental and physical, was "Good."

The slight, five-foot-two-inch, one-hundred-pound immigrant first lived with her mother's brother, Isidor Meegdall, and his family at 125 Fifty-First Street, in Brooklyn. Then, securing factory work, she moved in with New York City friends for five or six years.

Chawa soon forsook that version of her first name and anglicized the Polish version, Ewa (pronounced "Eva"), to become Eve. But it would be seven years, evidence shows, before she took the American name Eve Adams.

In New York, Eve joined a group of anarchist organizers, speakers, and writers then working out of the office of the journal *Mother Earth*, at 55 West Twenty-Eighth Street. The anarchist *Mother Earth* was published monthly from 1906 to 1918 by Emma Goldman and Alexander Berkman, after the latter served fourteen years in prison for the attempted assassination of industrialist Henry Clay Frick.

In 1892, the young Berkman and Goldman had plotted secretly with other anarchists to assassinate Frick, chairman of the board of Carnegie Steel and manager of its Homestead, Pennsylvania, plant. The act was intended to inspire a workers' revolution, but after Berkman shot Frick yet failed to kill him, his actions were reviled by many anarchists and labor movement activists, as well as the general public. The attempted assassination divided anarchists into warring factions—those supporting propaganda by violent deed, and those arguing that

Emma Goldman at a Union Square rally, New York City, May 5, 1916.

Alexander Berkman, September 1912.

violence only turned people against anarchism. Emma Goldman publicly equivocated about the use of violence to ignite revolutionary social change, pointing instead to the everyday violence that working people suffered daily under capitalism. This mental and physical brutality, she argued, provoked some desperate rebels to respond with violence of their own.

At the *Mother Earth* office Eve also became friends with medical doctor and militant birth control advocate doctor Ben Lewis Reitman. He was then managing and publicizing Goldman's speaking engagements, a job at which he excelled and for which Goldman praised him. Reitman's work as her publicity director helped Goldman's talks reach large numbers, and he often joined Goldman on her lecture tours.

Reitman, in an unpublished memoir titled "Eve," described his friend as "a short, red-headed Jew girl," casually deploying a then common derogatory phrase. But his account of Eve's "affairs with the ladies" was, for its time, unusually positive. Adopting a short-line prose form, Reitman recalled that Eve

Ben Lewis Reitman, 1908.

had a pale, freckled, masculine face
With an ambitious nose and a restless chin.
For years she was an unwilling factory worker
And found comfort in the radical labor movement.
She got tired of New York factory life
And decided to tramp around the country.
She had several experiences with men
But soon found that they had no joy to give her.
Quite accidently she slept with a lovely eighteen year old
    [woman]
And suddenly life began to take on new meaning and purpose.
She worked like hell and horded her money
Until she found some female of the right type;
Then she would pursue and lavish presents and affection
    upon her.
She traveled around the country in search of types
And had about twenty affairs with the ladies.
She said, "Why do you object—what harm am I doing?"

Eve's question suggested that people (including Reitman) did sometimes
object.

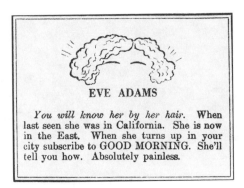

In this 1921 ad for Eve's sales services in *Good Morning*, her hair is styled exactly as it is in her 1925 family photo.

Reitman referred to Eve's hair as red, as do other witnesses, so she may have dyed it for a time (most sources list her hair as brown). If she dyed it, this was another sign of her self-making, her desire to stand out and be noticed, and, perhaps, her left politics. An ad for Eve's sales services, no doubt written by her, in the radical journal *Good Morning*, in 1921, stressed, "You will know her by her hair." Pictured complete with radiant symbols, Eve's hair was styled just as it was in a photo from 1925.

In a second unpublished description of Eve, Reitman called her "Olga," and began with a warning. The story of Olga and her woman partner "illustrate the ease with which a normal girl develops into a homo, and the serious consequences." Reitman then immediately switched to positive: "Olga was a charming young Russian girl":

> She was a healthy happy carefree anarchist, interested in labor
> propaganda, she often helped me in the office, and at meetings
> she was very valuable. She had a very beautiful love affair with
> a young [male] comrade and everything went along nicely. She
> became pregnant and had an abortion and almost died.

Reitman, as a medical doctor who performed abortions, certainly had personal knowledge of such histories.

Reitman's abrupt switch from "everything went along nicely" to "almost died" suggests an emotional disconnect that is repeated in his later letters to Eve. These abrupt tone shifts suggest his difficulty

Eve, center, with her brother Yerachmiel Zloczewer (later Zahavy) and, probably, her sister Tobe, during a 1925 visit with her family in Poland. Note Eve's pantsuit, daring for its time, her white shoes, perhaps the "white canvas oxfords" mentioned in her book—and of course her distinctive hairstyle.

empathizing fully with the experiences of Eve and others—perhaps, especially, homosexuals; perhaps, especially, lesbians.

Eve and Ben Reitman's long relationship, his written descriptions of her, and their letters, make him an absolutely central character in any telling of her life. So understanding Reitman, a complex, contradictory character, helps us understand Eve and their friendship. That Eve maintained a long relationship with the shape-shifting Reitman revealed her affection for him and her love for the rebellious, norm-challenging Americans he personified. Eve's long relationships with anarchists Emma Goldman and Alexander Berkman also made them important figures in her story.

In 1908, Goldman and Ben Reitman had begun a passionate though conflict-laden intimacy, the grand though tormented romance of Goldman's life. Goldman publicly rejected monogamy and supported lovers' freedom to choose multiple partners, but she was distressed to learn that Reitman made advances to almost every woman he met. When Goldman heard about Reitman's multitudinous propositions she was distraught, as bothered by his wandering penis as by her own profound attraction to him and it. His "Willie" and her "treasure box" were hot topics in the private porn notes they wrote to each other and preserved for posterity.

The month before Eve's arrival, in May 1912, the Goldman-Reitman intimacy was subject to a new strain. On the lecture circuit, Goldman and Reitman arrived in San Diego, California, to support free speech advocates against vicious, violent vigilante opponents. Reitman was kidnapped at gunpoint and almost murdered. Reitman described this harrowing experience in *Mother Earth* in June 1912. After he was carried by car to an isolated country spot, a "Respectable Mob" of fourteen men "formed a ring around me and commanded me to undress. They tore my clothes from me, and in a minute I stood before them naked." He was then" knocked down and compelled to kiss the American flag."

> When I lay naked on the ground, my tormentors kicked and beat me until I was almost insensible. With a lighted cigar they burned I.W.W. [for the militant labor organization Industrial Workers of the World] on my buttocks; they then poured a can of tar over my head and body, and in the absence of feathers, they rubbed handfuls of sage brush on my body. One very

Ben Reitman, center, at an Emma Goldman lecture in Butte, Montana, June 24, 1912.

gentle business man, who is active in church work, deliberately attempted to push my cane into my rectum. One unassuming banker twisted my testicles.

Let go but deeply traumatized by this terrifying near-rape-murder, Reitman responded by publicly pronouncing himself a coward who should have stood up to his attackers. To which Goldman privately responded to him with more ego than empathy. For a woman like her, "who has all her life faced persecution," to hear the man she loves "shout from the rooftops" that he is "a coward" is "a million times more painful than to have the rest of the World say so."

Reitman's experience newly challenged his manhood and perhaps contributed to his conflicted feelings about homosexuals, expressed in his later relationship with Eve.

Eve wasn't alone in responding "What harm am I doing?" when someone questioned her sexual life. By the late nineteenth and early twentieth centuries, a few rebel women had begun to speak out in defense of female and male homosexuals. In "A Note on Sexual Inversion in Women," in Havelock Ellis's pioneering book *Sexual Inversion*, an American woman physician, "Dr. K.," declared in 1897: "Current views on homosexuality are . . . cruelly unjust."

The 1901 edition of *Sexual Inversion* included a statement by an unnamed uppity female: "Inverts should have the courage and independence to be themselves, and to demand an investigation." She added: "All that I desire—and I claim it as my right—is the freedom to exercise this divine gift of loving, which is not a menace to society, nor a discrace to me."

Emma Goldman also publicly defended homosexuals. She recalled that, indignant at the "conviction of Oscar Wilde" in 1895 for sexual acts with men, she had "pleaded his case against the miserable hypocrites who had sent him to his doom." In a 1901 public lecture in Chicago on "Vice," she defended "any act entered into by two individuals voluntarily." She insisted:

> What is usually hastily condemned as vice by thoughtless individuals, such as homosexuality, masturbation, etc., should be considered from a scientific viewpoint, and not in a moralizing way.

Goldman's "scientific" rejection of negative moralizing actually constituted a form of *positive* moralizing. Starting in January 1915, Goldman's lecture tours sometimes included "The Intermediate Sex (A Study of Homosexuality)." Goldman's terminology (borrowed from the English socialist feminist Edward Carpenter) posited same-sex lovers as a third sex standing between men and women, helping those two opaque "opposites" understand each other and reject repression.

In Portland, Oregon, Goldman recalled, she spoke against war and for "freedom in love, birth-control, and the problem most tabooed in polite society, homosexuality." Censorship attempts, she remembered,

> came from some of my own comrades because I was treating such "unnatural" themes as homosexuality. Anarchism was already enough misunderstood, and anarchists considered depraved; it was inadvisable to add to the misconceptions by taking up perverted sex-forms, they argued.

Goldman's comrades' opposition to her sex talk only made her more determined "to plead for every victim" of "moral prejudice," and the responses were memorable:

The men and women who used to come to see me after my lectures on homosexuality, and who confided to me their anguish and their isolation, were often of finer grain than those who had cast them out. Most of them had reached an adequate understanding of their differentiation only after years of struggle to stifle what they had considered a disease and a shameful affliction.

One twenty-five-year-old woman told Goldman that she had never met anyone

who suffered from a similar affliction, nor had she ever read books dealing with the subject. My lecture had set her free; I had given her back her self-respect.

This woman was only one of the many who sought me out. Their pitiful stories made the social ostracism of the invert seem more dreadful than I had ever realized before. To me anarchism was not a mere theory for a distant future; it was a living influence to free us from inhibitions, internal no less than external, and from the destructive barriers that separate man from man.

Also in 1915, Margaret Anderson, a lesbian publisher and anarchist, spoke up publicly and unequivocally for homosexuals. Anderson, in her *Little Review*, criticized a public talk in Chicago by Edith Ellis, the lesbian wife of sexologist Havelock Ellis. Anderson complained that Edith Ellis had not explicitly defended homosexuals:

She had nothing to say about the difference between perversion and inversion, nor did she even hint at [Edward] Carpenter's efforts in behalf of the homosexualist.

Anderson accused Edith Ellis of knowing

the workings of our courts; she knows of boys and girls, men and women, tortured or crucified every day for their love because it is not expressed according to conventional morality.

In 1916, "Anna W." reported in *Mother Earth Bulletin* that Emma Goldman, the "true friend of the ostracized," displayed "the daring spirit of the propagandist pioneer" by lecturing in Washington, DC, on the "Intermediate Sex." Rejecting the "strenuous general opposition to the discussion of a subject long enshrouded in mystery and persistently tabooed by all other public speakers," Goldman

> delivered a most illuminating lecture on homo-sexuality. A dignified, tense and eager audience crowded the hall to its fullest capacity. The frankness and celerity with which they questioned and discussed were evidence of the genuine and deep interest her treatment of the subject had aroused.

Anna W. ended:

> Every person who came to that lecture possessing contempt and disgust for homo-sexualists . . . went away with a broad and sympathetic understanding of the question and a conviction that in matters of personal life, freedom should reign.

Alberta Lucille Hart, twenty-six, "heard many lectures by Emma Goldman and became much interested in anarchism" in 1916. In the winter of 1917–1918, Hart had a full hysterectomy and afterward lived as Alan L. Hart, marrying a woman, divorcing, and marrying a second woman, becoming a medical doctor, and publishing four novels that critiqued injustice and the social systems supporting it.

The famous Ma Rainey wrote and recorded a blues song on June 12, 1928, that featured a butch woman-loving woman boldly proclaiming her sexual interest in women and challenging the world to "prove it on me."

Emma Goldman's positive political take on homosexuality extended to women friends. When Margaret Anderson was to visit Goldman, the envious Ben Reitman warned Goldman that Anderson "is crazy about you." To which Goldman replied ruefully, "Yes Margaret is coming and I am glad of that. But—I do not incline that way. I love your damned sex."

Goldman was primarily attracted to Reitman's "damned sex," but Goldman's love life did include one documented sexual relation with a woman. The details of this intimacy are relevant to Eve's story because

Goldman shared them with Reitman, and this provoked him to worry that Goldman would find sex with women more exciting than with him. Reitman's jealous reaction added one more reason for him to be judgmental about lesbians.

Goldman's liaison began after Almeda Sperry responded on March 4, 1912, from New Kensington, Pennsylvania, to an inquiry from Goldman about Sperry's past love and sex relations with men. Sperry and Goldman had met when Sperry attended a Goldman lecture. In her letters, Sperry impressed Goldman with her bold, intimate revelations—her experience as a prostitute, her conflicted relationship with her husband Fred—and her passionate expression of her intense feelings. Both of these women were drama queens who admired that quality in each other.

Goldman invited Sperry to visit her in a country house she was occupying in Ossining, New York, and a sexual intimacy developed between the women rebels—an intimacy more physical, urgent, and intense on Sperry's part, but an intimacy that Goldman actively encouraged. Later, in one of Sperry's self-dramatizing missives, she told Goldman:

> Dearest. . . . If I had only had the courage enuf to kill myself when you reached the climax—then I would have known happiness, for at that moment I had complete possession of you.

But, "after possessing" Goldman, the melodramatic Sperry also experienced a new will to live. She added:

> I wish to escape from you but I am harried from place to place in my thots. I cannot escape from the rhythmic spurt of your love juice.

Goldman showed Sperry's letters to Reitman, to punish him, it seems, for his flings with other women. She warned Reitman "not to make her [Sperry] realize you know of her feelings for me." But when Sperry arrived in New York to see Goldman, the predictably jealous Reitman, sent to meet Sperry and knowing of her past as a prostitute, treated her disrespectfully.

Sperry later denounced Reitman to Goldman:

He tackled the wrong woman when he tackled me. I have had a deep horror of him ever since he met me at the N.Y. station. . . . Please ask him, for the sake of the Cause, if he ever goes to meet another sin-laden woman who is beginning to see a glimmer of light—please ask him, for humanity's sake, and the woman's sake—not to begin "fuck" talk.

Writing to Goldman from her Pennsylvania home, Sperry also reported that Reitman

asked Hutch Hapgood to suck one of my breasts while he sucked the other so I could have two orgasms at the same time, and that was just after I had had the most divine conversations with Hutch. He [Reitman] also asked me how many men there are in this town that I had not fucked yet.

Reitman suggesting a threesome with Sperry and bohemian writer Hutchins Hapgood revealed mixed motives: jealousy and anger at Sperry's intimacy with Goldman, and a homosexual attraction to Hapgood. This is confirmed in a Goldman letter to Reitman:

You say you wanted Hutch. Believe me dear boy, I do not begrudge you Hutch, I am glad he at least can give you what I can not, peace. . . . What [is] more natural than to go with Hutch when you were not exactly famished for me.

Goldman added, in another letter to Reitman:

Yes, I have known for quite some time that if H would sleep with you, you would not need me, also that your passion since you are in NY is due to your association with Hutch and not so much your love for me. I am not eager to act as a substitute and therefore hope H will oblige you. Why not ask him?

Whether Reitman propositioned Hapgood is unknown.

3

1912

AMONG THE ANARCHISTS WHOM EVE joined in New York, Alexander Berkman was one of the first to speak publicly and positively in the United States about homosexuals.

In October 1912, four months after Eve landed in Manhattan, Mother Earth Press published Berkman's *Prison Memoirs of an Anarchist*, recounting his fourteen years in jail for the attempted assassination of Henry Clay Frick. Berkman's book received many positive reviews, even in the mainstream press, and was later translated into Yiddish, so Eve certainly heard it discussed and probably read it.

Prison Memoirs included three frank, pioneering passages on same-sex love and sexual attraction in prison between older and younger males. During Berkman's first year in jail an older prisoner, Red, a florid talker, told him, "You're my kid, see?" When innocent Berkman asked what Red meant, Red explained: a "kid" or "punk" was a "boy" prisoner who gave himself to an older "man" prisoner. When Berkman doubted that "there can be such intimacy between those of the same sex," Red replied, "Man alive, the dump's chuckful of punks. It's done in every prison, an' on th' road everywhere." Here began Berkman's prison-sex education—and, no doubt, the prison-sex education of his readers.

More personally, and more daringly, Berkman, in a section set about five years later, described his own growing love for Johnny Davis, a younger male prisoner. One day, Johnny, from his cell, anxiously told Berkman, "If you were here with me—I would like to kiss you." To which Berkman responded with an "unaccountable sense of joy," telling Johnny, "I feel just as you do." When Johnny sickened and died, Berkman mourned his loss. Though not sexually consummated, Berkman's love for another male was a rare early, positive personal account of male-male desire.

In a section titled "Passing the Love of Woman," set after another five years, Berkman reported his discussions with "Doctor George," a fellow prisoner, who recounted his growing "real, true love" for a younger prisoner, Floyd. The doctor "desired sexual relations" with Floyd, he told Berkman, "yet, somehow I couldn't bring myself to do it."

When Doctor George worried that Berkman was laughing at his story, Berkman replied, "I think it is a wonderful thing, and, George—I had felt the same horror and disgust at these things, as you did. But now I think quite differently about them." Berkman's wary move from condemnation to acceptance of homosexual love hinted to readers that they could make the same moral and emotional move.

Despite Berkman's equivocation about same-sex love versus same-sex sex, few other early-twentieth-century writers so clearly, forcefully, and eloquently spoke up for homosexuality. Knowing Berkman can only have encouraged Eve herself to speak out.

The bohemian sexual culture into which Eve had stepped provided one of the few social spaces in which an independent young woman might be encouraged to experiment with life's possibilities. "Most of these experimenters are young women," stressed sociologist H. W. Zorbaugh in 1929, writing of Chicago's Towertown and New York's Greenwich Village. "It is the young women who open most of the studios, run most of the tearooms and restaurants, most of the little art shops and book stalls, manage the exhibits and little theaters, [and] dominate the life of the bohemias of American cities." Though Zorbaugh probably overstated young women's power, he pointed to these arty ghettos' special import for women's free development, a freedom Eve celebrated.

When Eve arrived in the United States, she joined a group of anarchists, socialists, and bohemians actively pioneering the creation of a modern, newly linked "sex-love." That linking of sexuality and love would have shocked Victorian upholders of middle-class propriety. Before 1900, respectable middle-class "true love" was pure and spiritual, not sexual. The idea of women and men having a positive "sexual identity" and "sex life" would have horrified proper middle-class ladies and gents. Before the twentieth century, sensuality and love only met and properly mated in the dark, under the sign of marriage and procreation.

Anarchists and Greenwich Village bohemians were trailblazers in linking sex and love without reference to baby-making or marriage. They had just recently started calling this new sex-love, yes, "heterosexuality." That new heterosexuality named a supposedly universal, natural erotic—actually, a historically specific, political ideology of lust just starting to be used then to normalize the heterosexual and pathologize the homosexual, another new sex category. Pathologizing the lesbian was one response of men just then affirming their still new, fragile companionate heterosexuality. But Eve's friends' positive valuing of their hetero intimacies can only have encouraged exploration of her homo desires. For if nonprocreative heterosex was valued, why not also value nonprocreative homosex?

The bohemian sex-love pioneers that Eve encountered were also experimenting with a new, nonmonogamous "free love." Hutchins Hapgood and his wife Neith Boyce, for example, strove to realize in practice their opposition to monogamous middle-class marriage. But acting on their free-love ideal was definitely a strain, especially for the determined, emancipated Boyce. Hapgood, Boyce, and other early free-sex explorers often found their deeply held ideals of personal, sexual freedom conflicting with profound personal feelings of possessiveness. Boyce often found herself beset by jealousy at the sexual flings with other women that Hapgood reported to her.

Free-loving women, despite their anarchist ideal of individual independence, or their feminist ideal of women's independence, sometimes found themselves pining for a traditional Prince Charming. Free-loving men, like Ben Reitman, sometimes deployed the free-love ideal to justify a traditional male philandering.

When Eve arrived it was sex o'clock in America. It was the twentieth century—the Jazz Age, the New Age, the Age of the New Paganism, the New Morality, the New Psychology, the New Woman, the New Man, the New Negro, the New Criticism, the New Arts, the New Literature, the New Freedom, the New Nationalism, the New Society.

It was the best of times; it was the worst of times.

On January 11, 1912, Polish women textile workers in Lawrence, Massachusetts, walked out on strike when mill owners reduced the women's wages. After a long, hard, well-publicized struggle, the strikers won. Before Lawrence, said radical feminist Mary Heaton Vorse, she had "not got angry." After Lawrence, "I got angry."

In 1912, the owners of the Triangle Shirtwaist Factory were prosecuted in New York City for the manslaughter of Jake Kline, who died in the fire at their company's factory a year earlier. That blaze killed 145 employees, mostly young women immigrants like Eve. But since the owners had earlier been found not guilty of causing several workers' deaths in the fire, the judge ruled that they could not be tried again for Jake Kline's death.

Two months before Eve's steamer docked in New York, the *Titanic* hit an iceberg, killing more than fifteen hundred. A first-class ticket included the best chance of survival. Lifeboats were nearer the first class. First- and second-class passengers stood first in line for lifeboats. Many third-class passengers were locked inside the ship.

It was "not the number but the kind of immigrants that gives grounds for apprehension," the director of the US Census declared in 1912. "Our population coming from Russia includes very few Russians proper, but is composed chiefly of Jews and Poles."

"There is one factor in the prevalence of insanity in this country. That factor is immigration," declared Ellis Island psychiatrist Thomas Salmon in 1912. Dr. Salmon later cited the "remarkable tendency to suicide" in the Japanese "race," the "strong tendency to delusionary trends of a persecutory nature in West Indian negroes," "the frequency with which we find hidden sexual complexes among Hebrews," and "the remarkable prevalence of mutism among Poles."

In 1912, presidential contender Woodrow Wilson telegrammed a supporter: "In the matter of Chinese and Japanese coolie immigration I stand for the national policy of exclusion. We cannot make a homogeneous population out of a people who do not blend with the Caucasian race."

Jack Johnson, the first African American world heavyweight boxing champion, convicted of consorting with a (White) woman across state lines, skipped bail and the United States.

In Hamilton, Georgia, on the grounds of a Black house of worship, Friendship Baptist Church, a White mob lynched four Black people— three men and a woman—John Moore, Eugene Harrington, the Reverend Burrell Hardaway, and Loduska Crutchfield. Sixty-two African Americans were murdered by lynch mobs in 1912.

"Prohibit any of the old time barbarous dances," the US commissioner of Indian affairs told a superintendent in 1912. The sooner Native dances were abolished, "the more rapid will be their development toward model American citizens."

In 1912, US marines landed in Cuba to help the island's government violently crush an armed revolt by Afro-Cubans, mostly former slaves, and thousands of Afro-Cubans were killed. US troops invaded Nicaragua to stop any other nation from building a canal; a treaty ratified by Congress put the United States in charge of Nicaragua's financial system. US military forces intervened in China to protect American interests during revolutionary uprisings.

"Vast" numbers of women and a few men marched in New York City in 1912 to demand women's right to vote in US national elections. "If America is ever to become a government built on the broadest justice to every citizen," W. E. B. Du Bois, the Black scholar, told the National Woman Suffrage Association, "every citizen must be enfranchised."

"A little band of willful women, the most unruly and individualistic females you have fell among," held the first meeting of the women-only Heterodoxy Club at Polly's restaurant, 137 MacDougal Street, in Greenwich Village. A number of Heterodoxy members had affairs with women. Four constituted couples: Elisabeth Irwin and Katharine Anthony, Ida Wylie and Dr. Sara Josephine Baker.

In 1912, the term *lesbian* did not often signify sex between women. In Maryland, a Woman's College newspaper was called the *Lesbian Herald*; a headline declared, LESBIANS OF WOMAN'S COLLEGE GIVE FETE. In a medical journal, Douglas C. McMurtrie felt compelled to explain, "The prototype of the woman invert has usually been regarded as Sappho, the Greek poetess of Lesbos." From Lesbos, he said, "homosexual affection between females" was named "Lesbian love."

4

War Clouds
and a Fan Letter

JULY 28, 1914: Two years after Eve's arrival in the United States, leaders of Germany and Austria-Hungary challenged leaders of France, Russia, and Britain to battle. The men challenged agreed to fight. Initiating colossal violence, a multination war began in Europe, fought by seventy million grunts, and resulting in nine million combatant deaths and seven million civilian deaths.

NOVEMBER 7, 1916: President Woodrow Wilson, who ran on the campaign slogan "He Kept Us Out of War," won reelection. Seven months later, President "He Kept Us Out of War" Wilson urged members of the US Congress to declare war on Germany. They obeyed.

MAY 18, 1917: Congress passed the Selective Service Act, requiring males between twenty-one and thirty to register for the draft.

JUNE 15, 1917: Congress passed the Espionage Act, establishing large fines and twenty years in jail for those convicted of obstructing the draft.

THE DAY THE ESPIONAGE ACT passed, Emma Goldman and Alexander Berkman were arrested for organizing antiwar, antidraft meetings, at least one of which Eve attended. Goldman and Berkman were declared guilty, fined heavily, sentenced to the maximum two years in prison, and recommended for deportation when their jail terms ended.

NOVEMBER 7, 1917: In Russia, Bolsheviks led an armed insurrection by workers and soldiers that overthrew the existing government and transferred authority to community assemblies called Soviets. US owners worried: America's workers might get the same idea.

Six years after Eve landed in New York, on February 21, 1918, the twenty-six-year-old wrote a fervid fan letter to actress Fania Marinoff. The actress was the wife of Carl Van Vechten, writer, photographer, and White supporter of African American artists. Though Van Vechten was predominantly homosexual, the couple's complex, often conflicted marriage lasted fifty years.

Eve had written after enjoying a dinner with Marinoff, Van Vechten, and Marinoff's brother Jacob and his wife. Jacob Marinoff was the editor of the Yiddish-language humor weekly *Der Groyser Kundes* (literally, "The Big Stick," more expressively, "The Big Prankster"). The magazine published such accomplished writers as Sholem Aleichem, Sholem Asch, and I. J. Singer. Eve was probably working as sales agent for *Der*

Fania Marinoff, photo by Herman Mishkin, 1913.

Groyser Kundes, and the dinner suggests that she was on friendly terms with her boss and his wife.

Eve's letter addressed Fania Marinoff as "Фаня—Adoràbile." Eve bidded boldly for the actress's attention. She spelled Fania in Russian, the actress's native language, Adoràbile in Italian. When Eve wrote, she had twice seen Marinoff star in the play *Karen*, in Greenwich Village. She wrote on the stationery of the Waldorf Cottage, in New Jersey:

> I am taking my short vacation in Lakewood and amidst the quiet country life I am thinking of my latest adventure. And Karen comes up my mind. "Karen" the play and Karen more than the play Miss Fania Marinoff.

Eve's unspecified "adventure" probably referenced some free-love hetero experiment related earlier by Eve at dinner. The drama, *Karen*, described a free-love experiment.

In the play, Karen, played by Marinoff, has had two live-in love affairs with men without marrying. When these falter, she returns home to her judgmental, austere theology professor father, author of *Marriage and Christian Morality*. At the end of four acts Karen again exits Dad's house, "free, to be sure, and independent, but lonely and disenchanted," the *Nation*'s reviewer reported. Eve clearly found the play's free-love message inspiring, as she certainly did Marinoff. Eve must have cheered inwardly when Karen responded in the play to her father's denunciation:

> *Strumpet* of a daughter. . . . That's the way our liberalism thinks and feels—our "established" liberalism. It establishes men's liberty—oh, mercy yes! But believe me, the day will come when we, too, will demand it as our right—demand the chance to live our own lives as we choose and as we can, without being held worse on that account.

Eve continued:

> You will forgive me, Miss Marinoff if I'll try in my poor English, to tell you my appreciation of your acting and how much moved I was, when I saw you for the first time and second time.

When Eve "came down to see you after the play I could not talk; words were not enough to tell you how great you are, Miss Marinoff."

When Eve had looked at Marinoff, she confessed,

> I saw nothing else but your beautiful dark, big eyes which are hidden under these long long eyelashes, yet I saw your soul and it made me shiver and respect you so much more than an ordinary actor.
>
> You are not an actress Miss Marinoff, you are a great artist and may be compared with the world-greatest.

Eve listed other women greats. When she saw Isadora Duncan dance for the first time, Eve wrote, "I could not forget her for a whole year." When Eve heard Ethel Leginska play classical piano for the first time, "I did not miss one of her performances." When Eve saw "Emma Goldman come out on the stage" at an antiwar meeting "crowded with detractors, police, and soldiers" she had heard Goldman shout, "I have only one life to give, soldiers help yourself!" Eve then "adored" Goldman "for her braveness."

"And when I saw you for the first time," Eve wrote to Marinoff, "I must say it was one of my 'happy moments' of my life which are so rare." She explained her rarity of happy moments: "I see the truth of life, the naked truth so well, that seldom a thing moves me or inspires me." So "when an artist makes me shiver I am thankful to him with breath and soul, and I am thankful to you." Eve gushed, "One need not go to see you on the stage to see the artist in you, you seem to be the artist all the time."

Eve had talked to friends about Marinoff, and the play "and one girl with a beautiful soul and spirit tells me she has been down to see Karen five times and wants to see Karen more and more." Another friend of Eve's "saw you once only but she must see you again." A young man whom Eve took to see the play "was so thankful to me and was so impressed by your art, Miss Marinoff." Other friends of Eve's had seen Marinoff in *Karen* "and everybody says it's the play of the hour and they can't imagine how it would be without you."

Eve concluded her note, "for I am afraid if it will be any longer you'll put it aside."

Eve sent her letter to Marinoff in care of the Greenwich Village Theatre, where *Karen* was playing. At this theater in a grand building on Sheridan Square, starting in 1917, the Greenwich Village Players performed original works by Eugene O'Neill and other notable writers.

Also at this theater, in 1923, Eve was likely to have attended a production of Sholem Asch's *The God of Vengeance*, with its intimate kiss of two women in love. When the play moved to the Apollo Theatre on West Forty-Second Street, that kiss was toned down or eliminated.

Asch's play featured an Orthodox Jew, his brothel, and his daughter's love affair with one of his prostitutes. Despite its censoring, the production's twelve actors and actresses and two managers were indicted under the same obscenity law later used against Eve. Accused of fostering an "indecent, immoral and impure theatrical performance," the play's producer, Harry Weinberger, an activist lawyer opposed to censorship, contested the indictment and later conviction. After a long battle that conviction was overturned.

Most of the complaints against the play alleged that it was anti-Jewish, reported the *New York Times*, but the grand jury that indicted the play "did not consider the racial phase of the complaints." The play was indicted for its sexual content: prostitution and same-sex eros, the *Times* hinted. In 1923, Sholem Asch defended the Jewish characters in his play, calling them "as good and bad as any race."

Eve ended her letter to Fania Marinoff "With love and appreciation," signing herself "Eve Zlotchever." She was not yet the Americanized "Eve Adams." What Marinoff made of Eve's bid for attention is not reported, but she or someone wrote on the envelope, "Very fan."

Marinoff's play closed in March 1918 after eighty performances. On October 4 of that year, New York City health officials publicly declared the existence of an influenza epidemic.

5

Spied On

November 11, 1918: German leaders signed an armistice with US, British, and French officials, ending "the war to end all wars." But US labor union leaders and members had gained ground during the war, and postwar labor militancy was common. The postwar years were big on strikes, Red scares, and Red raids. Corporation owners, politicians, government bureaucrats, conservative preachers, and status quo journalists blamed outside agitators for working-class discontent.

In 1919, seven years after Eve's arrival, she was tramping around the United States selling anarchist, socialist, communist, and radical labor publications, including Jacob Marinoff's *Der Groyser Kundes*. As traveling saleswoman, Eve joined a group of migratory women who worked their way from New York to San Francisco, making a small living. In 1926, sociologist Nels Anderson reported an increasing number of "hoboettes," women "bored to death with conventions, anxious to do something new," "'emancipated women,'" who resisted "living according to the clock." Eve Adams was cited as a former "hoboette," the only time in any document, private or public, that somebody gendered Eve femme.

As traveling hawker of left periodicals, Eve lived an adventurous, mobile life. But years later, a depressed Eve recalled, "What a price I paid for my courage and perhaps foolishness!" She had underestimated the punishment a noncitizen immigrant could receive for associating with notorious radicals, selling radical periodicals, and publishing a book affirming "lesbian love."

On July 14, 1919, a Waterbury, Connecticut, police official telephoned Bureau of Investigation agent Warren G. Grimes in New Haven: "Eva Adams" was in town, the earliest dated report of Eve using her new last name. She was "believed to be an agitator," an organizer for the Industrial Workers of the World, the militant labor organization that US government officials had already taken active, largely successful steps to crush. Agent Grimes and agent J. W. R. Chamberlin that day traveled to Waterbury and searched Eve's hotel room and confiscated some of her belongings, including "considerable printed literature and subscription blanks to a radical publication."

The First Amendment to the US Constitution had, since 1791, prohibited Congress from making any law "abridging the freedom of speech or of the press; or the right of the people . . . to petition the Government for a redress of grievances." So Eve's peddling of radical periodicals should have been protected against surveillance. The Constitution's Fourth Amendment also provided "the right of the people to be secure in their persons" and "papers," protected "against unreasonable searches and seizures." This right to security was extended to all "the people"—formally, at least, including noncitizens like Eve. But Grimes and Chamberlin mentioned no search warrant; they just searched and seized.

In Eve's room, Grimes and Chamberlin found, took away, and deposited with the Waterbury police a large amount of IWW literature, including membership cards, and some texts in Russian. The agents also took from Eve's room, and distributed to the Bureau of Investigation, a list of names and addresses found in her suitcase. The list included "Margaret Anderson," 24 West Sixteenth Street, New York City. Just a year earlier, Anderson and her romantic and creative partner Jane Heap had begun to publish in their *Little Review* James Joyce's sexy, genre-bending, modernist *Ulysses.*

A week after government agents broke into Eve's room, agent Grimes received from the Waterbury police a batch of papers taken from Eve. But Eve had never inquired about her papers and had "slipped away from town," probably figuring it was useless to protest.

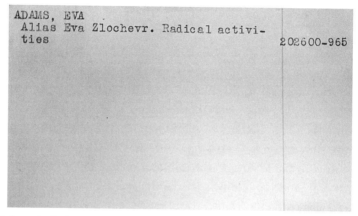

Eve Adams's index card in the files of the Department of Justice, circa 1919.

On August 1, 1919, the month after the first known surveillance of Eve, US attorney general A. Mitchell Palmer officially created a new "Radical Division" within the Bureau of Investigation to collect data on militant labor organizers, leftists, liberals, pacifists, and other dissenters. A twenty-four-year-old, John Edgar Hoover, was appointed head of the division and created a new "Radical Activities Index."

A card referring to US Department of Justice files, probably dating to 1919, was headed "ADAMS, EVA / Alias Eva Zlochevr. Radical activities." I'm told that Justice Department file 202600-965, to which the card referred, could not be found in the National Archives, but files of the Bureau of Investigation, a division of the Justice Department, do exist, and refer tellingly to Eve.

The Bureau of Investigation's "radical activities" included the acts of IWW members and other militant trade union organizers, anarchists both violent and pacifistic, socialists, and the small, warring, opposed factions of communists. "Radicals" comprised any activist critics of the capitalist system, its elected political representatives, or its unelected businessmen.

Eve's own radical politics, never explicitly defined by her, probably included an evolving, amorphous mixture of anarchist, socialist, communist, left-libertarian, and militant labor ideas about work, class, and the economy, culture, gender, and sexuality. Eve's politics are probably best described as left radical.

Eve's public association with leftist periodicals continued, probably provoking further Bureau of Investigation interest. On October 11, 1919, the *Liberator*, a socialist "Journal of Revolutionary Progress," assigned "Eve Adams" to cover a peace conference called by President Wilson in Washington. This is the first public report of Eve Adams using that name, the first to name her a reporter, and the first evidence of her association with the *Liberator*, the militant journal founded by its editor, Max Eastman, and his feminist journalist sister, Crystal.

As a saleswoman of left periodicals, Chawa Zloczewer certainly needed a name her US customers could pronounce and recall. But her chosen appellation also hinted playfully at her androgynous persona, combining a bit of Eve, a bit of Adam. Eve's self-naming expressed, in addition, a desire to break with family, tradition, and Poland, to play down her immigrant and Jewish roots, to assimilate and Americanize, like many others. It suggests her desire to define for herself the woman emerging on her exploratory American journey.

"Eve Adams" did not immediately supplant other versions of her name. A spelling of her Polish last name appeared with her new name in publicity for her sales services. In December 1919, the *Liberator* told its readers that "Eve Zlotchever-Adams" was traveling for the paper and taking subscriptions. "Please give her YOURS when she calls upon you."

Four months after Bureau agents broke into Eve's hotel room, Attorney General Palmer authorized simultaneous raids on the Union of Russian Workers in twenty-three US cities. This first big Red scare raid occurred on November 7, 1919, the second anniversary of the Bolshevik Revolution. Over ten thousand suspected radicals were arrested, and often "badly beaten by the police," as happened in New York City.

The following month, at five in the morning on December 21, 1919, Emma Goldman and Alexander Berkman were deported to Russia. With them were 184 members of the Union of Russian Workers, 49 other anarchists, 8 persons found likely to become public charges, 3 aliens found guilty of moral turpitude, 1 procurer, and 1 undocumented alien. Nobody had warned the deportees or their lawyers, families, friends, or lovers of their immediate expulsion, so Eve and Ben Reitman missed the

chance to say good-bye to Goldman and Berkman. But a deportation alert
had gone out to a number of reporters and congressmen, who roused
themselves in the middle of the night to observe the enforced departures.

Among the deportation viewers was John (now J.) Edgar Hoover, "a
slender bundle of high-charged electric wire." Hoover had made it his
crusade to see Goldman banished, and he and the other invited witnesses
actually joined the deportees on the tugboat to the ship that would
take the exiles to Soviet Russia. A congressman among the deportation
voyeurs recalled Goldman's last words:

> Time was when this country had professed to welcome the down-
> trodden of other lands.

Although the attorney general's "Palmer Raids" are recalled by that name,
the Bureau of Investigation operations were actually efficently managed
by Hoover.

On January 2, 1920, a second series of Palmer Raids resulted in the
arrest of 2,585 alleged radicals in thirty-three US cities. These arrests
focused on noncitizen immigrant members of the small, warring Communist Party and Communist Labor Party. On New York's Ellis Island,
arrestees were held in cold, unsanitary, overcrowded cells, and several
died. Ellis Island assistant commissioner Byron Uhl, who later signed
off on Eve's fate, insisted that no arrestee would be paroled until all
were paroled. New York politicians spoke of building a "concentration
camp" to hold the Reds.

Eve herself was back in the Bureau of Investigation's sights on February 11, 1920. That day, Agent J. T. Suter, in Washington, DC, advised
Agent E. Murray Blanford in the Bureau's San Francisco office:

> Eva Adams alias Eva Zlotchevr, who is known to have been a
> close associate of Alexander Berkman and Emma Goldman, is
> now on a tour of the United States, soliciting subscriptions for
> various radical magazines. . . . She expects ultimately to reach San
> Francisco, from where she will sail for Poland. She is described as
> having bright red hair bobbed. She can undoubtedly be located
> thru the general delivery window at the General Post Office in

your city, as she has been receiving mail in that manner in the various cities she has visited.

The notion that Eve was planning to sail for Poland in 1920 was the first rumor of many distributed by government agents—in effect, a US government rumormongering campaign against the radical Eve.

Agent Blanford informed J. Edgar Hoover and the Justice Department on November 9, 1920, that Eve had arrived in San Francisco. Blanford helpfully added, "Any action desired." Blanford also reported that a "Dr. Charles T. Baylis" had walked into the San Francisco office of the Bureau of Investigation to inform on Eve. Baylis had received a secondhand tip about Eve from "a lady" while all three were on the boat from Portland, Oregon. Baylis had "forgotten" the lady's name but promised to relay it to the Bureau. That lady had, at Baylis's suggestion, "pretended to be a convert to the Jewess' radical doctrines."

The "Jewess" Eve, Baylis said, had declared herself to be an organizer for the "Revolutionists," a term used then for radicals of all stripes. Eve had been in Butte, Montana, "the headquarters for the Revolutionists in the west." In Portland, she had just "finished organizing the 'Revolutionists.'"

In San Francisco, Baylis reported, Eve was expecting to receive names of local "Revolution" leaders, then go on to Los Angeles, Salt Lake City, and eastward. She would then go to England, France, Poland, and "Russia, where she would report to the 'leaders.'"

> She claimed to be working for the love of the cause, but admitted receiving liberal expense money from a headquarters in New York. At Portland, she said, she had received a check for $250 [about $3,300 today].

Eve reportedly boasted that she had used many aliases and had been arrested many times, under many names.

> She stated [that] she never carried any "Radical" literature in her baggage for fear of a "raid," but that it was always sent ahead of her.

How should we understand Eve's braggadocio as reported by a lady informant to informer Baylis? Is this just another fake fact? Or did Eve perhaps get a bit tipsy on the boat from Portland and exaggerate her radical exploits to a woman she found attractive? That was possible. But more likely, Baylis's secondhand report was greatly distorted by his blatant prejudice against radicals, Jews, and gender-benders. As Baylis described Eve to the Justice Department, she "has short fuzzy red hair; dresses mannishly and is dirty, greasy and Jewish in appearance." Baylis, and "a majority of the passengers" on the boat from Portland, considered Eve "a dangerous radical," he said.

"Dirty" and "greasy" were standard anti-Jewish, anti-immigrant slurs: "I for one won't stand for a lot of fat Germans an' greasy Russian Jews tellin' me how to run my country," said Billy, the Anglo-Saxon protagonist of Jack London's 1913 novel *The Valley of the Moon.* "When you catch me in a socialist meeting," Billy added, it will only be "when they can talk like white men."

Baylis was no random citizen informer. In 1919, he was making transcontinental lecture tours on "Making a Better America." He cast out radicals and immigrants—anyone who didn't conform to his particular American patriot ideal. Talking to a California Rotary Club, Baylis advocated, "Deport the 'alien' red, put the native born traitor in jail, restrict immigration to desirable persons and teach Americanism in the public schools."

Responding to Baylis's charges, Bureau agent F. W. Kelly, in Butte, Montana, reported that Eve had limited her activities there "to secret conferences with members of the Russian Soviet Metallurgical Bureau." (Eve's expertise in metallurgy is nowhere else mentioned.) Eve had also solicited subscriptions to the *Liberator,* but she had not been "openly active in the dissemination of other radical propaganda." Butte's alleged "Revolutionists" were not mentioned.

Eve was "reputed to be a niece of Emma Goldman"—Kelly passed on false rumor as if it might be fact. The agent also reported that Eve had stayed in Butte with one Albert Keene, "whose wife is an illegitimate offspring of Emma Goldman's." A lie. Goldman, the well-researched birth control advocate, had early made a conscious decision not to bear children, and never did. Rumor and unverified fact claims mixed promiscuously in US agents' reports.

On December 14, 1920, Los Angeles Bureau agent E. Kosterlitzky made "a complete search" of Eve's hotel room and belongings and read her mail, a second violation of her Fourth Amendment rights.

Kosterlitzky reported, "No papers of a compromising nature were found." Eve was "obtaining subscriptions for radical papers"—*Novy Mir* and *Russky Golos* (Soviet papers), *Il Martello* (an Italian paper), *Die Naye Welt* and *Der Groyser Kundes* (Yiddish periodicals), and *Good Morning* and the *Liberator* (American socialist papers).

A Los Angeles Bureau agent named Sturgis reported on January 14, 1921, that Eve's activities there consisted of "securing subscriptions to radical publications." He then commented on Eve's appearance:

> Age: 30; Height: 5′ 2″; Weight: 110; Jewish type; hair cropped, medium dark; Complexion: Medium; Not attractive. Wears nose glasses.

Despite the many references to Eve's "cropped" hair and gender-bending clothes and demeanor, it's hard to know how radically she rejected the day's feminine norms. Eve's "mannish clothes" were never fully described in any document. She probably wore slacks and rejected frilly blouses when tramping around the country. Agents cited her gender-confounding clothes as indications of her nefarious character. A stereotype of the butch, sexually predatory lesbian colored such judgments.

Agent Sturgis's assessment of Eve and her appearance was passed on to other Bureau offices by Agent Fred I. Keepers in Denver. Eve left that city on January 12, 1921, Keepers noted, with a forwarding address in Chicago.

One more US government official had his say about Eve. Matthew C. Smith, a colonel in the US Department of War's Military Intelligence Division, discussed Eve on January 15, 1921. He had "information from a reliable source that Miss Eva Adams . . . a cousin of Emma Goldman and a close relative of Alexander Berkman," had appeared in Los Angeles. More false claims about Eve's family links to famous anarchists—passed along this time by a colonel in the Military Intelligence Division's Negative Branch, dedicated to countering information impairing "military efficiency."

It "is rumored" that Eve is an organizer of "revolutionist activities" and a representative of *Revolution*, a New York radical paper, said Colonel Smith. The officer noted pointedly that Eve "is getting most of her subscriptions in the vicinity of Los Angeles from Italians, Mexicans, and Spaniards."

Smith's and Baylis's nativist prejudice contrasted with Eve's deep feeling for America. Six years later, at Eve's deportation hearing in 1927, she would plead to remain in the United States: "I learned to love this country with heart and soul and everything about it." This was not just strategic, an appeal to derail deportation. Eve deeply cherished the freedom she had experienced in the United States and the ideal of freedom Americans professed.

Eve added, "The reason I have not become a citizen in all these years, the only one I can give, is through neglect." The profound, even patriotic love Eve felt for the United States led her to underestimate the danger posed to a radical alien by enemies embedded within the US surveillance state.

Eve's failure to become a citizen may also have originated with her and her anarchist friends' rejection of the state as legitimizing institution. Emma Goldman, for example, rejected state-sanctioned marriage, sex, and love. Eve's failure to become a "naturalized citizen" may have also reflected her religious belief that the she and her lesbian desire had been "naturalized" at birth by God.

Five months after Colonel Smith sent his nativist memo, in June 1921, the New York satirical journal *Good Morning*, edited by the radical leftist artist Art Young, reported:

> Eve Adams takes subscriptions to GOOD MORNING. She is now enroute through the north-western states.

In August of the same year, *Good Morning* published a welcoming story describing a mythologized Eve Adams, reprinted from the *Truth*, a socialist paper in Duluth, Minnesota:

> Eve Adams, the celebrated hiker, who sets out for a seventy-five mile stroll in the morning and winds up with a swim across the English Channel in the evening.

Eve was "on the trail of the artists and students and housewives and farmers and all other workers to give them the inspiration of a lifetime by putting The Liberator and Good Morning and Soviet Russia and Truth into their hands for a year or so."

> Miss Adams has the reputation of having gotten more subscriptions for these publications than any other living Bolshevik in captivity. When you see her you will be sure to subscribe.

"This rebel girl is successful for the one reason that she knows what to select that is worth reading," the Minnesota paper added.

> She is in Duluth just now and while she is there she invites you into the select reading circle of the most advanced intellects of this country.

Years later, Eve fondly recalled the *Truth*'s heroic account of her as a super saleswoman of leftist periodicals, a larger-than-life people's heroine. Eve's drama-filled American life lent itself to mythmaking.

6

Chicago, the Grey Cottage, Ruth

FROM ABOUT THE WINTER OF 1921 to the fall of 1923, Eve settled in Chicago, where she continued as a sales agent for *Der Groyser Kundes*. Eve also tried to teach, and in April 1921 she placed an ad in the *Liberator*:

> LEARN RUSSIAN!! EXPERT INSTRUCTION BY RUSSIAN COL-LEGE GRADUATE. For full particulars, apply by mail to EVE ZLOTCHEVER, c/o The Liberator.

Eve was probably fibbing when she called herself a college graduate, but Russian was certainly among her language skills, along with Polish, German, French, Yiddish, Hebrew, and English, which she tried to monetize as she struggled to make a small living.

After "primary school" in Mława, Eve later testified, she "graduated in Plotzk," Yiddish for Płock, now in Poland, then part of the Russian Empire. Exactly what sort of school Eve graduated from is unclear; it was unusual at the time in Poland for a young Jewish woman to receive an advanced education. But a historian of Jewish culture in the late Russian Empire, Jeffrey Veidlinger, points out, "Women were often permitted to study foreign languages, including the languages of the surrounding populations, so they could tend the family store or conduct other business with non-Jews while the men studied."

The "static view" of Russian small-town life "propagated in American popular culture" is mistaken, Veidlinger stresses. Tevye, "the quintessential shtetl Jew" of Broadway's *Fiddler on the Roof*, wrestled with "the introduction of modern ideas into the shtetl." In the Sholem Aleichem story *Tevye the Dairyman*, the musical's source, "each of Tevye's daughters represents a different dimension of the new social norms." His daughter Chava, for example, eloped with a non-Jewish paramour. Chawa Zloczewer also took to her heart a quantity of unsanctioned paramours.

What in Russian Poland could have encouraged rebellion in the young Eve? In 1910, in Eve's hometown, Mława, political, religious, and cultural ferment was common. This town of 15,702 included 7,017 Jews. Zionists, on the left and the right, both secular and religious, envisioned a return to Palestine, while the secular, socialist General Union of Jewish Workers (the Bund) opposed the Zionists, arguing that Jews should stay in Poland, remain culturally distinct, and organize for social justice. Two socialist political parties recruited members, as did nationalists, liberals, and anarchists. Poland just before Eve's departure in 1912 was seething politically and culturally.

When Eve was fourteen, in 1905, a strike of discontented workers in Łódź, Poland, spread to Warsaw and other cities, resulting in a Polish Revolution against Russian autocratic rule. The czar granted some political reforms, which for a time quieted the most radical demands for change. But Polish political groups began more openly agitating for change.

Debates about educating village girls like Eve made up one aspect of the "woman question" in Poland. In 1907, the Union of Equal Rights for Polish Women initiated the country's first legally organized feminist organization. Rejecting that organization's focus on voting rights, one radical Polish feminist leader even called for women's sexual freedom. Another radical feminist defended the fictional females who sought new forms of love in the "erotic" literature of the younger generation. But Jewish women were alienated from the Union of Equal Rights in 1912, when the organization supported nationalists' anti-Semitic boycott of Jewish businesses.

Eve's family may have been one of those from a small Polish town that broke with Jewish tradition to honor their daughter's desire for higher education. Consider two other Jewish female immigrants to the United States from Poland in the early twentieth century—Fannia Cohn and Rose Schneiderman—who became longtime labor union activists and supporters of women workers. Both came from families that provided their daughters more education than was typical, as did the Lithuanian family of women's labor activist Pauline Newman. A fourth Jewish émigré, Clara Lemlich, from Ukraine, fought her parents for an education and went on to become a dedicated US women's labor activist. Eve's access to an unusual education may have encouraged her own form of activism: making lesbian lovers visible in a book.

Three of these women's labor activists—Cohn, Schneiderman, and Newman—never married and had intimate, live-in relationships with women. Late in their long lives, as researchers began to ask Schneiderman and Newman new questions about how their private lives had supported their public activism, both women shut down the inquiries. The elderly Schneiderman, working on a memoir, fired an assistant for asking about her sexual life and later destroyed her personal letters to a longtime woman partner. After a young historian asked Newman if she and Schneiderman had been lovers, Newman stopped cooperating with such inquiries. She did, however, leave an archive containing revealing personal diaries and letters to another longtime woman intimate.

Keeping their private lives private allowed these women activists to maintain respected positions in the labor movement—in Schneiderman's case, as a nationally recognized spokesperson for working women. Their late-life refusal to publicly discuss their personal intimacies reflects their earlier strict segregation of private and public, discouraging close scrutiny of their home lives. Some of these women may have never have fully come to terms with their private norm-breaking.

In 1925, women in the United States could quietly live and love together without worrying that their intimacies would be branded as erotic and scandalous. But Eve's *Lesbian Love*, and the reports of her arrest and trials, threatened this private world with exposure—this loudmouth had gone public, tattling about women's sexual and affectional intimacies with women. The working-class, anarchist Eve had no respectable public reputation to uphold. Even when Eve's own intimacies floundered, she continued to publicly affirm her desire for women and participation in the lesbian community.

Another young Jewish working-class girl's burning desire for knowledge and a substantial education was described in *The Promised Land*, the autobiography of US émigré Mary Antin, published the year Eve first arrived stateside. Antin's book became a bestseller and its author an immigrant rights activist, so Eve was likely to have heard of Antin and her book. Eve and Antin had unusual histories in common, and Antin's book could have encouraged the book idea in Eve.

Eve's Polish hometown, Mława, produced five ambitious sisters from the Wolfe family who immigrated to the United States in the early twentieth century. One Wolfe sister became a sculptor and one a writer for radio, two wed university professors, and another, Adele, taught Yiddish at the Workmen's Circle School and married the well-known Yiddish writer Joseph Opatoshu.

Born five years before Eve in the Słupsk Forest near Mława, Joseph Opatoshu included a number of explicit references to Mława in his books (one was titled, in Yiddish, *Mława Stories*). Opatoshu's fiction dealt frankly with thieves, smugglers, anti-Semitism, pogroms, prostitutes and their patrons, and sexual yearning and betrayal. Eve was likely to have heard of and read his stories, providing another possible inspiration for her own writerly ambition.

In Chicago, Eve comanaged a tearoom called the Grey Cottage. Located at 10 East Chestnut Street in the Near North Side neighborhood of Towertown, it was first publicized in the *Chicago Tribune* on April 1, 1922. That notice promoted a lecture "before the Chicago literati" by leftist writer Konrad Bercovici, born in Romania, who won accolades for the quality of his stories, many about Romanies (Gypsies).

A month later the Cottage was advertised in the *Liberator* as

> Chicago's Greenwich Village Tea Room.
> Eve Adams and Ruth Norlander in Charge.

In the American Midwest in 1922, "Greenwich Village Tea Room" signi-fied high bohemia and a refuge for leftist rebels.

In Chicago's Towertown, as in New York's Village, groups of political radicals, writers, painters, intellectuals, and sexual and gender non-conformists joined their like-minded peers to form bohemian ghettos. In 1926, a song proclaimed, "Way down south in Greenwich Village, in this Freud and Jung and Brill age" visitors discovered "Modernist complexes, And the intermediate sexes—Fairyland's not far from Washington Square."

The Grey Cottage ad's no-nonsense "Eve Adams and Ruth Norlander in Charge" also provided a hint of welcome to same-sexers, specifically lesbians. It certainly conveyed Eve and Norlander's determination to maintain standards. Those standards were evoked with a critical eye in a memoir of the Grey Cottage written many years later by poet Ken-neth Rexroth. As a youth of sixteen in 1922, Rexroth hung out at the Cottage, and later recalled:

> The proprietresses were Ruth Norlander, a Cézannesque painter, and Eve Adams, who wore men's clothes and for years traveled about the country selling Mother Earth, The Masses, and other radical literary magazines. Eve and Ruth didn't serve meals. They started serving coffee and cake and pie and setups along about nine o'clock at night.

"Setups" provided patrons who brought their own alcohol with everything required for a nice mixed drink—a contravention of Prohibition, which had been the law of the land since 1920.

The Cottage was "much the most bohemian of the bohemian tea-rooms of the Chicago North Side," Rexroth remembered. He contrasted it with the Green Mask, where he read his poetry to jazz along with poets Maxwell Bodenheim and young Langston Hughes.

That Hughes is one of the few African Americans mentioned in this biography reflects the profound racial segregation of the 1920s United States, even among progressives. Race mixing was unusual and noteworthy. In New York, the adventurous Mabel Hampton, an African American lesbian, heard that Greenwich Village was "where other lesbians hung out" and traveled downtown from Harlem to look for them. The Black homosexual writer Richard Bruce Nugent made forays to the predominantly White, queer Village. The bisexual Black leftist writer Claude McKay walked the Village streets with *Liberator* editor Max Eastman and leftist writer Mike Gold. Some White Greenwich Village masqueraders traveled uptown to Harlem to the famous old Hamilton Lodge Ball. Among the attendees, said a Harlem newspaper in March 1926, were "masculine women and feminine men," "men of the class generally known as 'fairies,'" and many Bohemians from the Greenwich Village section." Presented by a "colored organization, there were many white people present and they danced with and among the colored people." The Ball drew huge crowds, said a later report, including "Homo-sexual women, attired in men's clothing," though "female impersonators" predominated.

In Chicago, the Mask was run by June Wiener, Kenneth Rexroth recalled. Wiener had "been a carnival performer, burlesque queen, chorus girl, and snake charmer. Her partner, Beryl Bolton, had been the leading lady of the famous old heavy Frank Keenan," an actor who played grave, somber roles.

The Mask attracted a show business crowd, including some of "the great female impersonators." Rexroth met impersonator Karyl Norman, who performed as "the Creole Fashion Plate" but was known to friends as "the Queer Old Chafing Dish."

Rexroth recalled the Grey Cottage as

> a great deal more intellectual and radical than the Green Mask. Both Ruth and Eve were convinced libertarians and part of the movement. They attracted few customers from show business and almost no one from the world of carnival, cheap vaudeville,

and burlesque . . . and none of the tough homosexuals who came into the Green Mask. Ruth and Eve were principled young women and they objected to such people. Their friends were cast more on the pattern of Edward Carpenter or Inez Milholland than lady prizefighters and drag queens and cheap burlesque girls.

Milholland was an American labor lawyer, journalist, and public advocate for women voting. Carpenter was, as mentioned earlier, the pioneering defender of "the Intermediate Sex."

Eve and Ruth's standards were probably not as snooty-strict as Rexroth suggested. Sociologist Nels Anderson, who did fieldwork on urban culture at the University of Chicago, observed a White male prostitute one night at the Cottage trying to pick up "a fine-looking Negro"—the one reference to interracial mixing at the Cottage. Anderson also watched a "well-dressed young fellow" wander through a crowd at the Cottage, talking "only with the men." This hustler reported that, for the going rate of two dollars, he would play "either the active or the passive role," and cater to "trade that might be one way or the other." He told Anderson, "You'd be surprised how many of these artists are fagging."

Rexroth recalled poet Maxwell Bodenheim frequenting the Cottage with his wife Minna, who worked as a secretary for the IWW. When Rexroth "first started to hang out" at the Cottage, Minna and their new baby were staying in the Cottage's back rooms.

When the first customer would come in the gate we would all run around and pull down the strings [clotheslines], take down the baby's diapers, fold them up and put them in the folding bed, fold the bed up and push it in the closet, and take the crib and push it, baby and all, out beyond the pantry into what had originally been a coalbin. Then the place was open for business. The windows had blue and white tied-and-dyed curtains, which Minna said looked like bed sheets from a Martian abortion. The tables and chairs were flimsy secondhand dining-nook furniture painted in bar-mirror cubism. The place was always short of food and always running out of coffee.

Eve testified that she was once arrested at the Cottage, "together with a few other people who had brought some liquor into the place. I was released on bond of fifty dollars and subsequently the case was dismissed. It was a liquor case."

The *Chicago Daily News* reported on November 17, 1922, that the police had broken up a "free-for-all fight" outside the Cottage and found "three young fellows inside around a bottle of wine." The "wagon has to go over there three times a week," a police sergeant complained to a judge, and the judge "wagged a warning finger" at Eve, threatening that if he received any more complaints against the Cottage, that "stronghold of Bohemia would be closed forever." The paper concluded, "The youths declared they had chanced upon the place by accident, and all denied knowledge of the bottle of wine."

The last ad discovered for the Cottage, dating to December 8, 1922, promised "Southern Cooking" (really?), "After Dinner Tea Until 1 a.m." (code for setups served till closing), and "Lectures Tues."

Though the Cottage existed for just about eight months, its reputation as a bohemian hangout spread three hundred miles to Dayton, Ohio, where a newspaper columnist reported that the men "who foregather at the Grey Cottage . . . sit with chins cupped in hands looking into somewhat overmade feminine eyes . . . [and] know the cosmic urge and express it in words amusingly febrile"—a veritable hetero heaven.

A friend of Ben Reitman's, George H. Snyder, shared "some very pleasant recollections of the discussions over which you presided at Eve Adams' Grey Cottage." Numerous Chicago newspaper ads for the tearoom refer to Reitman as "Chairman" of talks on "Vice and Virtue in the Village" (a talk by Reitman with "Hot Discussion"); Sensuality in American Fiction" (by Maxwell Bodenheim); "Young Chicago Poets" (by Samuel Putnam); "Morals Versus Art"; and "The Penalties of Love."

One unhappy visitor to the Cottage called it "that refuge of thwarted intellect" whose "artistic atmosphere" consisted of "1 unsanitary frame house; 4 pine tables; 4 uncomfortable benches; 4 candles; 1 disgruntled piano; 3 men with dirty fingernails, two of whom are drunk and swearing profusely; 1 soiled menu card and 1 frousy-haired proprietress who borrows cigarettes."

Another even unhappier Cottage visitor, Marie Cramer, called by the *Chicago Tribune* the "butterfly of Chicago's bohemian quarter," left a party at the Cottage, walked to a nearby drugstore, bought sleeping tablets, and tried to commit suicide over unrequited love for a male writer with whom at least two other women were in love.

While living in Chicago, Eve participated in Ben Reitman's family life, years later fondly recalling that she served as "Master of Ceremonies" at a birthday party for Reitman's son Brutus, when he was four or five (February 23, 1922 or 1923).

Reitman recalled that Eve visited Chicago's Dill Pickle Club, the hangout for bohemians, anarchists, radical labor agitators, and assorted dissenters founded by Jack Jones, a former organizer for the IWW. Over the years, speakers at the Pickle included Margaret Sanger on "Birth Control" (1916); the German homosexual emancipation leader Magnus Hirschfeld on "The Intermediate Sex" (1931); and "Miss Elizabeth Davis" reading "her paper from Lesbos" titled "Will Amazonic Women Usurp Men's Sphere?" (1931). Ben Reitman described Davis as "Queen of the Hoboes," a Wobbly (IWW member), Chicago soapbox speaker, and notorious heckler at the Dill Pickle Club, who hitchhiked to Florida, California, and New York and "always came back with more money than she had when she left"—she turned tricks, Reitman hinted.

Eve also befriended Eulalia Burke, who worked for the IWW. During and after World War I, many of Burke's comrades were jailed for antiwar activities. In the 1930s Burke would be employed as a correspondent for the Federated Press, a leftist news service, providing stories for union newspapers.

Eve's partner in the Grey Cottage, Ruth Norlander, was at the time using her married name. She was born Ruth Olson, in Minnesota, about 1889, so she was just about two years older than Eve.

A 1911 report by Emma Goldman in *Mother Earth* praised "the zeal of our Comrades," including Ruth Olson, whose anarchist organizing in Minneapolis had led to six well-attended talks and a group to carry on propaganda. Goldman added:

> Groups of young artists, living a careless Bohemian life, with
> ideals for breakfast, paints and brushes for luncheon, and sunsets

for supper, are the usual thing in Europe. But to find such a circle in America, living their ideals and caring naught for dollars and cents, is indeed a great event.

The spirit of this extraordinary little band in the Studio of Minneapolis is an American girl, though of foreign parentage, Ruth Olson. At her age the average American girl dreams only of a good match and nice clothes. Not so our young artist. Breezy and free as the western plains, she is yet deeply absorbed in the most serious problems of life. She is on familiar terms with the best literature of the world and passionately devoted to art.

With her are two other girls and several young men, the insurgents of the Minneapolis Art School, which they have left in protest against its lack of freedom. As Ruth justly says, all great art is Anarchism, the freedom of expression. These young rebels have their own studio where they paint, dream, plan, and live on sandwiches and spaghetti in the most exquisite spirit of mutual helpfulness and solidarity. With more of this idealism, the youth of America, too, may some day, even like the heroes of Russia, give life a different meaning than what it has with us to-day.

When Goldman arrived to lecture in Minneapolis in 1915, she "felt a little doubtful of success in that city because our good worker," Ruth Olson, "had been called out of town." Goldman diplomatically added that other competent comrades took over the organizing.

In Ben Reitman's essay "Homosexuality," in which he discussed Eve as "Olga," he also described Ruth Olson, calling her "Bernice." He remembered her as

a splendid young American girl who I first met in Minneapolis. She was a promising artist and the sketch she drew of me showed evidence of talent. She was an anarchist in her art and in her living. She married a splendid young American and had a beautiful daughter. She lived a happy sex life. She drifted to New York [actually Chicago] to join the art colony and there she met Olga and the other Lesbians and soon become one of them. She lost her husband and is now hoboing around the country as an itinerant artist. Her child is now fifteen, and let us hope she will be an improvement on her mother.

Reitman's description of Olson as "splendid" veered suddenly into hoping daughter would improve on mother. Reitman's conflicted feelings about lesbians kept asserting themselves.

Eve herself recalled Ruth Olson Norlander in a letter to Reitman more than a decade after her intimacy with Ruth had ended. Norlander was a "teacher and friend of mine, the one great friend. When some one would come along in the Grey Cottage days and complain to Ruth about me, she would say 'There is good and bad in all of us.'"

When Ruth's daughter Joan was "only 4," Eve recalled,

> I would take her out boat rowing. Most of the time she herself handled the oars at that tender age. I was the captain watching out, and suddenly she would exclaim, "Oh, Eve, look at the pink clouds." "Pink clouds!" What a beautiful child's imagination— now a grown-up serious young woman.

Eve recalled that on another fishing trip,

> when Joan was no more than 5, I would take her out in a bright sunny winter morning on the lake. We would chop a hole through the ice and get away with a dozen silver perch, and Joan would hold one fish pole and I another, and suddenly she would scream, "Eve, Eve, quick, I got a fish; quick, pull it out; it's jumping."

Eve helped little Joan but sometimes missed catching the fish.

In a letter to her former partner about a decade after they had parted, Eve called Ruth "my beloved," adding, "I love you Ruth and the memories of our beautiful friendship and love keeps me young."

7

Greenwich Village, Eve's Place, Trouble

By September 11, 1923, the thirty-two-year-old Eve had parted with Norlander and returned to New York City. There, "Eve Zlotchever" signed a US government declaration of intention to become a citizen. Eve swore "to renounce forever all allegiance and fidelity to any foreign prince, potentate, state, or sovereignty" and that she was "not an anarchist" or "polygamist." It was her intent "to become a citizen of the United States . . . and to permanently reside therein." She signed her declaration with her individual flourish.

Robert Edwards, editor of the *Quill*, a popular little magazine distributed in Greenwich Village, published the first reference to Eve in New York City, in November 1924. For the next three months, "Mr. Quill's Guide" to Village businesses listed "Eve and Ann's," at 129 MacDougal Street, as "open evenings," with "Books, Batik, Art, etc." Eve transferred her Grey Cottage experience to a Greenwich Village enterprise.

Eve also experimented with another way to make a small living. In an ad in the *Quill* in December 1924, "Eve Adams, Director," urged potential artists to "Study the Human Figure as it is" in a "Life Class" held at 64A West Ninth Street on Tuesday evenings for two hours. Eve was also probably the artists' model—work she had performed for Norlander, as she later recalled.

44

No. 325779

UNITED STATES OF AMERICA

DECLARATION OF INTENTION

☞ **Invalid for all purposes seven years after the date hereof**

State of New York, } ss: *landed as*
County of New York, } *Chawe*   In the Supreme Court of New York County.

I, *Eve Zlotchever*, aged *32* years,
occupation *commercial advertiser*, do declare on oath that my personal
description is: Color *white*, complexion *fair*, height *4* feet *11* inches,
weight *100* pounds, color of hair *brown*, color of eyes *brown*
other visible distinctive marks _____
I was born in *Poland Russia*
on the *31* day of *March*, anno Domini 1 *891*; I now reside
at *308 E. 19*, New York City, N. Y.
I emigrated to the United States of America from *Antwerp Belgium*
on the vessel *Vaderland*; my last
(If the alien arrived otherwise than by vessel, the character of conveyance or name of transportation company should be given.)
foreign residence was *Poland*; I am *not* married; the name
of my wife is _____; she was born at _____
and now resides at _____
It is my bona fide intention to renounce forever all allegiance and fidelity to any foreign
prince, potentate, state, or sovereignty, and particularly to *Republic of Poland
or present Gover. of Russia*, of whom I am now a subject;
I arrived at the port of *N. Y.*, in the
State of *N. Y.*, on or about the *4* day
of *June*, anno Domini 1 *912*; I am not an anarchist; I am not a
polygamist nor a believer in the practice of polygamy; and it is my intention in good faith
to become a citizen of the United States of America and to permanently reside therein:
SO HELP ME GOD.

Eve Zlotchever
(Original signature of declarant.)

Subscribed and sworn to before me in the office of the Clerk of said Court
at New York City, N. Y., this *11* day of *Sept.*
[SEAL]   anno Domini 19 *23*

JAMES A. DONEGAN

Clerk of the Supreme Court.
By *MADuppe*, Special Clerk.

Eve Zlotchever's signed "Declaration of Intention" to become a US citizen, 1923.

Eve reestablished herself as a participant in New York's bohemian and radical community. Ben Reitman listed Eve among the regular attendees at the "popular" parties held in a seven-room apartment on Christopher Street in Greenwich Village. The host was Edith Adams, whom Reitman recalled as "a good-natured, whole-hearted, full-fledged anarchist. With her the sky was the limit. She disregarded religion and conventionality and whooped it up for the Revolution."

Edith Adams's apartment was "a combination hobo boarding house, hobo college, hobohemian hangout, and certainly a training school for female roughneck anarchists." It "was crowded day and night," Reitman recalled. Visitors included writers, hobos, poets, sculptors, and propagandists like Elizabeth Gurley Flynn, labor organizer for the Industrial Workers of the World, founding member of the American Civil Liberties Union, feminist advocate for birth control and women's suffrage, and Communist. Other guests included Anna Strunsky Walling, socialist, journalist, and lecturer; Margaret Sanger, international feminist activist and founder of the US birth control movement; Romany Marie, legendary Greenwich Village tavern and restaurant owner; Eugene O'Neill, honored playwright; Sadakichi Hartmann, American art critic, novelist, poet, journalist, and friend of Walt Whitman; and Robert Edwards, the Greenwich Village eccentric who would play an influential role in Eve's life.

Early in February 1925, Eve published *Lesbian Love*, and in March the first listing for Eve's own "Eve's Hangout," 129 MacDougal Street, appeared in Mr. Quill's guide to Greenwich Village businesses, in the monthly edited by Robert Edwards.

Eve had registered her intent to apply for US citizenship in 1923 but had not taken further steps toward naturalization. So in 1925, when she planned a trip to visit her parents in Poland, she asked the US Immigration Service for a permit to leave the United States and return. But Eve was on federal officials' watch list of leftist activists, and they flagged her travel plans. On May 26, 1925, William Walter Husband at the US Immigration Service referred to "File No. 68309" re: "Eve Zlotchever alias Eve Adams" regarding the agency's intentions of "denying vise [visa] and requesting information in re entry into U.S."

Despite Husband's ominous note, on September 25, 1925, the US Immigration Service issued Eve return permit 74702. Did immigration officials issue Eve a permit to leave so that they could prosecute her on her return?

In the autumn of 1925, Eve took her trip. Her traveling out of the United States without obtaining naturalization papers left her without the legal protections guaranteed citizens. She was vulnerable to prosecution and deportation under the US Immigration Acts of 1917 and 1924—a vulnerability whose seriousness Eve did not apparently consider.

The 1924 immigration law preserved and expanded the provisions of the 1917 immigration law, which restricted the influx of persons convicted of a felony "or other crime or misdemeanor involving moral turpitude;" and persons who "believe in or advocate polygamy; anarchists, or persons who advocate the overthrow by force or violence of the Government." The law also prohibited persons from entering the United States "for the purpose of prostitution or for any other immoral purpose," and persons associated with "any house of prostitution or music or dance hall . . . frequented by prostitutes." A "female of the sexually immoral classes" who married an American citizen did not thereby gain citizenship.

The law restricted the immigration of "persons of constitutional psychopathic inferiority" and those "certified by the examining surgeon as being mentally or physically defective" in a way "which may affect the ability of such alien to earn a living." Immigration doctors examining arrivals had wide legal latitude for rejecting or accepting aliens. Reflecting rising White nationalist, anti-Catholic, anti-Jewish, anti-Polish, anti-Italian, anti-immigrant fervor, the Immigration Act of 1924 set quotas on immigrants from Eastern and Southern Europe (Chinese and Japanese immigrants were already excluded). Supporters of the law cited as its rationale the principles of eugenics, the junk racial science devoted to breeding "fit," "superior" humans.

Into this bigoted environment stepped Jay Fitzpatrick, the Greenwich Village artist who informed on Eve to US Immigration agents. On June 23, 1925, Fitzpatrick presented himself to Inspector W. W. Brown on Ellis Island. Fitzpatrick brought a letter of introduction from James C. Thomas, a lawyer in the New York City office of the US Justice Department (ironically, the first Black person appointed assistant US district attorney), suggesting that Thomas, Fitzpatrick, and immigration officials were collaborating against Eve.

Fitzpatrick swore that he had seen William Husband's May 26 letter asking for information about Eve's request for a reentry permit. The letter had come to Fitzpatrick's attention, he testified vaguely, "through information reaching me through a servant" in Eve's building. How Fitzpatrick came to see this official document was never clarified, and I've found no evidence documenting his collaboration with Husband himself.

The artist told his tale of Eve's "illicit relations," her efforts to seduce and corrupt "decent girls," and his own determination to "put a stop to it" by spurring the authorities to act. His active animosity toward Eve suggests that he was the unnamed informant whom policewoman Margaret Leonard encountered on her third venture into Eve's tearoom:

> A gentleman came to my table, very Bohemian-like and asked me if I knew Miss Adams. I said, "No," and he said, "I thought you didn't, you are not the type that frequents here often." He said, "Do you know that Miss Adams is a known Lesbian? I said, "What is a Lesbian?" He said, "It will take a long time to explain, if you will take a walk, I will explain it. I told him that it was late and he walked to the subway station with me and in the meanwhile I learned what he knew of Miss Adams.

What about Fitzpatrick might explain his rancor toward Eve, focused in particular on her alleged oral sex with girls and women? At thirty-seven in 1925, Fitzpatrick was unmarried. It's a cliché to suggest that sexual repression leads to jealous anger at others' erotic expression. But this cliché may begin to explain Fitzpatrick's animosity toward Eve.

In addition, in the fall of 1928 Fitzpatrick would move into an artist's studio on the top floor of 129 MacDougal Street, the building in which Eve's tearoom had formerly occupied the basement. This suggests a link between Eve's landlords and Fitzpatrick, who worked for several years as an appraiser and real estate broker.

In 1925, the owners of 129 MacDougal Street were Harold Gilmore Calhoun and his wife, Dorothy Donnell Calhoun, a prominent married couple who invested in Greenwich Village properties and were, perhaps, worried about the notoriety of Eve's tearoom depressing their building's value. One well-informed New York police source reported that a "matron of social prominence" had complained about Eve's tearoom to the city's district attorney, setting in motion the events that would lead to Eve's arrest. Did the Calhouns contact friends in the US government and ask them to initiate legal action against their notorious, noncitizen, radical lesbian tenant? Did Fitzpatrick plot with the Calhouns to inform immigration officials of Eve's lesbian activities?

In Greenwich Village, starting in 1920, a neighborhood property owners association supported "a clean-up campaign to establish the respectability of the district." The New York City police obliged them by launching raids to shut down lesbian and gay male bars, restaurants, and tearooms. In May 1925, *Variety* reported that a new police drive had closed "Greenwich Village 'joints' catering to the 'temperamental' element"—period slang for homosexuals—with the object of keeping "this class out of the neighborhood." Parents of "wayward 'boys'" had initiated police action, worried about their sons "frequenting the places without knowledge of the parents."

The Village, said *Variety* had once "boasted at least 20 of these resorts [for homosexuals], since reduced to three." Dolly Judge's Flower Pot, on Christopher Street, had closed "after the coppers stepped in and frightened away the mob." Two of the "most notorious" resorts were "snuffed out by the police several weeks ago, with one of the proprietors now serving a term in the penitentiary upon conviction of a disorderly house charge." The other proprietor had received a suspended sentence if she left town.

So the police raid on Eve's was but one incident in the history of police harassment of establishments welcoming to homosexuals. Such harassment produced the desired results for property owners. By 1927, the *Christian Science Monitor* would headline a story GREENWICH VILLAGE TOO COSTLY NOW FOR ARTISTS TO LIVE THERE: VALUES INCREASE SO THAT ONLY THOSE WHO CAN WRITE FLUENTLY IN CHECK BOOKS CAN AFFORD IT.

One of those apparently well-off enough to remain was Jay Fitzpatrick. The occupancy by Fitzpatrick, an "artist, sportsman, and big game hunter," of the top-floor studio at 129 MacDougal was described by an awe-struck, gullible Greenwich Village newspaper reporter:

> [Fitzpatrick] has fitted up his top floor studio in the most gorgeous manner possible, installing a magnificent pipe organ (hidden away) to charm visitors; having spent some years in Egypt, Arabia, Africa and vicinity he has built within his immense studio the most truly oriental retreat to be found anywhere in New York City.

Fitzpatrick was known as the "Ambassador of Greenwich Village," the paper claimed, and "his Egyptian rendezvous is a sight worth seeing." In this abode Fitzpatrick entertained "some of the 'higher-ups' of our city."

Fitzpatrick's higher-up hobnobbing was detailed in the *New York Times* on February 2, 1933, the day after he hosted a testimonial dinner at 129 MacDougal Street honoring Philip Elting, retiring as a federal customs collector for the Port of New York after many years. Fitzpatrick had been an associate of Elting's for ten of them. Other "notables" at Fitzpatrick's dinner included New York City's police commissioner, two US State Department officials, the assistant commissioner general of immigration, and Assistant Secretary of Labor William Husband, whose actions at the Immigration Service nearly a decade earlier had played an important role in determining Eve's fate.

Back then, in November 1925, Eve concluded a brief visit with her family in Poland and boarded the steamship *Minnekahda* in Boulogne-sur-Mer, France, to head back to the States. On November 28, she responded to a US Immigration Service questionnaire. Her "Race or people" was now "Polish," not "Hebrew" as she had answered in 1912. Jews were second-class citizens in Poland, Eve later complained bitterly to Ben Reitman, and she was determined not to be slighted as Jewish in the United States.

Eve's occupation was "Commercial Advertiser." Asked who paid for her passage, Eve answered "Self." She possessed fifty dollars—she wouldn't become a state charge. Eve had never been in a "prison or almshouse, or institution for the cure and treatment of insane, or supported by charity." Her "health, mental and physical," was "Good," and she wasn't "Deformed or crippled." Eve of course answered "No" when asked if she was a "polygamist" or "anarchist" or advocated the over-throw by force of the US government.

Most significantly, when Eve was asked "whether alien intends to return to the country whence he came?" she answered "No." She intended to become a citizen and stay in the United States "always."

On December 8, 1925, Eve landed at the port of New York. She had no hint that US immigration officials, the New York City police, and an artist were colluding against her—along with a certain local editor.

At Eve Adams's deportation hearing, the immigration inspector asked if she had "ever incurred the enmity of anyone" in Greenwich Village.

> EVE: No, except the editor of the *Quill* is an enemy of mine. He
> issued something filthy about my tearoom in his magazine
> just before I was arrested.
> INSPECTOR: What is his name and address?
> EVE: Robert Edwards, 146 MacDougal Street.

Robert Edwards.

Edwards, born in Buffalo, New York, in 1879, moved to the Village after graduating from Harvard and attending Chase Art School. He advertised himself as a jack-of-all-trades: a musical instrument maker, painter, poet, movie actor, singer, illustrator, and portrait photographer, and he who made "Restaurants Famous." Edwards edited the popular Greenwich Village magazine the *Quill* between June 1921 and June 1926, the month of Eve's arrest.

Edwards presented himself as an unconventional, arty type, but one openly and vehemently opposed to politically and sexually radical bohemians. In the June 1919 *Quill*, for example, Edwards praised "the great craving for ideas among the aristocracy" of "idle rich" who subscribed to the *Quill* and sought culture in the Village:

> Most people, at least the Radical element, do not understand the more or less idle rich; probably the very pleasantest people in the world are those rich who have got tired of being it. They, only, are more unconventional than the Bolsheviki. They are more intelligent than the Kike intellectuals. They are the best read and noblest of mankind.

In the *Quill* in 1922, Edwards responded to the jokey misandry of Dorothy Parker's "Men: A Hate Song," published in *Vanity Fair* in 1917. Edwards's jokey misogyny was evident in his poem's third stanza:

> I hate women—
> They frazzle my serenity:
> They are necessary without being important:
> They have so many ubiquitous admirers—
> Or none at all.
> They only understand the outward semblance of listening
> They think with their sex and see personal allusions in abstract discussion:
> They are always interrupting themselves:
> They are a foe to concentration.

In 1925 in the *Quill*, Edwards targeted Paul and Joe's, a long-established local restaurant popular with homosexual men and lesbians, calling it a "hangout of dainty elves and stern women." Caught up in the police purge of queer-friendly establishments, Paul and Joe's had moved out of the Village to Nineteenth Street the previous year. It would close altogether in 1927.

As a gender-bender, lesbian, woman, radical, and Jew, Eve fit five of Edwards's disparaged categories. In June 1926, the *Quill* included a list of Greenwich Village businesses, among them Eve's—with a new description:

> Eve's Hangout—129 Macdougal St., Where ladies prefer each other. Not very healthy for the she-adolescents nor comfortable for he-men.

129 MacDougal Street, 1940, the basement of which housed "Eve's Hangout" in 1926.

One he-man did indeed feel uncomfortable after wandering, unknowingly, into Eve's. David George Kin (birth name Plotkin) whose writing identifies him as an anti-homosexual heterosexual, recounted his adventure in his book *Women Without Men: True Stories of Lesbian Love in Greenwich Village*, published in 1958. Plotkin recalled

> "Eve's Place," a lesbian hangout on Macdougal Street which I mistook for a legitimate, respectable tea-room. The name had attracted me: I had visions of the Garden of Eden where I, a lonely Adam, could find solace in the company of a beautiful daughter of Eve.
>
> There were quite a few men in the dimly lit, sub-cellar tea-room, and it was only when one of them ogled me amorously that I realized I had blundered into the wrong place. Fairies and lesbians often mixed in the Village, both for social and strategic reasons.

Eve's Place "had a mixed clientele," Kin joked, "mixed in more ways than one"—another critique of somebody else's gender presentation.

Yet Kin's discomfort in Eve's did not stop many other he-men from dropping in and carousing. On the night of June 12, 1926, for example, a probably intoxicated John Rose Gildea, a twenty-five-year-old poet with a documented interest in women, entered Eve's crying, "Who'll put the first penny into this keg for the abolition of prohibition?" Another he-man, poet Maxwell Bodenheim, "threw in the first dime." Poet Henry Harrison, a married man about to replace Edwards as the editor of the *Quill*, "threw in four pennies."

Three days later, on June 15, several he-men participated in a packed poetry reading at Eve's. An impressionistic account of this raucous event by Harrison set the scene. It listed seven men participants and one woman, Harrison's wife. One he-man was poet Eli Siegel, later the founder and chief guru of Aesthetic Realism, a cult claiming that believers could convert from homosexuality to heterosexuality (conversion from hetero to homo was not discussed). Others were bohemian poet Maxwell Bodenheim, a Mr. Beltrome, a Mr. Zam, a Mr. Dave Rosenberg—and the outgoing editor of the *Quill*, Eve's nemesis Robert Edwards.

Harrison read several of his own poems and one by his wife, greeted by "silence" and then "applause." Mr. Beltrome read "a caustic long poem. Met with laughter and applause." Eli Siegel

> reads his bad verse. Very much noise. Mr. Bodenheim tries to quiet the audience by banging on the table with a boiler-factory hammer. Silence. The hammer goes on. So does Eli. The place is jammed.

Then, Eli Siegel said "he must read another poem."

> Everybody, nearly everybody yells for Eli to read. Nearly everybody yells for Eli not to read. Dignity is not present. . . . Finally, after a good deal of haggling, disorder, hammering, quarreling, Mr. Siegel reads the pretty poor poem. Triumph. Mr. Zam follows. Mr. Rosenberg follows—with a fair burlesque on Siegel's poetry.

Just two days after that boisterous poetry reading, on Thursday, June 17, 1926, Eve was arrested in her tearoom by policewoman Margaret M. Leonard, two other policewomen, and two policemen.

The fullest description of Eve's arrest was published in October 1926 by "Mrs. Mary Sullivan," the director of New York City's policewomen, who sent Leonard to entrap Eve (unnamed in the piece). "Drastic measures are being taken to clean New York of vicious moral perverts," wrote Sullivan in the bulletin of the International Association of Women Police. Sullivan had investigated a tearoom "advertised . . . as a 'hangout—where ladies prefer each other,'" her first false assertion. "Where ladies prefer each other" was not Eve's advertising slogan but the derogatory listing by Robert Edwards in the *Quill*.

After an "attractive policewoman" visited the tearoom several times, Sullivan wrote, the "proprietress" asked this woman to the theater the next day, and in a taxi had "embraced and caressed her." During intermission, the proprietress had "passed her business cards" to "pleasing young women" in the "women's lounge"—more sinister spin over Eve's efforts to promote her tearoom.

After the show, Sullivan went on, the policewoman had accompanied the proprietress to her room, received an autographed copy of her "vicious, immoral book," and been the object of the proprietress's attempted "indecent act." The policewoman arrested her victim for "disorderly conduct" and for publishing "obscene" literature.

Another account of Eve's arrest was published in 1931, five years after the event, in the sensation-mongering *Broadway Brevities*, "America's First National Tabloid Weekly." It included fanciful inventions, evidence that Eve and her arrest had become the stuff of urban legend. This is mythology worth recounting as such, and for a few possible grains of truth. The report displayed some sympathy for Eve, but it was a mixed, jaundiced sympathy for a "sharp-looking Jewess," "one of the Village's most interesting characters." Eve had run what was then called a "personality club," a place whose founder lent it a unique, positive, customer-attracting character:

> For two or three nights previous to the raid, two exceedingly fat women of no pulchritude, presented themselves at Eve's. Eve, never, to be exacting in her amours, immediately played court to both of them. There was nothing unambitious about Eve. About the fourth night one of the ladies was distressed, and inquired the whereabouts of the dressing-room. Eve indicated an upstairs room. The lady, unable to find the light, begged Eve to assist her. Ever helpful, Eve proceeded to accommodate her. When Eve reached the level of the dressing-room, the lady crudely pulled Eve inside, and blew a police whistle. Instantly, the halls swarmed with police, and screaming and cursing, the hoarse voices of the Lesbians assaulted the night air as the patrol wagon careened around the corner to bear a screaming, cursing Russian Jewish Lesbian off to durance vile.

In 1938, Mary Sullivan, in her second report on Eve's arrest, presented new, intriguing clues about Eve's surveillance. In her memoir, Sullivan recalled Eve (under the pseudonym "Billie") in a chapter on "Strange People"—"degenerates," a category that included child killers, child abusers, masochists, sadists, and "mashers" (men who harassed girls and women). The "woman with homosexual tendencies" was one of the "most difficult types of degenerate with which we have to deal," Sullivan began.

The before-mentioned "matron of social prominence" had complained to the district attorney about a tearoom where "indecent literature was on sale and the proprietress tried to entice girl students from a nearby college to visit the place after school hours." Eve's tearoom was across from New York University.

Sullivan assigned "one of our youngest policewomen" to investigate, and, this undercover agent, provided "with textbooks, a brief case, and a girlish tweed suit," appeared in the tearoom late one afternoon. A few minutes later Billie appeared, "a wild-looking individual, with cropped hair that was combed back in a ragged pompadour, and a mannish suit supplemented with a collar and tie." Billie talked with the decoy for over an hour, urging her to return the next evening.

Sullivan herself also cased the tearoom, recalling "dark beams overhead, pieces of shining pewter on the mantel, and andirons that might have dated from the American Revolution." She found Eve's "really attractive though a bit arty"—oddly positive words about a degenerates' den.

The supposed college student returned the next day to the "dimly lighted" tearoom, "received Billie's undivided attention," and was promised "an autographed copy of one of the improper books distributed on the premises." Billie asked the policewoman to a matinee and then supper the next day, and on the way to the theater kissed the undercover policewoman "so ardently in the taxi that several traffic policemen became interested, and the policewoman had to wave her handkerchief as a signal not to interfere." At intermission Billie passed her tearoom flyers to "all the young girls she saw." Returning to the tearoom that evening, the policewoman found an excuse to slip away and call headquarters, and patrol wagons soon "clanged up the street."

"The raid created tremendous excitement," said Sullivan, and in "a few minutes the narrow street was filled with hundreds of spectators. Officers went through the old rattletrap building very systematically, taking out a number of men who seemed mistaken as to their sex, along with Billie."

Billie was jailed and her tearoom closed, but Sullivan felt that Billie and "her ilk" should be "treated primarily as medical and psychiatric cases," though officials still had much to learn about how to treat "degenerates."

A few days after Eve's arrest, on June 23, 1926, *Variety* headlined:

"EVE'S TEA ROOM" BOSS
RAN INTO POLICEWOMAN
Result, Arrest on Two Charges
—Had Immoral Book Called
"Lesbian Love"

The second charge was "disorderly conduct"—Eve's "alleged sex attempt on the policewoman." Arraigned in the Tombs Court at the city prison in Lower Manhattan, Eve had pleaded not guilty to both charges. Unable to provide bail of $2,500 (about $37,000 today), she had been "remanded to the Jefferson Market Prison," in the middle of Greenwich Village, once next to today's Jefferson Market Library. The seemingly high bail suggests US immigration officials may have asked New York court officials to keep Eve locked up prior to trial.

Variety added, "Four young men and a young woman, of the student type, all friends of Miss Adams, were in court and accompanied her to jail after the arraignment." The names of Eve's friends are, sadly, lost to history.

After Eve's arrest she was fingerprinted and her prints photographed. The unique twirls on Eve's fingertips provide an oddly intimate image, an eerie artifact of her physical existence.

Eve Adams's fingerprints.

Eve's first trial, for "Indecent Book," was held in New York City's Court of Special Sessions, in the Building for Criminal Courts, on July 2, 1926, before a three-judge panel, Thomas J. Nolan presiding. No transcript was made of the trial, because Eve or her supporters would have had to pay for it.

The New York State "Obscene Prints" law under which Eve was charged declared criminal anyone who "sells, lends, gives away or shows," or even possesses, "any obscene, lewd, lascivious, filthy, indecent or disgusting book, magazine, pamphlet, newspaper, . . . picture, drawing, [or] photograph." This law was grouped among several provisions originally drafted by Anthony Comstock, head of the New York Society for the Suppression of Vice. These provisions also criminalized "Exposure of person," "Obscene play or exhibition," "Indecent placard or poster," and "Keeping disorderly houses." Also criminalized was any "instrument of indecent or immoral use"—that is, "any slot machine or other mechanical contrivance with moving pictures of nude or partly denuded female figures"—denuded male figures were not declared illegal. Obscene publications also included those "principally made up of criminal news, police reports, or accounts of criminal deeds, or pictures, or stories of deeds of bloodshed, lust or crime." (Shakespeare's *Hamlet* and *Macbeth* clearly fell under that definition, but no matter.)

The law never defined "obscene, lewd, lascivious, filthy, indecent or disgusting," the omission suggesting that every upstanding New York State citizen would readily agree on the meaning of those loaded terms. When a case came to trial, judges' and juries' decisions were guided by a British court's ruling in 1868, the case of *Regina v. Hicklin*. This defined obscene works as those that tended "to deprave and corrupt those whose minds are open to such influences, and into whose hands a publication of this sort may fall." This definition remained the standard in the United States until its rejection in 1933 in a case involving James Joyce's *Ulysses*.

Eve did not consider her book "immoral," the *New York Times* reported the day after her trial. Her book was "a scientific literary contribution," she argued, and it "related to her own experiences." The title of Eve's work was unprintable in the *Times*. Eve had told the arresting policewoman that she received five dollars for her book, the *Times* said, though Eve later testified that no copies had been sold. The crime of publishing an obscene book did not require the book to be sold, but the accusation of selling an obscene book made Eve's alleged crime sound more mercenary, more reprehensible. The police "had received many complaints about objectionable persons visiting" Eve's tearoom, the *Times* added.

A second story in *Variety*, subtitled "Boss of Eve's in Village Sold 'Dirty' Book—Man-Hater Besides," also reported Eve's "indecent book" trial. Eve, said the paper, "who assumes mannish clothes and is a self-confessed 'man-hater,'" had been investigated by the police for "complaints received concerning the actions of young girls." The arresting policewoman had testified that Eve "started to 'flirt'" with her, and "advised her to read" *Lesbian Love*. Eve was recommended for deportation, the paper added—the earliest reported public reference to the exile threatening Eve.

Despite Eve's defense of *Lesbian Love*, Judge Nolan found her guilty of authoring an "indecent book." Nolan then privately requested that the secretary of the New York State Parole Commission, Thomas R. Minnick, ask the commissioner of immigration at Ellis Island, the Honorable Benjamin M. Day, to "take up the matter of deporting" Eve after she had served her prison sentence—the first official communication to initiate Eve's deportation hearings.

Eve's "indecent book" was punishable according to law by a minimum of ten days in jail and a maximum of one year—the actual prison time to be decided by members of Minnick's Parole Commission. His group found that Eve's foul crime deserved the maximum one year. It was an unusually harsh outcome. Just six months earlier, on February 26, 1926, Esar Levine had been sentenced to three months in the workhouse—"a stiff sentence" for the crime at that time, according to a historian of erotica—for publishing and selling Frank Harris's memoir *My Life and* [Heterosexual] *Loves*. A legal scholar who analyzed the enforcement of New York obscenity laws in 1928 concluded, "Few types of books are considered sufficiently harmful to be tabooed." *Lesbian Love* was considered sufficiently harmful.

Eve received the especially harsh sentence for a reason: the Immigration Act of 1917 provided for the deportation of any alien sentenced to "one year or more" for a crime of "moral turpitude" committed within five years of entering the United States. Because Eve had left and returned to the States in 1925, immigration officials claimed that her one-year sentence for publishing an "indecent book" constituted "moral turpitude" and grounds for deportation. If Minnick's Parole Commission had not given Eve the maximum sentence, her deportation would not have been possible—yet the authorities had begun to plot her exile before the sentence was handed down. The moral turpitude did not reside with Eve but with Minnick, Judge Nolan, Commissioner Day, and the other officials (almost all men) who conspired against her.

On July 6, Eve was admitted to prison on Ellis Island to start her one-year term as prisoner 684 for publishing her "indecent book." The following day she was escorted out of prison temporarily to be tried for "disorderly conduct"—her alleged attempted sex with policewoman Margaret Leonard, the chief witness against her.

New York State's disorderly conduct law prohibited a wide list of vaguely defined acts: (1) acting offensively on any means of public transport, (2) eavesdropping, (3) using threatening, abusive, or insulting language, (4) loitering about "any public place soliciting men for the purpose of committing a crime against nature or other lewdness," and (5) acting "in such a manner as to annoy, disturb, interfere with, obstruct, or be offensive to others"—apparently the clause under which Eve was charged.

Judge Andrew Macrery presided over Eve's second trial in New York City's Magistrate's Court, and again, no transcript of this trial was made. Eve denied attempting sex with policewoman Leonard, and Judge Macrery found her guilty. In addition to Eve's earlier sentence of a year in prison for obscenity, served on Ellis Island, Eve was to serve six months in the women's penitentiary (or workhouse) in Manhattan's East River—named, with cruel irony, Welfare Island (today Roosevelt Island).

The policewoman whose testimony convicted Eve went on to a long and decorated career in New York's police department. In 1934, Margaret Leonard arrested a man who offered to provide her with an abortion. In 1935 she was promoted to detective and became the first woman appointed to the narcotics squad. As an undercover operative she helped to break up narcotics rings and received awards in 1941, 1949, and 1951 for her service as a pioneering woman professional.

Policewoman Margaret Leonard at retirement, 1954.

In 1954, Leonard, sixty-two, was nearing the required retirement age, and several news items recorded her transition to "fulltime housewife." In a story headed GRANNY QUITS THE FORCE: WARRED ON DOPE 19 YRS., the *Daily News* reported, "Mrs. Margaret Mabel Leonard is finally catching up with her house work." She loved "cleaning closets," and "I love my kitchen," she said. A photo showed Leonard at her stove. Leonard's retirement was not her idea. After twenty-nine years on the police force, "the only reason Mrs. Leonard retired, she said, was the age limit." Like many other women after World War II, Leonard was shifted from paid wage work into unpaid housework.

But in 1957, thirty-one years after Leonard served as decoy to entrap Eve, Leonard cast aside unpaid kitchen work to become a presumably paid technical adviser to the creators of *Decoy*, a trailblazing TV series about a woman cop, New York City policewoman Casey Jones, who goes undercover to fight crime and save many women crime victims.

On July 8, 1926, the *New York Times* reported Eve's guilty verdict for acting "insultingly" to policewoman Leonard. The exact conduct for which Eve was imprisoned remained unspecified in the *Times*.

The same day, a front-page newspaper report of Eve's trials and sentencing appeared in the *Journal* of Milwaukee, Wisconsin—890 miles west of the Manhattan crime scene. "Greenwich Village Eve," the "proprietress of Eve's tearoom," had been found guilty of unspecified "disorderly conduct" and "distributing 'Lesbian Love,' a book which she wrote." Eve's brave missive, launched from New York, landed in Wisconsin, asserting the existence of a derided eros.

On July 17, 1926, Eve's convictions for "selling an obscene book" and acting "insultingly" toward a policewoman made the front page of the *Tablet*, a Catholic newspaper in Brooklyn.

"Eve's Tea Room has had a cop present since the conviction of its proprietress," *Variety* reported on July 21, 1926. The story detailed police crackdowns on Greenwich Village businesses serving liquor. But *Variety*'s most sensational story about Eve appeared one week later. New York City district attorney Joab Banton and the police believed that Eve "was being financed as a procuress" for a RING OF RICH CULTISTS, as *Variety*'s headline proclaimed. The district attorney was "ferreting out a supposed ring of wealthy women cultists known to be operating" in Greenwich Village. Calling lesbians "cultists" demonized them; calling cultists "rich" played on class resentment.

A "report" by Eve's "probation officer," *Variety* alleged, questioned how Eve had been able to pay the rent on her tearoom and apartment—sinister financial backing was insinuated. Investigators had asked Eve who was financing her, but she had "refused to talk." Eve's determination not to inform on others is several times documented; *Variety* presented it as a sign of her cupidity: "Reports around the Village are . . . that she has stood pat throughout the proceedings upon promise to be taken care of liberally."

The disparagement continued. Shortly before launching her tearoom, *Variety* reported, Eve "had effected masculine attire and became a regular at the various resorts catering to 'temperamentals' [homosexuals] until a police drive chased most out of the district." When Eve opened her tearoom on MacDougal Street, the paper alleged, she had given "the tip-off of what kind of a joint it was through placarding the main entrance with a sign which read 'Men are admitted but not welcome.'"

That sign probably never existed—it is not mentioned in any other source, and its words suspiciously promote the stereotype of lesbians as "man-haters." The same stereotype inspired Robert Edwards's earlier description of Eve's tearoom as uncomfortable for "he-men," probably the inspiration for *Variety*'s supposed sign.

The opening of Eve's place, *Variety* continued, had brought a "big parade of close-cropped women in mannish attire on again in the Village. In most cases the mannish ladies were accompanied by girls of tender years and some not so tender." *Variety* actively circulated folklore in which butch lesbians preyed on young girls. Eve sometimes rounded up "unattached females" and invited them to her tearoom, the paper reported, again giving Eve's solicitation of tearoom customers an evil spin.

Before Eve's conviction, said the report, "someone had seemingly assured a coterie of her disciples that she would be liberated on a reasonable doubt certificate. A gala celebration had been set at the tea room to welcome back their 'martyr.'" But Eve did not show up at the planned party: "She dined at Blackwell's Island instead." (Blackwell's had been renamed Welfare Island five years earlier—fact-checking was not *Variety*'s strength.) A "cop was on hand to see that the celebration to the absent honored guest was kept within bounds of decency," and this agent of the state had stayed on duty at the tearoom ever since.

When Eve was sentenced, *Variety* said, it was recommended that, when set free, she "be deported back to Poland."

Despite these few reports of Eve's arrest, trials, and imprisonment, the mainstream press paid her and her book little attention. This contrasts with the wide publicity received a couple of years later by Radclyffe Hall and *The Well of Loneliness*. In 1928, Hall's novel, a plea for the toleration of sexual inverts featuring a lesbian protagonist, would be published in the United States. The following year the New York City police seized copies, charging that it violated the state's obscene literature law. A judge upheld the charges, but his ruling was overturned.

One more publication sheds light on Robert Edwards' role in Eve's fate. The month after her conviction, in July 1926, Edwards published an essay in the *Quill* about his "ideal of the Village," which had been realized "before the advent of the dirty radicals." His ideal was "a clean

Bohemia: a place where young people . . . could work uninterrupted by senseless and outworn conventions." He gloated, "Now that radicalism is dead, the Village . . . seems to be returning to that happy state."

> Now that Freud is forgotten, Bolshevism and its practical expression in "free love" have passed out, the Village may have time to get something done.

Edwards, known in the past, he said, as "the ruler" of Village bohemians, had suffered "the smart of the continuous abuse . . . we received from press, pulpit and police." But he "did not see how I could protest effectively." The "police would only add to the odium and wreck the wrong people."

> Many times I longed to cast all radicals, Freudians, androgynes, narcissi, etc., into the bottomless pit, but I was no Mussolini nor Savanarola [sic].

Benito Mussolini, leader of Italy's National Fascist Party, had solidified his dictatorship a year earlier. Girolamo Savonarola, the puritan fanatic, had done the same in Florence, Italy, 432 years earlier. Bringing up unflattering comparisons only to deny them, Edwards certainly seems defensive. Had he heard angry rumors circulating in the Village about his role in Eve's arrest?

Rumors that Edwards had sparked Eve's troubles were documented five years later in *Broadway Brevities*. In 1931, *Brevities* referred to Edwards's "crusade against lesbians in the Village." The scandal sheet wasn't suddenly protesting lesbians' persecution. Its charge against Edwards was only one sensational angle of a story that also took aim at "dikes and fags." Edwards, the paper charged, had "turned the eyes of the ever-willing public on Eve's notorious hang-out. Bobby's exposure led to a police crusade to clean up the Village that shortly threw its net over Eve."

Two months after Eve's arrest, Edwards took another swipe at the now incarcerated Eve. He responded in the *Quill* to an earlier essay by George Bogner, who complained that he found "no romance in the Village," only "homely women." Bogner lamented the Village's "emasculated men, unfeminine women, an absence of decorum, a flaunting [*sic*] of convention . . . everything but romance." In response, Edwards imagined "none but the emasculate staying to endure Mr. Bogner. Perhaps he strayed into Eve's. Certainly the idea that Village girls are homely is the distortion of the bilious eye."

But Eve's was no more. In September 1926, the *Quill* reported, "Eve's place is gone; and Anne Martin's has succeeded it." The publication's new editor, Henry Harrison, approved: "What a contrast! The walls are now richly decorated with painting by Archie Sinclair, and good paintings they are too."

The following December, Harrison's *Quill* published a symposium on "The Greatest Need Now in the Sex Life of the Nation." Participants asked how society could "assure normal lives" to women when "the great majority seldom if ever have their sex needs fully gratified." Authors discussed interracial marriage, birth control, prostitution, and the "drastic punishments" handed out to "abnormal men and women . . . of the intermediate sex." Eve haunted this symposium, an unnamed ghost.

Five months later Robert Edwards was still taking potshots at his old targets: "The Quill will be excellent when all such tiresome things as prostitutes, androgynes, gynanders, sex and vers libre are cut out."

How Eve experienced her year and a half in prison was suggested by the few words a fellow prisoner, pickpocket May English, wrote to their mutual friend Ben Reitman: "They led her a hell of a life" (English reported the words of a prison matron). Eve "got along a little better after I left," English had heard. She added, "My heart ached for her many times, and I tried to be kind to her."

8

Eve Adams's *Lesbian Love*

THE BOOK THAT LANDED EVE a long prison term was short, just seventy-two pages. Published in February 1925 with the help of a friend whose name she refused to reveal, it was "Printed for private circulation only," and "limited to 150 copies"—words meant to assure potential smut prosecutors that its small influence was not worth their bother.

Lesbian Love was published under the pseudonym "Evelyn Addams," suggesting that Eve knew it was risky for a noncitizen immigrant to claim authorship of such a title, or even to publish such a book at all. Just how risky Eve seems not to have realized. She also probably wanted to ensure that US relatives did not get wind of this particular author debut. Adopting a pseudonym, Eve also followed a common practice of Jewish writers in the late Russian Empire from which she had emerged.

The text's typos and imperfect English indicate that no one edited Eve's book for her, defects that prove to be blessings, for *Lesbian Love* preserves Eve's own voice. Divided into nine short sections, Eve's book refers either in passing or in a bit more detail to twenty-five women given fictional names. One more woman goes unnamed. All the characters were based on women Eve had known, she later testified.

While traveling around the United States, Eve was said by Ben Reitman to have met and romanced a quantity of ladies. Comanaging a queer-friendly Chicago tearoom had also introduced Eve to a large cast of characters, reflected in her book's socially, though not racially, varied group of women. Casing the competition in New York before opening her tearoom, Eve probably visited other tearooms and lesbian and gay male bars, observing how these establishments functioned as welcoming spaces to meet and greet.

Characters closely resembling Eve appear several times, under several names, in different sections of *Lesbian Love*. Eve's book contains more autobiography than is immediately apparent. Little Jimmie, for example, is "a working girl, of the Russian Inteligentzia," who labors in a "ladies waist shop" (a women's clothing factory) and belongs to the associated union. Eve's contribution to a little-known working-class lesbian history remains one of her book's most valuable accomplishments.

When Jimmie's union rents a hotel in the Pennsylvania countryside, she takes a vacation from the "sweat-shop" and finds other vacationers "just to her fancy—they were all radicals, and were free and unconventional in their attire and speech."

This Pennsylvania hotel was probably Unity House in Bushkill, Pennsylvania, bought in 1919 by two locals of New York City's Dress and Waistmakers Union, an organization of radical Jewish women garment workers. Working-class solidarity would be enhanced, these women had insisted to doubting male comrades, if members had a country place to dance.

Eve's knowing narrator says, "Little did Jimmie know of herself; little she knew of the masculine spark within her—all she did know was that she felt far more comfortable in boyish clothes. She could run better, climb trees better, and feel unhampered in every action." That "masculine spark," a male-typed yearning to run, climb, pursue boys' activities, wear boys' clothes, and feel free, is a repeated, poignant theme in several early narratives of persons born female who rejected restrictive feminine norms. Although Jimmie is the only girl at the hotel "enjoying this boyish freedom," no one frowns on her clothes or activity, so she is "perfectly at ease." Elsewhere, it seems, Jimmie's clothes and swagger have elicited criticism.

At a Saturday-night party, Jimmie requests a dance with "a little girl, with a youthful, eternal spring-like form." The girl smiles and asks Jimmie to lead—which Jimmie loves to do when dancing with girls. As they waltz, Jimmie realizes that her partner is "not a working girl" but "a dancer"—suggesting a vast divide between proletarian and professional. Jimmie's partner—Bellina, it turns out—dances with a Philadelphia ballet company.

The two young women quickly develop an intense romantic friendship, and three weeks later Jimmie is invited to Bellina's family home in Philadelphia. There Jimmie announces that she has left New York City and is going out west: "I am going to work my way circulating for a publication" (like Eve's work selling radical papers).

That night, after Jimmie joins Bellina in bed, "they nestled closer, silently kissing each other, and finally discarded their night clothes, against the rules of mother." Discarding the rules of the mother with her clothes nicely describes the unfolding of Eve's libido. A romantic friendship between two women leads here to sex, as it did in a number of bed-sharing intimacies between women (and between men).

"Neither of them knew what it was all about," Eve's narrator reports. "All they felt was that they were happy, and lay awake until dawn in each other's embrace."

Another character, Miki, a "wanderer" (like Eve), is "unconscious of her feelings toward her own sex," but knows she likes "boy's clothes" (like Little Jimmie and Eve). On a Labor Day trip to the country, Miki dresses in "a Palm Beach suit . . . borrowed from a boy-friend before leaving the city, white silk sport shirt, windsor tie, tan silk stockings, and white canvas oxfords." (Eve wore what look like white canvas oxfords in her 1925 family photo.)

In the country Miki meets a "charming," "feminine" woman, Dr. M., dressed in "tailored blouse with a white turn-over collar, [and] a blue silk windsor tie." Dr. M. may well have been based on Dr. Marie Equi, the anarchist lesbian doctor in Portland, Oregon, photographed with a "white turn-over collar."

When the two Windsor tie wearers meet again a year later, Dr. M. asks Miki to her home, and that night offers Miki "tender, intoxicating soft kisses . . . trembling . . . thrills . . . joy . . . ecstacy [*sic*] . . . sweet pain" (ellipses in the original). Miki, the wanderer, wanders off the next day.

Eve briefly describes other women:

Jonnie is rich. She is rumored to have "kept six women in her apartment and treated them all royally!!!!" She is "tall, broad-shouldered," and wears "strictly tailored clothes."

Ann comes from the West Coast, "has a charming deep voice, almost masculine," and is "able to impersonate a hundred other voices." Ann is a "magnet" but is "only attracted to virgins," and "she always leaves behind some victim."

Sara, "a slip of a girl," plays the piano in a little "tearoom" ran by May ("known as Jim"). One night, after the single male customer leaves, "six or seven girls" exclaim, "Thank God," and Sara plays a song she had composed for Ann:

> I love to have parties with you,
> I know it's not right, but I do!

The song, said to be "full of passion," depicts "two nude girls, in ecstacy [sic] of love, fondling and kissing each others [sic] breasts, murmuring words of love"—the sex in Eve's book is never more explicit than this.

The women's relief when the single male leaves suggests these women's strong desire for lesbian-only space and documents tension between lesbians and men over such space. But that tension does not signal lesbians' animosity to all men, as the man-hating lesbian stereotype suggested. In addition to the male friend who lends Miki a suit, another male friend brings dinner to a lesbian waiting anxiously for a date. Homosexual and heterosexual men are documented as visiting and enjoying Eve's tearooms.

Another woman, Willie, is about eighteen, "loves to wear knickers, collar and tie," and "rolls her shirt sleeves up with a pair of garters." Willie loves it when the "all feminine" Jackie tells her she looks "masculine." This couple "really believe they can have a baby, and talk of getting married to each other"—perhaps the earliest published account of the desire for lesbian parenting and marriage.

Sulamith (called Sol) is a "Goddess" with a "body made carefully by the hand of God. A model of His great heavenly work." Eve's palling around with militant atheists hadn't destroyed her belief in a Divine Maker.

Dawn, a "little Jewish girl with a mass of golden hair," had "struggled ... in old and new Russia." Dawn "has worshiped" Sol, but Sol loves Ann. So Dawn, who "has a tender heart, caused by much suffering and disappointments [*sic*]," settled for a "beautiful friendship" with Sol and Ann.

Juliet (called Julius) and Ottilia (called Otto) meet in a café and make a date to meet again in Otto's room. There, Julius makes love to Otto ("I shall kiss each part of your body separately, and you must let me!"). Then Julius rushes off. She calls Otto the next day saying that she can't see Otto again. Her previously unmentioned "wife" has "found out where she was the night before." And so "another page of sorrow was added to Otto's life."

Another pair, Sammie and Dottie, "got tired of back stage life and applause," and in a basement, in a famous neighborhood, open the Flowery Tea Pot. The two are often written up in the press "and are generally called 'husband and wife.'" Some lesbians in Eve's circle simply decreed themselves married.

Dottie is "pretty and stout" and always "wears sleeveless gowns, while Sammie 'struts' her tightly fitting tailored suit, and the inevitable attached collar and tie, which means so much in the life of a Lesbian." The butch Sammie is the "Lesbian"; the sexuality of Sammie's femme partner remains unnamed.

Eve had absorbed her culture's idea of the "sexually inverted woman." The "true," "real lesbian" was the masculine lesbian—"the mythic, mannish lesbian" named by anthropologist Esther Newton. The femme partner was lesbian by association. If the "real lesbian" was assertive and masculine, the "real woman" was retiring and feminine—a Victorian ideal. Eve had not yet adopted the new idea of a "female homosexual"—a woman defined by her female object of desire, not by her gender-nonconforming behavior.

Sex-typed clothes, mentioned throughout Eve's sketches, play an important role in defining these women as masculine or feminine, just as gendered costume played this role in the lives of Paris-based American lesbians in the 1920s—and, indeed, in the lives of most of us who inhabit a gender-polarized society.

The Flowery Tea Pot, reports the narrator, becomes a popular rendezvous "for loving couples of the same sex, mostly the fair sex." There, women lovers "look into each other's eyes" and "lonely ones" sway together "to the melody of a dreamy waltz."

Eve named the Flowery Tea Pot after the Flower Pot, the "gay" place in Greenwich Village operated by Dolly Judge. The Flowery Tea Pot may also stand in for the Green Mask, located in a Chicago basement and hosted by a former actress and retired burlesque queen.

Another character, Diana Thornton, has "wicked blue eyes" and is the "perfect woman vampire of women." She discards ex-lovers and says of the distraught notes they write, "My maid reads them first, and if she finds something worth while, I let her read a passage or two for me."

Diana honeymoons in hotels in New York, Miami, Bermuda, and Paris, and expresses her class privilege without embarrassment: "What I want, I take." Her current lover, Gracia, is just as beautiful as Diana, and "just as fickle." But their "honey-moon" is lasting unusually long, Eve warns, "so girls, your chance is gone!!"

Eve dedicates *Lesbian Love* "to my last love Rosalie O. N.," who has the same initials as Ruth Olson Norlander, Eve's former romantic partner in Chicago. Perhaps Rosalie was a secret lover's name for Ruth, or her friends' nickname.

One section of Eve's book references her onetime lover. In this story, a woman named Sorine meets a romantic partner, Irene. The details suggest that Sorine is Ruth Norlander, and that Irene is Jean Cambpell, the partner who apparently supplanted Eve. Sorine, like Ruth, grew up in the Midwest among Norwegians and is a visual artist who also loves music and books. At twenty-four, Eve writes, Sorine conceived a "child of passion," a girl. The married Norlander, when she was in her late twenties, gave birth to her daughter, Joan.

Described in *Lesbian Love* by an "unhappy disciple" (Eve's stand-in) Sorine is a teacher of ascetic ideals with a small following: "She tried to awaken a good and beautiful soul in each one that crossed her path"— "the body meant nothing."

But one night in Chicago, the austere Sorine unaccountably puts on a costume and attends an "Arabian Nights Ball." At this masquer-ade a dancer appears, "a girl dressed in a tramp's outfit, half under the influence of liquor. She began to entertain the crowd by exhibiting a negro dance with all the life and passion there is in the black race."

Eve certainly meant to praise the vitality of African American dancers, but the terms of her appreciation included the stereotyping of a whole people. The same racial typecasting was evident in 1928, in a New York reviewer's praise of "negro dancing" revealing the "simplicity and deep earthiness of their race's hold on life." Loaded language about "the black race" was not uncommon in the mid-1920s, even in comments by White progressives meant to be complimentary. At the time, a number of White leftists and liberals supported eugenics. The dire perils of this pseudoscience only became fully clear after revelations about how Nazi race theory was actualized in Nazi race practice.

Praising a special talent of the "black race," Eve positioned herself as White, a judgment questioned by the era's guardians of American racial purity, who categorized immigrant "races." Members of the Polish "race" were "darker than the Lithuanians" but "lighter than the average Russian," declared that official US government document *Dictionary of Races or Peoples* in 1911. It added, "In temperament" Poles "are more high-strung than are the most of their neighbors." Distinguishing Jews from Poles (rather than Jewish Poles from Catholic Poles), the report added, "These are the races now coming in greatest numbers to America"—except for Italians, another disparaged group. A secretary of the federal commission that published this race dictionary was Eve's future antagonist William Walter Husband.

Eve's story continued with her narrator grudgingly admitting of the girl in the tramp's outfit, "She danced well, we must say." The dancer is Irene, "twenty-three and boyish, with big, penetrating grey-green eyes." Irene, we learn, was brought up in an orphanage and then "took to the freedom of the road," so performing as a tramp replicates her own experience. Irene is "boisterous" and tough. Irene "has fought men and can prove it by several scars on her body." When Irene "wanted something she got it, and when anything or anybody was in her way, she brushed them aside with ease"—apparently the complaint of a superseded lover.

Sorine and Irene now live "far away in the North-West, by a lake," in a little cottage once owned by Sorine's husband. Sorine, Eve's narrator reports, was earlier "the dominating type, the master." But present-day

Sorine "no more rules. That mystic power of hers is gone. She is silent and obeys Irene. She no more preaches love for all humanity, and even expresses hate to a few, for Irene has influenced her."

The narrator adds, "At moments you may see that [Sorine's] soul is tortured by some thought of the beautiful past, but soon it is forgotten." Eve's text again expresses the jaundiced judgment of a jilted lover.

My guess is that Eve, as a proud new author, sent Ruth Norlander a copy of *Lesbian Love*, oblivious to the degree of unconscious rancor it expressed. If Norlander and Cambpell read this story, they must have found it a profoundly hostile critique of their relationship and their character. Eve later complained that Norlander failed to answer her letters, a failure that seems explained by Eve's overt profession of love for Norlander and covert expression of hostility.

The revelations about Eve in *Lesbian Love* continued in her last section, "How I Found Myself." The most psychologically astute and accomplished section of her book, it provides the first glimpse we have of her early life and blossoming sexuality. The "I" of the title and the account's details, of a young wanderer traveling for her work, clearly identify the unnamed narrator as Eve. This younger Eve is nineteen years old, Eve's age in 1910, two years before she immigrated from Poland.

As the section begins, the young nomad is traveling into the countryside by herself. Stopping for a while at a house in "a colony of artists," she is already seeking out the arty set. She also seeks peace, for "I was so tired of people and talk with which I had to contend in the business world." Taking off her traveling clothes, the young woman puts on "overalls and sandals" and looks "very much like a boy of fourteen." Transmuting her sex with her clothes, this girl-boy opens herself to new possibilities.

Several days later, at the end of an evening walk, the narrator arrives back at the dark, empty house, and hears "a soft woman's voice" say, "Hello, little boy." Spying a woman on the porch rocker, the narrator explains, "I am not a boy." To which the woman responds, "in a sweet voice," "I know you are not a boy, but just a lonely little girl; won't you sit down on my lap?"

Feeling "a bit lonely that night," the narrator has long "dreamed of a woman's motherly caresses." She is also tired of the men she meets through her work, who, on social occasions, "all tried to caress me." She exonerates these men of offense—they did not try "to take advantage of me in any way" and were "gentle and very comradely." She explains, "They were of a radical type, and sincere men, they admired my work and helped me, but to one thing, even a kiss, I could not respond. I did not know why."

The passing reference to "radical," "comradely" male friends suggests that in Poland as a teenager, Eve was already active in anarchist, socialist, or radical labor politics. Eve's quick acquittal of her male associates for what now sound like persistent unwanted advances may be explained by her support for their political cause. The problem, she seems to have concluded, was her lack of interest, not the repeated caresses.

On the dark porch, the narrator yields to the woman's suggestion, sits on her lap, and talks with her for a long time. She feels "gentle, tender caresses" and is "happy." Invited to the woman's room, the narrator notes her age, "thirty, or a little younger." The narrator says, simply, "I remained with her."

Held tight in the woman's arms, it seems to the narrator "as if our nude bodies melted into one, and a sudden fear came over me that I could never be separated from her body." The narrator whispers her fear to her partner, and the woman smiles and calms her anxiety with "kisses and ardent caresses." The narrator recalls this "beautiful" experience as one of the "most significant events of my life." That Eve dared to recount the experience in a book likely to be labeled "obscene" and criminal is evidence of how important it was to her.

Eve's inaugural, desire-defining intimacy with a woman apparently occurred before her immigration to the States. So her adventurous New World journey can be seen as her search for a place to explore her desire. Eve joined those few early immigrants to America known to have fled their countries due to the discovery of their same-sex intimacies, or to investigate where desire might lead—one of those "huddled masses yearning to breathe free," or just yearning.

Eve's book expressed the same ardent desire—to speak publicly of her love, and to see herself, her friends, and their eros represented in the world. Her title, "Lesbian Love," boldly named a love "among Christians not to be named," affirming the diversity of human affection. Her book's introduction quoted lines from nineteenth-century English poet Algernon Swinburne's "Sapphics," including its reference to "Lesbians kissing across their smitten / Lutes, with lips more sweet than the sound of lute-strings." Persons identified as lesbians loved, kissed, and connected in Eve's book.

That old word—*lesbian*—had by the early twentieth century begun to signify the emerging personal and group identity of women-loving, women-lusting women. For women such as Eve, same-sex desire and acts had coalesced into a sense of self shared by a community. As the earliest portrait of the lesbian community released in the United States by a lesbian author, Eve's book was groundbreaking. Its publication constituted a unique, major event in lesbian resistance history, a political protest against invisibility, making Eve one of the country's first lesbian justice activists.

Eve's book presents empathetic, sometimes critical, sometimes amused snapshots of a large cast of characters drawn from life. Writing about them, Eve was acting as a learn-by-doing sociologist, an investigative reporter in training, a self-made anthropologist. A participant observer, Eve created the first, informal US lesbian community study.

The community study, as a literary and sociological genre, appealed to other pioneering authors who reported on networks of sex- and gender-variant people emerging in cities in the late nineteenth and early twentieth centuries. A lesbian, Mildred Berryman, in an unpublished study, described a group of twenty-three lesbians and nine homosexual men in Salt Lake City in the 1920s and '30s, based on interviews and personal observations. *The Stone Wall*, the 1930 autobiography of Ruth Fuller Field (writing as "Mary Casal"), depicted a community of professional woman-loving women, along with the author's life story.

In 1914, a Russian Jewish activist, Shloyme Rapoport, claimed for Jews "the honorific title of People of the Book." He referred to the written Torah, but he also pointed to a tradition by which Jews had passed down stories of their "long, difficult, and tragic historical lives"—an oral tradition that he and other Jewish ethnographers were starting to record in books. As an apprentice ethnographer, Eve participated in this long Jewish tradition but detailed little-known lesbian lives.

Eve boldly defended lesbians and their loves. While doctors diagnosed "sexual inversion" in women, the inverse of a supposedly natural, proper, biologically ordained female sexuality, Eve responded that women like her were ordained by God or nature with an inverted sexual desire natural to them. When religious leaders condemned "immoral, indecent" acts of women with women, Eve countered by judging these intimacies right and good. Eve affirmed an inverted ethic, celebrating what others condemned.

But Eve's affirming of lesbian "love" also promoted a particular romantic story that traditionally defined the basic worth of a person—especially a woman—in relation to a romantic partner. This old "love story" denied many women's sense of their own, independent value. When Eve publicly affirmed "lesbian love" as good, she did so using the same vocabulary by which many women were traditionally disqualified. She adopted a "reverse discourse" that continues in the twenty-first century; it's much more "respectable" to affirm homosexual love than homosexual sex! That old "love" talk was one powerful weapon available to Eve, and she wielded it with courage.

The phrase "lesbian love"—referring to sexual affection—had first begun to circulate in US medical journals in the late nineteenth century. In 1883, Dr. P. M. Wise, assistant physician at the Willard (NY) Asylum for the Chronic Insane, published "A Case of Sexual Perversion," describing as "Lesbian love" the intimacy between inmate Joseph (born Lucy Ann) Lobdell and wife Marie Perry. In 1892, the *New York Medical Record* reported the "Lesbian Love and Murder" of Freda Ward by Alice Mitchell, in Memphis, Tennessee. And in "Sexual Perversion," a paper on presented to the Medico-Legal Society in 1895, Dr. William Lee Howard cited the case of Mrs. W., thirty, "a chronic masturbator" who had "practiced lesbian love at boarding school."

In the late 1920s and '30s "lesbian love" began to move slowly out of doctor discourse into US newspaper reports of crimes and scandals, and reviews of novels and plays, usually accompanied by disparaging judgments. Surprising are a few positive references to "lesbian love" appearing in papers outside the main urban centers often stereotyped as culturally "backward." Novels played a major role in asserting the existence of this love, a fact of lesbian resistance history noted early on by pioneering lesbian bibliographers.

For instance, in 1935 a reviewer in the *Lexington (KY) Leader* explained that Claudine, the narrator of the new novel *The Indulgent Husband* by French writer Colette, "finds herself falling into Lesbian love with an acquaintance, Rezi, who is even readier than she to pursue an unnatural affair." But Claudine, quoted from the novel, refutes the reviewer's "unnatural" judgment:

> "If I take a lover without loving him, but merely because I know it is a wicked thing to do—well, that's unnatural. But if I take a lover—someone I really love or whom I merely desire—I am obeying a sound law of nature and I consider myself the most virtuous of women."

Though Claudine finally returns to her husband, the reviewer pointed out "nothing she says indicates that she has rid herself finally of her Lesbian impulses."

> Indeed, she seems to accept that emotional distortion as if it were almost normal, as if it were not out of the ordinary for woman to be attracted by woman. That assumption is one of the qualities of this book that will bewilder readers in America, if not on the continent where abnormalities are popularly supposed to be commoner.

In 1935, Rowena Wilson Tobias, writing in the *Evening Post* (Charleston, South Carolina) reviewed Gale Wilhelm's novel *We Too Are Drifting*. Tobias called it a "frank and unashamed Lesbian love story," presented with a "tender hand," making it "a thing of beauty and artistic distinction," on a par with or even better than Radclyffe Hall's *The Well of Loneliness* or Lillian Helman's play *The Children's Hour*. Wilhelm's central character, Jan Morales, stood forth, said Tobias, "shining and unashamed. There can be no question of morally condemning Jan: she is a serenely calm personality too big and powerful to be judged by any ordinary standards."

The idea of love and lust between women was moving inch by half inch, step by tiny step, into the mainstream media, forging a new moral universe that included diverse forms of human sexual affection. This was not, to be sure, an uninterrupted movement toward greater and greater

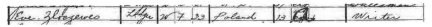

"Eve Zloczewes," identified as a "Writer" in the New York State Census, June 1, 1925.

acceptance. There were hemmings and hawings, steps forward and back, progress and retreats, failures of love, suicides, murders, renunciations, and voluminous negations by doctors and psychologists. It would be many, many years before Eve's brave, troublemaking title publicly signified an equal eros. But she had paved the way.

When Eve was asked her occupation by a New York State census taker on June 1, 1925, she declared "writer." This bold scribe had indeed written herself and her friends into history.

9

The Bureaucrats Attack

THREE MONTHS AFTER EVE'S IMPRISONMENT, on October 7, 1926, the case for her deportation was outlined by V. F. Jankovski, in a letter to Henry H. Curran, commissioner of immigration for the Port of New York, Ellis Island. Jankovski, an inspector in the commissioner's office, probably could not have initiated Eve's deportation hearings on his own authority but was likely following orders from boss Curran, who may have been following orders from Assistant Secretary of Labor William Husband or Harry E. Hull, the US commissioner general of immigration.

Jankovski alleged that Eve, by attacking policewoman Margaret Leonard, "attempted to commit the crime of conenlinguism [*sic*], which is a form of prostitution, and which she practiced on the unsuspecting young women visiting her tea room in the Greenwich Village section of the city." Linking Eve's "conenlinguism" with "prostitution," this federal official maintained that Eve's "disorderly conduct" was a crime justifying deportation. Jay Fitzpatrick's earlier, fraudulent sworn testimony acquired greater import with each repetition.

Jankovski also relayed false information reported by Eve's probation officer: "The alien had served terms in prison in Chicago and was deported from there." An "Eve Adams" and an "Evelyn Adams" had been arrested in Chicago on "disorderly conduct" charges, reported Jankovski, though no records had been found of either's deportation. He presented no evidence that those common names referred to Eve.

But on the basis of this alleged conduct, Jankovski recommended that officials initiate a hearing to consider Eve's removal. How Jankovski, a Jewish émigré from Lithuania in 1892, felt about Eve's possible deportation is unknown.

The second call for deportation hearings was made two days later by Inspector W. W. Brown, who had earlier received Jay Fitzpatrick's sworn testimony against Eve. Eve's crimes—practicing prostitution, managing a house of prostitution, and entering the United States for an "immoral purpose"—were proved, he said, by her guilty verdicts for "Disorderly Conduct" and publishing "an indecent book."

The document actually initiating Eve's deportation hearings was the one signed by William Husband on October 16, 1926.

At Eve's first deportation hearing, at the women's penitentiary on Welfare Island on November 24, she asked that her lawyer be present, and the proceedings were postponed. Eve had a right to be represented by counsel—at her own expense.

At Eve's second hearing on November 30, she was represented by Manuel Rosenblum of the firm Turk & Eilperin. Rosenblum was twenty-three and just six months into his law practice, so it's unlikely that he had any experience that would have prepared him to defend a radical activist, alien immigrant, gender-bending woman found guilty of attempted lesbian sex and publishing an obscene lesbian book. In addition, Rosenblum's ethical standards were later shown to be questionable. Seventeen years after defending Eve, in 1943, he was suspended from practicing law for three years for "professional misconduct" after several clients accused him of overcharging, passing bad checks, and other financial misdeeds.

The prosecutor at Eve's hearing, Inspector Thomas J. Conry, focused on the alleged evidence of Eve's crimes. He read aloud Jay Fitzpatrick's testimony about watching Eve having oral sex with young girls, and Eve called it false.

Conry asked, "Did anybody ever accuse you of practicing Sapphism?"

"What is that?" Eve responded, pretending she didn't understand. (She had included that bit of Swinburne's "Sapphics" at the start of *Lesbian Love*.) Eve then acknowledged, "I know," adding, "I always worked hard for a living"—a bumbling attempt to reject the prosecutor's linking of Sapphism with prostitution. Eve stressed that she had "never practiced prostitution in all my life" and never managed a house of prostitution. "I have always lived in my own furnished room and alone." As a "Dweller in Furnished Rooms," Eve represented a recognized 1920s "Urban Type."

Eve protested her obscenity verdict as "unjust," saying, "If the court had read my book carefully I would never have received such a sentence." She added, "There is a play now going on in New York City called *The Captive*, and it bears exactly upon the same subject. The author of the play was not molested, and I can't see why I should be singled out and sentenced to imprisonment for writing my book."

The Captive, a melodrama by Édouard Bourdet, translated from the French, was described by a *New York Times* critic as

> the tragedy of a young woman, well-bred and of good family, who falls into a twisted relationship with another woman. For nearly half the play this loathsome possibility, never mentioned, scarcely hinted at, hangs over the drama like a black pall, a prescience of impending doom.

Though her fiancé marries the heroine "to save her from her warped infatuation," just before the final curtain, the young woman "succumbs." Depicting a wife succumbing to an irresistible lesbian, the play summed up hetero men's anxieties about their own attractiveness to women. This play opened at the Empire Theatre, on Broadway, on September 29, 1926, and ran for 160 performances.

A week after *The Captive* opened, George Jean Nathan, a famous theater critic, condemned other reviewers' failure to name the play's "Lesbian motif." Instead of telling "without evasion" what the play was about, "the timorous gentlemen hem and haw." Nathan found it difficult to understand "what there is to offend any newspaper reader in the word Lesbian." Yet reviews seemed to be written for the *Christian Herald* or the *Youth's Companion*.

Three months after Eve's reference to *The Captive*, at the end of February 1927, the play was shut down by the police, under the same New York "indecency" law used against Eve. A section of this law criminalized

"Obscene, indecent, immoral or impure" productions, shows that "would tend to the corruption of the morals of youth or others." That year this law was expanded to criminalize theater owners whose houses presented plays dealing with "sex degeneracy, or sex perversion." The night *The Captive* closed, newsboys peddling papers at the theater reportedly shouted, "Lesbian Show . . . off the Boards," defeating vice crusaders' attempt to keep the word *lesbian* out of public circulation.

Bemoaning the success of Broadway plays dealing with "Lesbian love," novelist Upton Sinclair worried in the Communist *Daily Worker* near the end of 1927, "Drama courses in young ladies' finishing schools in New York now include an explanation of what this is and how it works."

The Captive was not the first play on Broadway to deal with lesbianism. In 1921, Harry Wagstaff Gribble's *March Hares* had flirted with a barely coded homosexuality, both female and male. Janet, annoyed by her live-in fiancé Geoffrey's lack of amorous interest over a three-year engagement, brings home Claudia. So Geoffrey brings home Fuller, "a very normal young man," according to the stage directions. But Fuller arrives carrying a "handbag," a knowing reference to Oscar Wilde's *The Importance of Being Ernest*, and a homo-alert for audience members in on secret sex signals. Hetero sex-love triumphs in the end, of course, but the titillating homo hints were clearly intentional. They extended even to the printed edition of the play, titled *March Hares (The Temperamentalists)*—the homosexuals.

As Eve's deportation hearing continued, Inspector Conry asked her, "Were you ever afflicted with a venereal disease?"

> EVE: No.
> CONRY: Are you a drug addict?
> EVE: I don't even drink liquor. I only smoke a cigarette.

Cigarette companies had convinced women by 1926 that smoking was sophisticated, satisfying, and healthy.

> CONRY: What effects have you?
> EVE: Two suitcases and clothes at 38 Washington Square.

Asked why she should not be deported, Eve answered:

> I have always conducted myself properly in this country, I love this country with my whole heart and soul, and I have made application for my final papers. I want to become a citizen. If I am deported, my life is ruined, because Poland is a poor country and my parents are dependent upon me for their support.

Eve's uncle Alexander Migdall bravely testified, in person, in her defense. A Hartford, Connecticut, businessman and naturalized citizen with a wife and two children, the owner of an amusement park and the manufacturer of candy vending machines, he "surely did not believe" Eve guilty of prostitution. About Eve's book, he said,

> I never read it, and from what I have heard there is nothing to it. I vouch that any book written by my niece, according to her good character and reputation, could never be immoral. I have kept in close touch with her ever since she came to the United States, and she has always worked hard for a living in one capacity or another.

If Eve was released after her prison term, Migdall agreed that he would pay her requested bond of $1,000 (nearly $15,000 today). Eve's lawyers tried repeatedly to offer bond to delay her deportation after her prison term, to buy her time to further contest her removal or even stay it.

At Eve's third deportation hearing, on February 10, 1927, Inspector Conry asked her, "How long did you reside at 38 Washington Square West, first floor?" Eve immediately answered, "Off and on for about two years," for thirty-five dollars a month.

> CONRY: Were you in the habit of receiving women guests in that room?
> EVE: I had friends call in my room.
> CONRY: Males or females?
> EVE: Female sometimes, male other times.

Conry asked Eve to cite her friends' names, and Eve answered, "No, I don't care to."

Conry asked if women telephoned Eve to meet her alone in her room. Eve replied, "I had a telephone and people called up to make an appointment to come to dinner or so, the same as anyone else."

Conry inquired, "Did you have two steady customers who would telephone you, make an appointment with you, to be alone in your room . . . ?" He asked whether these women paid five or ten dollars to "have immoral relations with you."

> EVE: No, it is not true.
> CONRY: Have you ever managed a house of prostitution?
> EVE: No.

Policewoman Leonard testified to attending the theater with Eve on June 12, then going to Eve's room, where she alleged Eve tried to sexually assault her. She rejected Eve's attempt, Leonard said, adding: "We went to the tearoom. . . ."

Leonard then added, "We put her under arrest about eight thirty," implying that Eve was arrested on June 12. All other evidence, including Leonard's later testimony, documented Eve's arrest on June 17. This mistake in a major witness's testimony raised questions about the truth and accuracy of other details. But neither Eve's lawyer nor Eve caught Leonard's mistake.

Eve's lawyer asked Leonard how long she had been a policewoman when she arrested Eve. "About seven months," she answered.

Having established Leonard's inexperience, Rosenblum continued: "You say that when you came into the tearoom you saw a lot of degenerates there." Leonard had described "degenerates of male and female type." Rosenblum asked, "How do you know they are degenerates?"

> LEONARD: My own judgment.
> ROSENBLUM: How are you qualified to state they are degenerates?
> LEONARD: They were the type.
> ROSENBLUM: By gazing upon these people you form your conclu-
> sions by their dress and manner that they were degenerates?

Eve's inexperienced lawyer fed the prosecution's witness details that made her testimony more credible. Leonard simply answered, "Yes."

ROSENBLUM: "You never charged that defendant, Miss Adams, with being a prostitute?"

LEONARD: No.

ROSENBLUM: You never paid her anything at all, did you?

LEONARD: No, what would I give her money for?

With that, Leonard contradicted federal officials' attempt to picture Eve as money-grubbing whore.

ROSENBLUM: To your knowledge, did she commit an act of prostitution with you?

LEONARD: Thrusting me on the bed.

Inspector Conry asked Eve about any cash transactions with Leonard:

EVE: When we got to the theater, I wanted to pay the bill and she said, "I will pay it." At dinner, the bill was three dollars and we both paid. Miss Leonard attempted to pay and I said, "Let us each pay our own share," and we did pay our share. . . .

CONRY: What did you sell your book for?

EVE: It wasn't for sale, I just distributed it to friends.

CONRY: What did it cost you to print it and edit it?

EVE: Somebody took it over and published it, a friend.

CONRY: Who was the friend?

EVE: I don't care to give it.

CONRY: While you were in Europe in December 1925, did you try to bring several young girls to the United States with you for an immoral purpose?

EVE: No.

CONRY: Do you recall having lived one time at the Rice Hotel, 755 North Dearborn Street, Chicago?

EVE: Yes. . . .

CONRY: Mr. Kingbell, the proprietor of the Rice Hotel, was interviewed by an immigration inspector recently and he testified that . . . he was compelled to request you to leave the hotel because you were receiving men in your room.

EVE: No, it is false. You cannot receive men in a room in a hotel
even if you want to. . . . I never had any unpleasantness in
that hotel.

The following day, February 11, Inspector Conry summarized Eve's
hearings, concluding that the prostitution charge had *not* been sustained.
But the indecent book charge was proven, he claimed. He recommended
"the alien's deportation to her native country at the expense of the
steamship company bringing her hither."

On April 12, a memo by Ellis Island commissioner Byron Uhl labeled
Eve a "High Deportable"—referencing, apparently, an Immigration Service hierarchy of deportables. But two weeks later, on April 21 and 25,
two immigration officials recommended that Eve's case be reopened.
Their hearts had not suddenly been moved by Eve's plight; the officials
worried that an earlier federal appeals court decision might free Eve.
In that 1925 case, a judge had freed an alien facing deportation after
officials cited one crime as the basis for deportation but then provided
evidence of a different crime. Acting Commissioner George J. Harris
declared that evidence supporting Eve's indecency conviction and details
regarding the length of her sentence had to be added to the record, and
Eve and her lawyer had a right to inspect that record.

Eve's last hearing was convened a month later, on May 23, 1927,
with Inspector Thomas Conry again presiding. Ruth Tashman, a secretary, transcribed the testimony, becoming the second female state
employee named in the proceedings after policewoman Leonard.

When the hearings began, Eve's lawyer was absent, and Inspector
Conry asked her, "Have you heard from your attorney recently?"

EVE: No.
CONRY: You are advised that he was notified to appear here at
the reopening of this case . . . but he has failed to appear. Are
you prepared to answer any questions without the presence
of your attorney?
EVE: I would rather wait until he appears before answering any
questions, because I do not know what it is all about. I was
unaware of the fact that he was to appear today.

> CONRY: You are advised that ample opportunity has been given
> your attorney to appear here if he still represents you, and
> the hearing will be proceeded with.

The hearing that would decide Eve's future proceeded without her counsel present—due process be damned. Conry later claimed that Eve's lawyer had asked for that particular hearing date—suggesting that he was to blame for not appearing. His guilt apparently extended to Eve.

Eve had served six months for attempted sex with policewoman Leonard, Conry said, and had begun a prison term for her "indecent book." Eve interrupted: "Yes, they call it an indecent book, [but] if they read it carefully, nothing indecent would be found in it."

The inspector then held up a slender volume and asked:

> CONRY: Is this the book referred to of which you are the author,
> *Lesbian Love . . . ?*
> EVE: Yes.

A copy of Eve's book was made part of the record.

Conry asked when Eve had published the book, and she answered, "Early in 1925," in February, before leaving for Europe. She had "left a few copies in Paris," she volunteered. "I just distributed it to a few friends."

> CONRY: What printer published the book for you?
> EVE: I forget, I don't remember."

Conry asked Eve to respond to the legal grounds for her deportation, her convictions for "Disorderly Conduct," an "indecent book," and "moral turpitude"—a response requiring legal knowledge. She did her best:

> I never realized that the book was indecent. If I did, I would have
> never written it or printed it. I merely wrote this group of short
> stories of people I observed in my travels out west and mostly in
> Greenwich Village. I merely intended to describe these characters
> with the aim to help them, to show them the truth of their lives.

All the persons portrayed in *Lesbian Love*, Eve said, "are living characters of today, living their lives unaware that they are committing a crime
against the law of man. . . ."

Eve denied knowing it was "against a law and against this country"
to tell "the truth of these so-called unfortunate people, whom God chose
to create different, and willed them to be so." If she had known of such
a law, Eve explained,

> I would not have told the truth, I would have kept silent about
> it. If one chooses to read the book with a pure mind, he will find
> nothing vulgar, vile, or obscene or indecent. I could not write
> anything indecent if I wanted to, for my life and associates in
> this country have been at all times with people of high culture,
> such as prominent artists and writers, etc.
>
> I also want to make one statement, that I am more than
> positive that the judge of Special Sessions, Magistrate Nolan,
> has not read my book through prejudice, because I believe his
> religion does not allow him to read this book. He was merely
> told it was indecent, and this heavy sentence was imposed on
> me unjustly and unfairly.

Judge Nolan's Catholicism prevented him from reading her purported
porn, Eve implied.

Eve also compared her sentence to another recently in the news:

> The play *Sex* on Broadway was pronounced indecent, and Miss
> Mae West, the producer and star artist, who was charged with . . .
> writing the play, and also acting indecent, came here to the work-
> house for ten days and a $500 fine. I have met Miss West here and
> I have spoken to her, and she wondered why I was given such a
> heavy sentence on a similar charge, practically the same. All I can
> say is I did not have a proper attorney and I was misunderstood.

When Mae West's three-act comedy/drama about a working-class
prostitute—titled, provocatively, *Sex*—opened at Daly's 63rd Street Theatre on April 26, 1926, the *Daily Mirror* called it "Offensive . . . Plucked
from Garbage Can, Destined to Sewer." The *New Yorker* spoke of "street

sweepings." The *Herald Tribune* said, "We were shown not sex but lust—stark, naked lust." Yet *Sex* was a long-running hit, giving 375 performances before closing in March 1927. But the following month, on April 19, West was sentenced to ten days in prison for her supposedly immoral play. She spent one night in the Jefferson Market Prison and was then sent to the Welfare Island workhouse. She served her time as a prisoner with special privileges and was freed two days early for "good behavior."

Mae West did not mention Eve when she published an account of her time in the women's workhouse. And on first thought, the meeting between the bawdy, earthy, funny West and the serious, arty, high-minded Eve boggles the brain. But on second thought, Eve Adams and Mae West were both daring rebel women imprisoned for their media activism, for pushing the boundaries of what could be said publicly about sex. (West's account of her imprisonment also pushed the day's race boundaries, describing an "intelligent" matron, "a colored woman, with a gold badge, in charge," and including empathetic portraits of several "colored" women prisoners.)

It was at this point that Eve pleaded to remain in the United States and become a citizen. In addition to affirming that "I learned to love this country with heart and soul," the patriot Eve requested "a chance to prove myself a worthy resident of this country," a "chance to become a citizen of this country, America, which I feel it is my home." She stressed, "I think in the language of this country."

She added:

> I never committed an act of prostitution in any manner since I have lived in this country or accepted money in any form for any immoral act. If any person made such a charge against me, I beg that I be confronted with the witness and I am most certain that no such witness could be found, for I am not guilty and I never was of any such act.

Inspector Conry asked Eve:

> Upon completion of your present sentence, and if the Government should decide to place you on parole for a year, do you believe your uncle could supply a bond of $1,000?

Eve: Yes, he visits me and is interested in me.

Ten Days
and *Five Hundred Dollars*

(Reading time: 14 minutes.)

[Editor's Note: The author of this article was the author and star of the play, Sex, which was suppressed after eleven months on Broadway. Miss West and the two producers of the show were sentenced to pay fines and serve short terms in jail. She describes here her experiences as an inmate of the Workhouse on Welfare Island.]

The Experiences of a Broadway Star in Jail

An Article by

MAE WEST

A photographic study of Miss West *(above)* and *(at left)* the Women's Prison, Welfare Island, New York City.

Picture by Arthur Little

Mae West, author and star of Sex, as she appeared in an enforced sequel — ten days in jail.

THE court attendant leaned toward me and said, "Are you feeling all right, Miss West?"

I replied, "Quite all right."

He then escorted me to the side of the courtroom, through a cage effect, then out a door, where there were a few steps leading down to another door. That door was opened and two gentlemen who stood there said, "Right this way, Miss West."

They were most courteous; they didn't want anything to happen to me before I got to Welfare Island, I guess. I was ushered into a waiting-room. There was a colored woman, with a gold badge, in charge.

She was intelligent, and during my half-hour wait I talked with her, asking her various questions regarding Welfare Island. I like to know something about a place I intend to visit.

Later, five women were brought into the room: the first a woman who appeared to be about sixty-five years of age. Later I learned she was only forty-one. She claimed she had lived alone for twenty years, without relatives or friends, and she was homeless and penniless. Her clothes were old and torn.

Number Two was a colored woman wearing a black knitted cap. She had a very deep voice and a comedy personality, with Bert Williams' speech and delivery. I learned later that she was a drug addict.

Number Three was a tall, thin woman with gray hair, a spinster type, with a long scar on the side of her face and her neck that looked like a burn. She spoke with an Irish accent. She had been sentenced to ten days for stealing a $3.89 pair of shoes at a sale.

Number Four was another colored woman— rather young and healthy-looking. I was surprised to learn that she also was a drug addict.

Number Five was the most pitiful of all: a woman about five feet five, weighing not more than seventy pounds. Her eyes were sunken; her face long and narrow—just skin and bones. A drug addict in the last stages of tuberculosis; a mental and physical wreck. The poor unfortunate! God—what a sight!

They all sat before me—one, two, three, four, five! All glaring at me; all filthy, dirty,

tattered and torn; human derelicts.

I forgot about myself completely. I forgot I was there. Their eyes were upon me with a sort of bewildered expression, and I sat there waiting for something to happen: for one of them to speak to me; for one of them to move. But not a word, not a move.

Then the door opened and a husky fellow in a driver's cap and a dark blue flannel shirt appeared. He was quite good-looking, and seemed to be in his early twenties. He pulled a few wise cracks to the five women and then took them out.

I figured that he must be the man with the Little Black Wagon.

He talked to another chap a few moments, and then added, "I'm coming back; I'm going to make a special trip." He glanced at me.

I was alone now with Mrs. Campbell, the colored woman with the gold badge. By this time all the newspaper reporters and photographers and various other people flocked outside the door. I could hear their voices crying:

[CONTINUED ON NEXT PAGE]

Essay by Mae West about her workhouse experience in *Liberty* (Rye, NY), August 20, 1927.

Alexander Migdall continued to actively support his niece in her plight, despite the criminal charges against her.

Eve's final hearing ended. On June 3, Inspector Conry wrote to Ellis Island commissioner of immigration Henry H. Curran, asserting that the indecent book charge had been sustained and again recommending Eve's deportation. "However," Conry added, "the Bureau's attention is respectfully invited to the plea made by the alien"—Eve's fervent, eloquent request to become a citizen.

Eve's senior lawyer, Harold L. Turk, wrote Commissioner General Harry Hull on June 13, requesting that Eve receive "probation for a year" and pointing out her uncle's promise to furnish bond. The following day, Howard Allen, of the Immigration Service's review board, determined that the prostitution charges against Eve "are not supported by any evidence whatever." But the "indecent book" moral turpitude charges had been sustained, he concluded, and the alien should be deported. Freeing Eve on bond was rejected.

Commissioner General Hull responded to Eve's attorney on June 22. Her case had been "very carefully considered," and "the alien's removal from the United States will be effected as soon as possible after she is released from prison."

Five months later, on November 26, as Eve's prison term was ending, her lawyers begged the commissioner general to delay her deportation. Howard Allen of the review board responded to them on December 3: "No adequate grounds for such exceptional consideration are given." He recommended immediate deportation.

Four days later, Harry Hull advised Eve's lawyers: a stay of deportation was denied. Commissioner Hull also answered Congressman Thomas H. Cullen, who had that day phoned Hull's assistant supporting Eve's lawyers' request for a deportation stay. He emphasized to the congressman that Eve had been found guilty of publishing an indecent book: "It is entitled 'Lesbian Love,' and is pictorially characterized in a highly suggestive manner. It is clearly a book of filth."

The alleged filthy pictures were four drawings included in Eve's original edition of *Lesbian Love*. None of these drawings of nude, seminude, and clothed women were sexually explicit, and none of them were more overtly sexual than illustrations in books then openly published in the

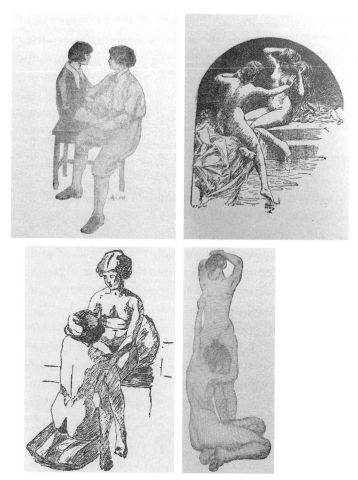

Illustrations from *Lesbian Love*, pp. 5, 20, 44, and 65 (171, 176, 185, and 195 in appendix).

United States. The drawings in the book, Eve had said at her deportation hearing, "can be exhibited in any place—nothing immoral about them."

Hull also told Congressman Cullen that Eve had been found guilty of "inducing girls to visit her apartment for immoral purposes," repeating Jay Fitzpatrick's unproven allegation that "on one occasion, at least, she was seen having illicit relations with another person of her own sex. This she denied, but . . . admitted that she often took boys and girls to her room." Hull considered Eve's testimony inconclusive, but when considered in relation to the whole record, it was "highly significant as to the immoral character of the alien." Eve would be deported.

On the same day, J. Friedman of the Immigration Bureau's warrant division in DC composed a memo to his boss. When the record of Eve's hearings had reached him that morning, "the envelope attached to the file did not contain the exhibit—a book entitled 'Lesbian Love.'"

George J. Harris, now the assistant commissioner general, responded that same day: "The book in question was in the envelope when the record was placed in the file box on my desk." Harris instructed Friedman "to institute a search for the book as it appears to be an important exhibit." But Eve's book had vanished, to be enjoyed in private by one of the US government officials who was expelling her for that book.

That same fateful day, December 7, 1927, an Ellis Island clerk executed a "Warrant for Deportation" on "Zlotczewer, Chawa Eva, Alias Adams Evelyn," sending her away from her adopted country on the steamship *Polonia*.

Daily News columnist Jack Kenny that day published MODERN EVE ADAMS DRIVEN FROM EDEN. Immigration authorities had deported Eve, "not on a ship manned by members of her own sex as her intensely feminine theories would command, but on the first boat sailing." Eve's problems had started "because of the lax way" she "picked her friends"—specifically, when she "started to hang out with policewomen." Her Mac-Dougal Street tearoom was supposedly organized "much after the style of a Quaker meeting house. The men kept to one room, the women in another, but its smooth-tongued steady customers were anything but Quakers." ("Smooth-tongued" again expressed anxious concern about lesbians' reputed skill at oral sex.)

The "lithe authoress," Kenny went on, had stopped in New York City "to introduce to it her new, well let's call it a book." The district attorney's investigation had revealed that "something had to be done." So the "youngest, slimmest policewoman in the city, disguised as a Columbia student, visited 'Eve's tearoom,' and Eve took her to her arms and heart. It was all three huskier policewomen could do to separate them." The young policewoman "had obtained an autographed copy of Eve's book, which contained things about Eve that Adam never dreamed of."

Eve had moved into an apartment at 38 Washington Square, the columnist claimed, vacated by her "intimate friend" the deported Emma Goldman, and there entertained Alexander Berkman, the "one-time radical lawyer." Berkman was not a lawyer; no evidence locates Goldman at 38 Washington Square.

Mixing truths, half-truths, outright falsehoods, and barely coded references to sex between women, Kenny called "red-headed Eve" one of "Greenwich Village's most famous and ultra-modern maids." Kenny's "ultra-modern" stood in for the unspeakable "lesbian." Kenny's jokey words painted Eve, the antimodernist, social-realist writer, as a specifically modern maid, even representing her as an iconic modernist—the newest of the new women. Just as the lady with a torch in New York Harbor personified liberty, so Kenny's Eve personified modernity.

Kenny's tale was one of several that presented Eve as antiheroine of Greenwich Village legend. His campy words belied the dead serious, nativist politics that justified Eve's deportation and its life-changing consequences.

The next day, a second but unsigned *Daily News* item summed up Eve's deportation: "The morals of this 35-year-old woman . . . were not what this country demands from a would-be citizen."

Hearing that Eve had been "transported," Eve's former prison mate, May English, thought that she "must have been heartbroken for she surely wanted to avoid that above everything else."

10

Eve in Exile

THE FIRST EVIDENCE OF EVE in exile is the letter she wrote to Ben Reitman on February 15, 1929, reporting that "cold and hunger" had driven her out of "the free state of Danzig" (now Gdańsk, Poland, on the Baltic coast). She had stayed in Danzig longer than she had wanted—to secure a Polish passport.

Eve had made it to Warsaw in January and was working as a governess for a five-year-old girl. She was "making a good governess," she said, "for I naturally love children." Eve received room, board, and laundry services, plus a small salary. But she was "too tired or too poor" to go to a concert or the theater. Her job reminded Eve of "the workhouse" in which she had been imprisoned in the United States, "except that the door is not locked." She wailed, "What a future, what a life!"

> Have no friends here—I feel a total stranger in my own country and in addition handicapped, because I am a Jewess—in Poland there are distinct two races—Christians & Jews and they don't mix. In all the world, a foreigner and in the country I was born a Jew.

She stressed: labor, in Poland, "is terribly underpaid in all branches," and "life here is only for the very few, the rich and the Christian—and a Jew cannot get any decent job here, because he is a Jew."

In a later letter, Eve listed for Reitman the many other ways in which she was struggling, in exile, to make a small living. During "the famous cold winter of 1929" in Danzig, Eve said, "I was earning exactly one dollar a week giving English and Hebrew lessons. Out of that I used to buy tobacco, bread, tea, sugar and out of the 4 necessities 2 would be missing most of the time."

Then, in the spring, she had "found a job as waitress in a big, seaside, open air café in Zoppot" (then in Germany, now Sopot, Poland). Later she'd worked collecting ads for the Zoppot Casino. Then she had been employed as a translator from German to English, and from English to Polish and German.

Next, Eve worked for a photography company—"developing, printing, and enlarging all in 10 minutes." She'd "learned all the tricks of the trade quickly and loved it." She'd traveled for the company to a Stockholm exposition—"and then I was off to Berlin and then Paris."

In her 1929 letter, Eve told Reitman, "I dreamed last night I was back in America," adding, "What horrors in awakening." She had been "dreaming of coming back to the U.S. illegally thru Canada." But she had read in the newspapers that if illegal immigrants were caught in the United States after returning for a second time, they received two years in prison and then deportation, and "it scared me a bit." She mused, "But to tell the truth if I had the chance—" The sentence trailed off but the wish was clear.

Eve said she dreamed of taking the train from Warsaw to Paris, but it cost thirty dollars. She thanked Reitman for earlier sending twenty-five dollars. She wondered if she could ask Reitman, her "dear friend," to raise her train fare "among friends?" She added, "I know how busy you are all there and how far away I am from you all and that makes you forget"—she nudged and guilt-tripped.

Eve wondered whether Reitman and their mutual friends had escaped "the influenza," which she read "was raging in Chicago and New York." Eve asked after her "beloved friend Violet Dixon," a Chicago artist. "I could never forget her." She added, "O, God, how I long for one of your friendly faces. How lonely I felt all this year in this land!—How many times I felt to end it all would be best!"

Did Eve actually contemplate suicide? Or was this her way of saying how deeply she treasured Reitman's letters? Eve's neediness and readiness to find fault seem to have kept other American friends at bay while Reitman's thick skin prevented him from being bothered.

Recalling life in America and the publishing of *Lesbian Love*, Eve said, "What a price I paid for my courage and perhaps foolishness! And still paying if I have to live a life as such I lived until now in Poland & Danzig."

She lamented, "How starved I am for music" and "things beautiful in life." During the past year, "my everyday worry was for a piece of bread. And now when I have the piece of bread I have to give all my time to it—14 hours each day and in the evening I am not supposed to go out." She did go out "sometimes," but if she went out too often she risked losing her food and shelter—"and it is such a cold bitter winter here. Siberian weather."

Eve entreated Reitman:

> I have written to you my dear beloved friend several times— twice or three times from Danzig but got no reply—Do not forget me again. A word from America from friends gives me hope & courage—and could you help me again? O, how I hate to ask, but there is no way out—I cannot steal and I am a stranger-Jew here.

Eve carried with her a Ten Cent Classics edition of Alfred Tennyson's poems, calling them "my bible." Saying these "few lines kept me alive," she quoted, "Have faith, have faith! We live by faith, / And all things move together / For the good." Recalling good times stateside, she shared another Tennyson quote: "The present is the vassal / of the past: / So that, in that I <u>lived</u>, do live."

"Ben," Eve recalled, "I remember you wrote me last year that I will have yet lots of fun in Europe—well not much fun up till now . . . ." She ended on a wistful note: "Perhaps the sun will shine again."

In New York, the same month Eve wrote to Reitman, *Variety* headlined a front-page story QUEER SHOW QUITS BEFORE COPS COP IT. A play, *Modernity*, a "dramatization of 'Lesbian Love' . . . by 'Jane Adams'" had been closed "on a tip off that the cops were ready to step in."

Modernity had played two weeks "to surreptitious patronage," at the Play Mart, "a cellaret playhouse on Christopher Street" in Greenwich Village. The Play Mart had "housed arty projects from time to time," and the playhouse had been sublet for four weeks to the troupe behind *Modernity*, who called themselves "the Scientific Players."

> Those who grabbed a load of the piece before it went self-sloughed, claimed "The Captive" and "Pleasure Man" were kindergarten stuff in comparison. The show drew mainly an audience of queers at $3 a ticket.

Pleasure Man, a revised, retitled version of Mae West's *The Drag*, a comedy/drama featuring homosexual characters, had opened at New York's Biltmore Theatre for two performances, October 1–2, 1928, after which it was raided and closed by the police for "indecent" content.

11

The Crash

NEARLY EIGHT MONTHS AFTER *MODERNITY*'S demise at the Play Mart in Greenwich Village, in September 1929, the New York City police prohibited the opening of "a new sex play," *The First Night*, at the same theater. A month later, on October 29, economic modernity reared its head as the New York Stock Exchange collapsed, setting off crises around the world, including Eve's world.

Almost two years after Eve's first letter to Reitman, on December 12, 1930, she had made it out of Warsaw and addressed him from the visitors' writing room of the American Express office, Paris. Eve apologized for not writing to Reitman for "a long time." She was "very happy" to hear from him, and to have "those clippings you sent of your doings in Chicago." (Reitman enclosed newspaper reports about himself and his family in at least two letters.)

"I am writing a group of prison stories," Eve reported, stories apparently based on her US prison experience. Two of the tales "were accepted here in Paris by Sam Putnam, for his magazine 'The New Review,'" and were scheduled to appear in March. "The Workhouse is Raided, Prison Sketch by Eve Adams" would be listed as forthcoming in the *New Review*, August–October 1931. As a writer in Paris, Eve was still using her American name, a sign of her appreciation for the freedom she had experienced in her adopted country and her continuing belief in the ideals the United States had promised, then torpedoed.

But Eve's story did not appear in the *New Review*, and that journal ceased publication before any of Eve's writing was printed. Eve's stories may have been lost to history when Putnam left Paris, placing mischief-maker Henry Miller and his high-jinks ally Alfred Perles in charge of the *New Review*. The boys, rebelling against Putnam, their friend and mentor, tried to discard much of the scheduled content.

Eve had also sent three other prison stories to Max Eastman, former editor of the *Liberator* and the *Masses*, "to place them," and she was "writing more." Eve's unjust deportation had disrupted her life for the past four years. But having now made it to Paris, she was starting to recover from that state-inflicted trauma and reactivate herself as writer.

Eve gossiped: the "crazy" poet Maxwell Bodenheim "is here in Montparnasse" and he's "a big snob!" Montparnasse, Paris's famous bohemian neighborhood of the mid-1920s and early 1930s, was recalled bleakly by Samuel Putnam:

> A weird little land crowded with artists, alcoholics, prostitutes, pimps, poseurs, college boys, tourists, society slummers, spend-thrifts, beggars, homosexuals, drug addicts, nymphomaniacs, sadists, masochists, thieves, gamblers, confidence men, mystic fakers, paranoiacs, political refugees, anarchists, "Dukes" and "Countesses," men and women without a country; a land filled with gaiety, sometimes real and often feigned, filled with sorrow, suffering poverty, frustrations bitterness, tragedy, suicide.

Eve's 1930 letter portrayed Paris on a quite different, upbeat note. She had "seen dear Sasha [Alexander Berkman] a few weeks ago and we had a nice talk. He looks splendid! When I get down south I will see Emma too." In 1926, Emma Goldman had first rented a small cottage in Saint-Tropez, a small fishing village in southern France. Samuel Putnam recalled seeing Goldman in Paris, most often on the terrace of the café Select "surrounded by a group of lesbians." Eve also anticipated a second trip south. She was "planning and hoping that I will be able to hop down to Nice for a month or so, during the winter."

Eve asked, "Ben, darling, Please send on to Violet [Dixon] my enclosure! I simply cannot afford the postage." She concluded, "I long to see you all," adding, "Write to me again soon Ben dear—you will make me very very happy."

About six months after her letter to Reitman, in early June 1931, Eve wrote to her former partner Ruth Olson Norlander from Mirmande, a little village in southern France. "Not far away from here," Eve said, "Cezanne used to paint."

Norlander's paintings were described by Kenneth Rexroth as "Cezannesque." Paul Cézanne's paintings were probably a major reason why Norlander visited Albert C. Barnes's art collection in Pennsylvania several times between 1926 and 1947. Once, with no prior notice, Norlander dropped by Barnes's house, he showed her his art collection, and the two had a long talk. Barnes said he would like to see Norlander's paintings, and asked her to return.

Eve's letter described Mirmande's "old stone houses" and "blue hills," calling the area "a silent country place that . . . fills my heart with a great sorrow and thankfulness to the Maker." Eve maintained her belief in a Divine Constructor.

"My thoughts are with you in Glenwood every moment of my existence," Eve told Ruth, in Illinois, "for my life is somehow similar to those days, except for the great love." Eve reminisced: "Dearest Ruth, years have gone by. Many hard years of suffering interwoven with a few beautiful moments."

She described her current situation: "Now here I am in a country place so beautiful, hard at work, not for the love of it, just a job." She had been "taken away from Paris in a Ford 400 miles out by a couple: woman painter and man writer." Eve was modeling for the painter and working as a secretary to the writer. "Charming people," Eve concluded, "he Rumanian she Russian, both Americanized i.e. American passports." The couple were "good people, both talented. His name is famous already and in a couple of years he will be one of the greatest."

The writer was Peter Neagoe and the painter his wife Anna Frankeul (who used the name Anna Neagoe). The bisexual Djuna Barnes, Peter Neagoe's onetime lover and friend, referred to him colorfully as "my little piece of Transylvanian sassafras, spitting in the prune keg."

Alexander Berkman was also in Mirmande with his "young wife"— his partner Emmy Eckstein—"thanks to my suggestion to get him to revise and edit manuscript." Berkman had earlier worked creatively as an editor of Emma Goldman's autobiography, and now, thanks to Eve, he was editing for Neagoe.

Contemplating her situation, Eve said, "Everybody with their love and work and I with my memories." She recalled "the time when I posed for you outdoor for the nude."

Norlander's painting of a nude Eve perhaps appeared in a Chicago show in which Norlander and other Swedish American artists participated. Norlander contributed "Nudes" and "Ploughing" to a "No-Jury Exhibit" in 1922, in the city's grand Marshall Field's department store. This surprising venue for "Nudes" is explained by the show's organizers, the city's rebellious No-Jury Society of Artists, whose rules allowed any creator to exhibit any two works after paying four dollars (about sixty dollars today). All works were arranged alphabetically by the artist's last name, and about two hundred artists exhibited in eight galleries on the famous store's second floor.

"Why you do not write to me I don't know, I am sure," Eve complained. They had last corresponded two years earlier, Eve noted pointedly.

When Eve wrote to Ruth, Eve had earlier visited Emma Goldman in Saint-Tropez, and had read the original manuscript of Goldman's autobiography. Having discovered a vivid passage about Norlander, cut for space reasons from Goldman's published book, Eve quoted it to Norlander: Goldman had described young Ruth in 1911 as "breezy and free as the Western plains" and as sharing a studio with other "artistic rebels" who "dreamed, painted and lived on sandwiches and spaghetti in the spirit of mutual helpfulness and solidarity." Goldman's autobiography was "powerful and most fascinating from the beginning to the end," Eve reported. Goldman's *Living My Life* was published in New York in June 1931, the same month as Eve's letter to Ruth.

That evening in Mirmande, said Eve, "the hills were a grey blue," with "pink clouds, as your Joan used to describe them." Eve had never dreamed that France was "so beautiful" when she was "so much in love with America." If Eve "had some money," she added, "I would send you enough to come over and see France and Germany and your beloved Toledo, Spain. These countries hold the greatest charm and the tourist never sees it, but you would be different."

Eve asked, "How are you, Ruth, my beloved? And little Joan? She must be big now and probably forgotten me entirely. And your dear Jean?" Eve remarked, again, on Norlander's silence: "At times I believe the world has swallowed you, for there is no one that I come across that knows anything of your existence or whereabouts."

Eve exclaimed, "Life is cruel sometimes, very cruel." She complained, "Most beloved and nearest to one's heart do not even take the trouble to let you know that they are alive and happy or unhappy, for what reason God only knows. It is not selfishness I am sure." Eve's comment was unlikely to encourage Norlander's reply. Though Eve clearly desired to hear from Norlander, her barely concealed hostility defeated her desire.

"It is night now," Eve wrote, and "I did not go out for my usual lonely walk tonight. Too beautiful was the sky and my thoughts were too full of you, Ruth." She added, "I love you Ruth and the memories of our beautiful friendship and love keeps me young, by God as young as ever—even my sinful body. The fact is I can earn my living as a model if necessary. My heart aches, my spirit is not touched." Eve set her sinful body against her sin-free spirit. That Ruth had once held such judgments echoed a passage about Norlander's stand-in "Sorine" in *Lesbian Love*.

Eve ended:

> Au revoir my beloved. Perhaps some day I shall be blessed with the great happiness of seeing your face once more and hear your deep voice speak.
>
> My love to you, my little girl Joany, and dear Jean.

She signed herself Eve, with her bold flourish.

Back in New York, in October 1931, four months after Eve wrote to Norlander, Billy Scully, a columnist in the *Greenwich Village Weekly News*, recalled Eve's tearoom as "one of the most delightful hang-outs the Village ever had."

A month later, in November 1931, *Broadway Brevities* headlined a front-page story SAPPHIC SISTERS SCRAM! This, the same article that provided a scandalous account of Eve's arrest and Robert Edwards's role in it, also made more general claims about New York's lesbian community. A subhead proclaimed an economic/sexual determinism: "Depression Drives Ladies of Lesbos to Normalcy," and those ladies were "Deserting Boat Boys for Jobs and Feminine Frills."

Since "the boy in the boat" was slang for the clitoris, "Boat Boys" were butch lesbians who performed oral sex on women partners. Translated into standard English, the headlines asserted that those partners were forsaking oral sex performed on them by masculine lesbians in order to make a living dressed like proper femmes. The story—authored, of course, by "Connie Lingle"—continued:

> Depression has hit Lesbos. Among the lyric lanes of this half-light land of sex the lutes of the lesbians are muted in minors.
> Eve Adams, once the queen of the third sex, has fled to Paris where her "Le Boudoir De L'amour" on Montmarte [sic] attracts the supple tongued sirens of the lesbian element.

While the actual Eve Adams struggled for a living in Depression-era Europe, in New York "Eve Adams" had become a fabled character. This sensationalist folklore crowned the leftist, radical Eve as Sapphic royalty, a lesbian queen, as well as the capitalist proprietor of a Parisian Love Bedroom. Eve opening a lesbian lust den in Paris's entertainment district was an Eve Adams myth, the creation of a thrill-mongering, prurient New York rag.

In contrast to Connie Lingle's mocking reference to lesbian tongues, such tongues were seriously celebrated in Djuna Barnes's 1928 novel *Ladies Almanack*. There, on the death of "Saint Evangeline Musset" (stand-in for lesbian hostess Natalie Barney), her acolytes burn her body. "And when they came to the ash that was left of her, all had burned but the Tongue, and this flamed and would not suffer Ash." This female saint's fire-resistant tongue symbolically combated the new century's interpreters of Freud, who prescribed penis as the sole source of mature women's pleasure.

The same *Broadway Brevities* feature mentioned Eve again in a fond though melancholy memoir of New York City's former lesbian and male homosexual haunts. The writer recalled Eve's, in its time, as the "most popular place in the Village": "Eve's was a great resort for the after-theatre crowd and chorus beauties. Eve was at that time one of the Village's most interesting characters."

Brevities' 1931 report ended: "With the closing of Eve's place," after her arrest, "the element began to scatter."

12

Fascism

In the early 1930s, the rise of the Nazi Party in Germany held ominous portents for Eve and millions:

January 30, 1933: Adolf Hitler was made chancellor of Germany; the Nazi Party assumed greater control of the state.

February 27, 1933: In Berlin, an arson attack on the German parliament building, the Reichstag, gave Hitler the excuse to suppress political dissent. The Nazi government falsely portrayed the fire as a Communist plot to overthrow the state—another Red scare used as rationale to shutter democracy.

March 20, 1933: In Dachau, near Munich, Nazi storm troopers opened the first concentration camp for political prisoners. The camp held German Communists, Social Democrats, trade unionists, and, later, Jehovah's Witnesses, Romanies, repeat criminals, "asocials," male homosexuals, and Jews. Lesbians were not declared criminal by the Nazis, though many lesbians suffered under the regime in ways that historians have only lately studied.

March 23, 1933: The German parliament abolished democracy and officially recognized Adolf Hitler as dictator.

April 1, 1933: The Nazis carried out their first nationwide action against German Jews: boycotting businesses owned by Jewish persons.

May 6, 1933: In Berlin, Nazi students attacked the Institute for Sexual Science, headed by Magnus Hirschfeld, a Jew, homosexual, and homosexual emancipation activist. They looted and a few days later burned the institute's library and archive, destroying some twenty thousand books and magazines, and thirty-five thousand photographs (a catastrophic attack on the lesbian, gay, bisexual, and transgender archive). Books like Eve's vanished in the flames.

FEBRUARY 6, 1934: In France, fascist groups rioted against the government's democratic parliament. Several French antifascist groups formed to combat the fascist threat.

On a passport, signed July 2, 1934, "Eve Chawa Zloczower" declared her occupation: "literatka—femme de lettres." She was not just a "woman writer" but "a woman of letters"—a classy woman scribe.

On August 15 of that year, while on "holiday" in London, Eve wrote to Ben Reitman, delighted to have received a letter from him with news about his work in Chicago, his wife and son, Brutus, Violet Dixon, and Ruth Norlander. Eve reminisced, "All that has such a great memory for me. It represents America and the past, beautiful active life of mine there."

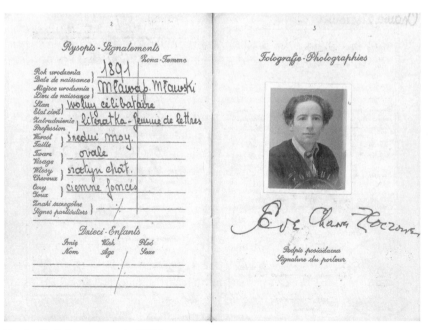

Eve's Polish passport, 1934.

A third-class train ticket had carried Eve from Paris, where she once again resided, to London. "I did not swim in the channel this time, as I did once, according to a Duluth radical newspaper," she wrote, recalling the 1921 report in the *Truth*. She was in England, she explained, because "I got too tired and exhausted of Montparnasse and continually selling Ulysses and Lady Chatterley's Lover to Americans." So "I packed my grip and off I went to London to take a rest from the famous Lady Chatterley, the best seller, and here I am."

In Paris, Eve made a living selling American tourists "dirty" books not yet openly available in the obscenity- and sex-obsessed United States—books including venerable porn like *Fanny Hill* and new sexy books by James Joyce, D. H. Lawrence, Henry Miller, and Anaïs Nin, today considered literary classics. Joyce's *Ulysses*, once called "the most infamously obscene book in ancient or modern literature," is now featured on college freshman reading lists.

Eve had become well known among American expatriate bohemians in Paris as a literary porn peddler. An American journalist in Paris, with the improbable name Wambly Bald, wrote an English-language column, La Vie de Bohème, for the *Chicago Tribune and the Daily News, New York* (published in Paris, despite its name). On January 3, 1933, Bald celebrated Eve Adams as "the active girl with bobbed almost-red hair" who "plucks your sleeve" and tried to sell you *Ballyhoo* (an American humor magazine), or James Joyce's *Ulysees*. Eve was also selling the "infamous expatriate anthology Americans Abroad," an essay collection edited by Peter Neagoe, for whom Eve had worked.

"Eve knows a few things," suggested Bald. "Forget about her red tie and gray suit"—a red tie signaled a homosexual inclination. Bald added: Eve "is one of the few females who never criticizes other women!" He advised his readers to ask Eve about "the famous Grey Cottage" and "how she did everything she could to make life pleasant for the Girl Scouts" camping nearby on the shore of Lake Michigan. In Chicago, Eve's Grey Cottage tearoom had competed with Ben Reitman and Jack Jones's well-known Dill Pickle Club, claimed Bald.

Bald then added: Eve had been "asked to leave America because she wrote a harmless little book called Lesbian Love." He concluded with a prophecy: "One of these years America won't act that way." That brief,

Drawing of Eve.

bold comment—those extraordinary words—are the single defense of Eve's book published in her lifetime. Bald's brave words accompanied an affectionate caricature of Eve.

Henry Miller and his wife, June, discovered Eve's porn service on a trip to Paris and bought a copy of *Fanny Hill* and a set of sexy postcards. Between 1928 and 1932, Miller worked on his early autobiographical novel *Lovely Lesbians* (later titled *Crazy Cock*). The original title perhaps referenced Eve's *Lesbian Love*, which Miller is likely to have first heard about after Eve's arrest and trial. In the novel, the central male character, Tony Bring (Miller's stand-in), becomes unhinged when his beloved wife falls in love with another woman and introduces her into their home (mirroring the Millers' history). When Bring's wife angrily suggests that he might have homosexual tendencies, challenging his fragile manhood, he responds furiously, ironically, and oddly by imagining himself a "homo": "I'm going to put on a red necktie and advertise myself. Maybe I could bring a little money in too if I were persevering. A homo to rent—by the week or month—moderate terms. A respectable homo, with a wife and family."

Eve's name and fame probably also inspired the working title of Parker Tyler's novel-in-progress "called something like 'Eve's Adam,'" according to a 1931 column in a Greenwich Village paper. That queer, campy modernist novel was published by Tyler and Charles Ford in 1933 as *The Young and Evil*. It opens with the androgynously named male protagonist, "Karel," greeted at the "Round Table" by "a fairy prince and one of those mythological creatures known as Lesbians." Joining the Round Table, Karel spied "the most delightful little tea-pot"—alluding, perhaps, to Eve's tearoom and her starring role as mythic-lesbian in several published pieces.

While Eve in Paris peddled "pornographic books and highbrow magazines in the Montparnasse cafés," Henry Miller's friend Alfred Perles recalled, she pointed out Miller, the porn author, to her customers. "She didn't sell many magazines; she used them, chiefly, to conceal the pornographic books from the vigilant eyes of the police."

Eve had decided, according to Perles, that "Henry Miller was a drawing card" because "he was even mentioned in the Press." The *Chicago Tribune*, in September 1931, carried Wambly Bald's piece about Miller and his story about a Parisian whore, "Mademoiselle Claude," published earlier in Samuel Putnam's *New Review*. Bald's account of Miller "wasn't much," said Perles, "but enough to impress a naïve creature like Eve Adams." Perles, I think, underestimated Eve's sophistication.

In 1934, Miller's sexy *Tropic of Cancer* was published in Paris, and its fame spread. Eve, the traveling Parisian literary porn peddler, sold copies to American and English tourists at Le Dôme in Montparnasse, the famous café and gathering place of travelers, intellectuals, and aspirants to intellect. Perles recalled *Tropic of Cancer* selling "fairly well under the counter and in the Montparnasse cafés where Eve Adams peddled it together with back copies of Norman Douglas' limericks."

A sample from Douglas's limericks anthology confirms his own description of the verses as "coarse" and "obscene," suggesting one sort of stuff Eve was peddling:

> That naughty old Sappho of Greece
> Said: "What I prefer to a piece
>   Is to have my pudenda

Rubbed hard by the enda
The little pink nose of my niece.

To help his friend Eve, Perles reported, Henry Miller supplied her with copies of *Tropic of Cancer*, which he bought from the publisher at the author's discount rate, "ostensibly to give them away to his friends." Miller's support of Eve was reciprocated. "Eve was always good for a touch," Perles recalled, "and Henry liked her for that. She always gladly forked out a few francs when he happened to arrive broke at the Dôme."

Perles recalled that Eve "was very fond of Henry who treated her with great gentleness and listened to her tales of woe." Eve had been deported from America, Perles recalled, "for being an anarchist, an accusation based on the fact that she was a personal friend of Emma Goldman's. Eve was delighted to be able to talk with Henry about Emma Goldman, for he too was a great admirer of hers."

Perles's claim that Eve was deported because of her anarchist associations corroborates evidence I have offered showing that US Justice Department and Immigration Service officials first targeted Eve because of her "Radical activities" and comrades. Perles's comment is also important as an account that he may well have heard directly from Eve, Miller, or another friend of Eve's. His comment suggests that Eve had surmised and publicly discussed US officials' persecution of her for her anarchist connections.

Henry Miller's friendship with Eve, and his sex writing, helped him process his feelings as an adult about his childhood homosexual experiments. Late in life, Miller for the first time casually admitted that his friendship, from age seven to twelve, with a boy named Joey Imhof had included "the habit of buggering one another." The two boys "thought nothing of it," Miller claimed, though Imhof's judgmental older brother, a serious Catholic, accused them of "committing a grievous sin."

Eve continued her 1934 letter to Reitman, relaying a bleak report on the Paris tourist scene: "In Montparnasse an American boy said to me one day not long ago 'Eve, you and I will be the last two Americans in Paris.'" (The American perceived Eve as American, a perception that Eve cherished and did not apparently correct.) "Montparnasse without the American students and hobos has lost its glamor," Eve continued.

> There is hardly any one left, as in the good old days, to come along and say "Eve, have you got a couple of francs for a French brioche—a cup of coffee at the Zink bar?" And if I did not have it, I would say "Wait here a minute. I'll rush around and see whether I can sell a copy of the Boulevardier; just stay here." And back I'd come in 5 minutes and we'd have a cup of coffee at the Zink bar. Or I'd say "Let's all chip in, get a taxi and run over to Hotel de Ville, and get a real Jewish meal." In the good days, there was a merry bunch of American youngsters and we all had a treat, a real dinner!

At the time, the Hôtel de Ville (the Paris Town Hall) was located in an area then home to many Jewish restaurants and a large Jewish population.

After the 1929 US stock market crash, Americans had begun to desert Paris, scrambling home, newly motivated by money worries. Eve's picture of Paris deserted by Americans was the first time her letters registered the economic collapse. The diminished demand in Paris for dirty books in English has not often been noted as an effect of the Great Depression.

Eve's perception of Americans fleeing Paris is confirmed in a syndicated newspaper report by Charles Estcourt Jr., appearing in many US newspapers in December 1934. Headlined INTELLIGENTSIA DESERT PARIS AND FLOCK BACK TO NEW YORK, the report described the Depression forcing "many of American art's advance guard" to leave France. The report nostalgically recalled the "more gallant if shabbier days in Paris" of Ernest Hemingway, "the dour James Farrell and the undefinable Eve Adams." Eve was one of three iconic names defining a lost era of American expatriate life in Paris. The Eve Adams legend was still aborning.

When the American writer James T. Farrell and his wife Dorothy made it out of Chicago and ventured to Paris in 1931, they were sailing against the tide. At the Deux Magots café they got to know Eve, and heard about her friendship with Emma Goldman, her anarchist links, the US publication of *Lesbian Love*, and Eve's deportation. Eve was poor, well known, and liked in the cafés, they reported. When James Farrell returned to Paris in the summer of 1938, he found Eve to be even more of a Paris bohemian institution.

Though well known in some Paris expatriate circles, Eve would not have been welcome at the famous salons of wealthy lesbian American expatriates, neither those of Gertrude Stein and Alice Toklas nor the rival salons hosted in the 1930s by Natalie Barney. Eve was a poor, working-class, leftist social observer and realist writer, which set her apart from the richer, modernist "literary" American lesbians in Paris. Some of them, like Stein, held anti-Semitic views, and some, like Barney, pro-Fascist, pro-Nazi views. And to lesbian bookseller Sylvia Beach, Eve was competition, hawking sexy books to English-speaking tourists in cafés while Beach sold modernist English-language texts out of her brick-and-mortar bookstore Shakespeare and Company.

Eve also represented trouble, just as she had in the United States—a walking, talking threat to the silent pact between "respectable" lesbians and their societies. That pact, adopted especially by professional, middle- and upper-class lesbians, meant "never talking about it," sometimes even among themselves. Speaking the word *lesbian*, clear and loud, as Eve did in speech and person, blew the cover off the old discretion, further- ing a new, modern, public sexual naming. Eve's positive, public name- calling seriously challenged the earlier constructed silence that allowed a number of lesbian couples to share years-long, live-together sexual love relations without community castigation. It's not surprising, then, that three of the known reports from Paris about Eve and *Lesbian Love* are by heterosexual men, none by lesbians.

In her 1934 letter from London, Eve reported to Reitman that his last missive had been forwarded to her from Paris by her "dearest friend" and "most beloved girl, Hella, a German refugee, a marvelous artist and singer and the most beautiful thing to look at." Thanks to "fate," Eve and Hella had "found each other" on July 1, 1933, the day Hella had arrived in Paris with twenty francs, "and we are the most devoted of friends." Eve added that Hella, her "adopted child, a grown woman of 28" who looked 19, had been ill during most of the winter "and we had hard times, and a bit of a struggle to make ends meet, but everything is fine—now." Eve's "dearest," "beloved" and "beautiful" spelled out her own attraction. Hella's feelings for Eve are undocumented, leaving this intimacy's exact character unknown.

Eve's self-described role as Hella's caretaker recalled Reitman's mem- ory of Eve lavishing "presents and affection" on attractive women. Eve, as her parents' first child, the oldest of several siblings, had, early on, helped her mother care for the others, adopting the nurturing role she later seemed to play in regard to others.

Eve's "dearest friend," Hella Olstein, was not in fact "a German refugee" but had spoken German in school in Basel, Switzerland. She had been born into a Jewish family in Łódź, in Russia-controlled Poland, in 1905, the year that Polish workers rose up against the Russian Empire. Olstein had lived and worked in France and London, and then returned to France. She made a living singing in French cabarets under the name Nora Waren (also Norah Waren). She is striking in a photo she sent to her brother.

Eve was planning to return to Paris in a few days, but was also thinking of a new migration later in 1934:

> My mind is on Moscow and Tel-Aviv, two new lands. Don't know yet which will be the first. Have not one dollar towards the trip, but it has to be in the very near future. Both countries, Russia and Palestine, are calling me, and there where I can make myself useful and do something to help along to build life, I shall remain until the wanderlust will call me again. I made up my mind to go together with my friend Hella. How and when we will do it I do not know as yet.

Hella Olstein Soldner.

Eve needed to leave France "in the very near future," she sensed, but international travel was difficult or impossible for two women without much cash. They did not know how rapidly grave danger was approaching.

Along with her letter, Eve sent Reitman two snapshots of herself, "one taken over 10 years ago on my wanderings in Yakima Valley" in Washington State, "the apple country, as I was dressed on one of my hitch-hiking trips towards Seattle." The other photo was taken in 1932, in the French Alps, "where I spent a few glorious days in the snows."

Reitman had asked Eve to contribute an autobiographical "chapter" to his book in progress on women migrants, and she responded, "Why, my dear man, if I wanted to write my experiences of my wanderings and people and adventures, which still continue with every blessed day, it would take me years to write and I could fill volumes, not chapters."

Eve asked, "Now, Ben, how can I begin writing my life story? It is two o'clock in the morning" and she had "an appointment at 10." She complained, "I am so far from everything I loved dearly—but not complaining."

> I remember, Ben, you wrote me once in my exile days, about 5 years ago, "There is lots of fun to be had in Europe." I did not believe you then, but I do now.

She ended: "It is three o'clock in the morning. I want to go to sleep."

On August 27, 1934, Ben Reitman responded encouragingly to Eve's "delightful long letter" of August 15, in which she had, despite her protests, apparently sent him samples of her writing. "I've told you before you can write and I hope some day you will write the story of your life."

But if Eve wrote her autobiography, Reitman warned, "make a better job of it than Margaret Anderson did in her THIRTY YEARS WAR or Emma Goldman in her LIVING MY LIFE, or even Gertrude Stein did in the biography of Alice Toklas. None of them were honest or satisfactory to me." Eve, in contrast, had found Goldman's autobiography "powerful and most fascinating from the beginning to the end."

Reitman had reason to dislike Margaret Anderson's memoir. In it he had read: Ben Reitman "wasn't so bad if you could hastily drop all your ideas as to how human beings should look and act."

Reitman then detailed for Eve his general critique of women autobiographers:

> No matter how free or frank or rank you women live you always have your pride and your complexes and your prejudices and it is extremely difficult for a woman to write an honest book. I hope you can do it. Go ahead and try. I don't think you will have the least bit of trouble in finding a publisher and, if there is anything I can do to help you, I will be glad.

Reitman was also glad that Eve was "getting by with such ease," though "ease" did not well describe Eve's daily struggle to make a small living. Referring to Hella Olstein, Reitman was pleased "that you are attracting such satisfactory friends or sweethearts, whatever you may choose to call them." It clearly irked Reitman that Eve had not specified the sexual character, if any, of her new relationship.

For Reitman's book in progress on hobos and migrants, he asked Eve to write an "intimate sketch of the various American girls you have met in Paris. I mean girls who are on the bum and earning their own living as they go along. Think you can mention real names without embarrassing any one." He urged her to describe how "American girl tramps, or English, or Russian girl tramps . . . live in Paris without money, where they sleep, eat, get their clothes, and what they do." If Eve's texts were included in Reitman's book in progress on women hobos, he would be "glad to recompense you in some way or another."

Reitman then gossiped about mutual acquaintances. Dill Pickle founder Jack Jones had become "a tramp printer" after being "thrown out" of the club he'd established. He'd refused to pay protection money to the mob, said Reitman, and the police had responded by shutting down the club.

Emma Goldman was in Canada, hoping for a US visa.

Reitman was "working with a group of University of Chicago students studying the minds of the men who are on relief." Twenty-two million Americans were on relief and ten million out of work, he told Eve. She would be "be surprised" that "so many of our old comrades and the radicals are receiving relief from the government and biting the hand that feeds them." He then claimed, "Whenever an anarchist, a communist, or an I.W.W. begins to take food and shelter from a government relief station, they begin to deteriorate and become less revolutionary."

He hoped "that no matter what hardships and panhandling" Eve had to endure,

> you will never become an object of charity. Your fertile mind and your ability to adjust yourself ought to provide for you in all sorts of situations. There is no hardship, no hard luck. Everything is all a part of life and I'm so glad you can look back to the hungry days in Poland and see they were very useful in developing your character.

Nowhere in her writings does Eve state that hunger developed her character.

Reitman sermonized, "You know, my dear Eve, that I am a preacher and I'm tremendously conserned [sic] in your further development and your welfare. Some day I hope to see and talk with you."

He then previewed for Eve

> that which I shall try to weave into my book BOX CAR BERTHA—that is, that the women on the road, the wandering American female hobos are becoming more and more homosexual, Lesbianism apparently is on the increase, and while a homosexual expression is just as moral and delightful as a heterosexual expression—and I don't think there is any sin or shame about it—I can't help but think that intellectually and spiritually homosexuality leads to retrogression and often disintegration. Especially does it lead to a narrowing of the individual person's interest. Most of the homo hobos that I see . . . are interested primarily in sex, and in themselves.

Reitman said that he saw "virtually hundreds" of homosexuals in his doctor's office, and had "met them in the joints" (prisons).

> Some of them write very well and a few of them are good poets and painters. But mighty few of them have an active part in the

radical or revolutionary movement. Few of them display any social consciousness outside of their own group or community interests and so I would say to you and any other woman with Lesbian tendencies, that if you want to serve humanity, if you want to be an influence for good in the world, you have to live as near a normal life as is possible. This is no joke, and is not a matter of pride or prejudice. I've watched happy variants for nearly 40 years and I can't help but say again that to live a great, big, large, useful, clean life it is necessary to "fall in line."

Reitman ended with an upbeat family picture: "I am leaving this afternoon with Brutus and my wife for a little trip."

How the renegade Eve responded to Reitman's advice is not recorded, but he was her main tie to the American life she still deeply loved. Eve also needed the cash Reitman had hinted he would pay for her writing. Eve did contribute to Reitman's book, sending him "a very fine glimpse of the female American hobo in Paris"—"a splendid article," Reitman told Emma Goldman.

Reitman's *Sister of the Road: The Autobiography of Box-Car Bertha* was published in 1937. As Gertrude Stein had in *The Autobiography of Alice B. Toklas*, Reitman penned someone else's "autobiography"—in his case, "Bertha," an invented composite of women he had known. Eve's contribution, however, did not end up in the book, the long editing process of which involved many hands.

Reitman's long friendship, mentoring, and correspondence with Eve were in part compensatory, his attempt to make up for the profound guilt he felt when, during his first marriage, he abandoned his daughter Helen as a small child. Despite an attempt on Helen's part, as an adult, to make contact with Reitman, father and daughter never established a close relationship.

Closely resembling Eve, Reitman's daughter was also an extraordinary, pioneering lesbian activist who initiated an early study of homosexuals that she hoped would lead to their greater acceptance. Like Eve, Helen renamed herself, taking her maternal grandmother's family name and calling herself Jan Gay, a self-naming that also asserted her identity as a lesbian and her alliance with the homosexual community.

Reitman's ambivalence about his own homosexual experience as a boy also contributed to his alternately positive and negative comments to Eve. Reitman was a child when, deserted by his father, he left home to ride the rails, the source of his fascination with tramps, hobos, and migrants of all types. Reitman was about twelve, he recalled in his essay on "Homosexuality," and "bumming around the battery in New York City" when he met a sailor who "took me home to sleep with him." He said no more about that sleepover, but immediately contrasted it with a "very terrible experience": when a "mob of crooks" tried to pass him sexually from one to another, he protested, and they threw him off a hayloft.

At thirteen, Reitman recalled, he "fell prey to the sexual will" of an older man, Ohio Skip, who ordered him to "do as I say. I'm your jocker [sexual boss] and I'll take good care of you" Rejecting the offered "care" and payback sex, the independent boy escaped.

Reitman cited youths who "experiment" with homosexuality "with satisfaction," then move on to a "normal sex life" but "never forget their experience. That is the terrible thing about sex. Any kind of an [sic] sexual experience they have had either in childhood, youth or old age, will be remembered and there is apt to come back a desire to repeat the experience." Homosexual desire lingered in the conflicted Reitman, a source of his interest in and ambivalent comments to and about Eve.

Reitman knew many persons who wrote about homosexuality, he wrote in his own essay "Homosexuality," "and all of them were suspicious"—suspect, that is, of not merely writing about it. Reitman coyly hoped he was "an exception, but there are many who will also have their suspicions." His own attraction to and rejection of homosexual desire is clear.

Reitman and Eve were also linked by their similar personal backgrounds. Reitman, born in 1879, the son of poor Russian Jewish immigrants in Saint Paul, Minnesota, was the only Jewish boy in his mostly Irish neighborhood. Taunted as "Sheeny Ben," he responded with his own on-off antipathy to Jews. Eve, born twelve years later, adamantly rejected the Christian Poland in which Jews were subject to slurs and physical attacks. As a Jew and lesbian, Eve identified with society's pariahs. As a Jew and hobo, Reitman identified with society's outcasts.

As a young woman, Eve's "wanderlust" led her to the United States and, later, to tramp around the country as a traveling saleswoman. As a boy, Reitman rode the rails, developing a deep appreciation of wanderers. Both these nomads, when tired, sought out or created safe houses. Reitman returned repeatedly to his mother's home in Chicago, and settled finally, on his fourth try, into marriage and family life. Eve created queer havens in Chicago and New York where she and other lesbians could, at least for a time, feel protected.

Both Reitman and Eve served time on Welfare Island for breaking New York's "obscenity" law, in Reitman's case by promoting birth control. He was also arrested for "vagrancy" as a boy and later served time, like Eve, for "disorderly conduct," leading a march of Chicago's jobless during the Great Depression.

Both Reitman and Eve were self-taught writers who published community studies. His first book was on pimps and their networks, his second on the hobo network of the apocryphal Box-Car Bertha. Writing as Bertha, Reitman assumed a feminine persona, just as Eve, in life, enacted a masculine one. Both aspired to publish more autobiography, turning their private, drama-rich rebel lives into public, creative nonfiction. Both were early, self-made sexologists: he as specialist in venereal disease and the complaints of prostitutes, madams, pimps, hobos, and homosexuals; she as observer of lesbian foibles and friendships. Both took pleasure in publicly speaking forbidden words: he, "vagina," "intercourse," and "birth control"; she, "Lesbian Love."

America "has no patience with the social pioneer," Reitman said. "It treats him with scorn, contempt, and bitter opposition." He could have been thinking of Eve.

13

War

AUGUST 19, 1934: In Germany, Adolf Hitler declared himself Führer.

ON AUGUST 24, 1934, Eve wrote a short postcard in Yiddish to her brother Yerachmiel, who had immigrated to Palestine with their brother Eliezer and changed his last name to Zahavy. Eve was staying for couple of days at a resort about forty miles from Paris and had that day "bathed in the river and rowed a boat."

"How do you expect me to come to Palestine so quickly?" Eve asked, responding to her brother's urgent plea to immigrate. First, she needed to be able to stop working. Second, she needed sixty pounds in hand. Palestine's British colonial administrators had established strict terms for tourists and limited the number of legal immigrants, a major issue after the rise of Hitler caused many German Jews to seek a safe refuge in what Zionists called "the Promised Land."

Eve said she'd write again when back in Paris and signed herself, affectionately, "Khavetshe," employing the Ashkenazic version of her first name, Khave, with a common Polish diminutive.

Ignoring ominous political developments, gossip columnist Butch Anderson reported on December 1, 1934, in the *Paris Tribune*, "Eve Adams is neglecting the book trade and making eyes at a new blonde." News of Eve's palling around with the fair-haired Hella Olstein was getting around.

Eve in Paris, September 1934.

SEPTEMBER 15, 1935: German legislators passed laws providing the legal framework for the persecution of the country's Jews.

Eve wrote to Ben Reitman from Paris on February 20, 1936. She and her "friend" (Hella) "were very happy to hear from you." Eve had "wanted to write long ago but always problems and worries." Life "is harder than ever now," she said, and Paris was "deserted by Americans," buyers of her sexy books.

Despite the hardship, Eve reported, "We spent a month in St. Tropez last summer" (probably visiting Emma Goldman). Eve was "dying to go for a trip somewhere again," she said, but "unfortunately cannot. Just working hard and existing from day to day." She wished that Reitman would make a trip to Europe—"it would be so good to see you."

Eve reported that Emma Goldman was in England, Alexander Berkman in Nice. She asked to be remembered to "all the friends" on Chicago's

Hella Olstein (performing as N. Waren), center, wearing a French tricolor ribbon and patriotic cap, probably representing Marianne, personification of liberty, equality, fraternity, and reason in a big, probably pre-occupation revue featuring eighteen saluting chorus girls and scenery displaying the tricolor and the Gallic rooster.

Hella Olstein (performing as N. Waren), in dark dress, seemingly in the role of a good woman imploring the return of her bare-chested man, torn between love for her and the charms of a bare-breasted woman, in a revue perhaps inspired by the Folies Bergère, popular in France in the 1920s and '30s.

Eve, right, and Hella Olstein, place and date unidentified.

North Side, Violet Dixon, Ruth and Joan Norlander, and Jean Cambpell. Eve complained that Norlander and Eulalia Burke had not written in years.

MARCH 7, 1936: Nazi troops invaded the Rhineland.

MARCH 11, 1938: Nazi troops invaded Austria.

JULY 6, 1938: Delegates from thirty-two countries met in Evian, France, and discussed which nations would accept German Jewish refugees. Officials from the United States and other nations refused to expand their immigrant quotas.

SEPTEMBER 28, 1938: Officials of Great Britain, France, and Italy, meeting in Munich, appeased Nazi leaders, agreeing to let the Nazis annex part of Czechoslovakia.

From Paris, on November 5, 1938, Henry Miller wrote to novelist Lawrence Durrell, "Eve Adams is just beginning to sell my water colors!! I might earn a little dough in this most pleasant way. Ho ho! What a joke!" Eve sold Miller's watercolors for 50 francs each (about $1.45 in 1938, $27 today). One of Miller's paintings was given to the poor young architect

Eve, left, Hella, center, with an unidentified woman and man, place and date unknown.

trainee Georges Olstein, brother of Eve's friend Hella, when he visited his sister and Eve in France in the summer of 1939. Eve added greetings to Hella Olstein's correspondence with her father, Jacques, and two brothers, Georges and André. Eve was clearly on good terms with Hella's family.

MARCH 15, 1939: Nazi troops seized parts of Czechoslovakia not earlier annexed.

In Saint-Tropez, on July 16, 1939, novelist and memoirist Anaïs Nin reported meeting Eve and Hella Olstein. Nin had just received a first copy of her second novel, *Winter of Artifice*. "Eve Adams saw me riding by. I showed her the book. We talked about [Henry] Miller. We arranged I would give her some copies to sell, that we would meet at the café one late afternoon."

Nin told her current lover, the temperamental Gonzalo Moré, about her plans to meet friends. Then, continued Nin, "I met Eve Adams. I was dressed in my Spanish cotton dress, with a flower in my hair. As we sat there, her friend came to sit with us, a sad little singer [Hella]."

The jealous Moré then walked by, "mouth compressed," an angry expression on his face. Nin, concerned about her possessive lover's fury, left the café to deal with him. By the end of 1939, Nin fled to New York with her banker husband.

AUGUST 23, 1939: Hitler and Stalin signed a nonaggression pact.
SEPTEMBER 1, 1939: German and Soviet troops invaded Poland. That day, the Nazis bombed Mława, hometown of the Zloczewer family. The town's center was destroyed. The Polish army fought the German army in the "Battle of Mława,"one of the opening conflicts of World War II. The Poles lost to the invaders.
SEPTEMBER 3, 1939: The Nazis occupied Mława. Physical attacks on Jews began immediately. Jews were required to perform forced labor. Jews were prohibited from walking on the town's sidewalks. Jews were required to wear a Star of David with the word "Jew." Baruch Goldstein, sixteen, recalled the terror the Nazi invasion caused his Mława family.
SEPTEMBER 3, 1939: French and British officials declared war on Germany. World War II officially began.
APRIL 9, 1940: Nazi troops invaded Denmark.
MAY 10, 1940: Nazi troops invaded Luxembourg, the Netherlands, and Belgium.

By June 14, 1940, the Nazis had occupied Paris. A mass exodus of frightened civilians fled south. That day, a German train carried the first prisoners—suspected members of the anti-Fascist resistance, Catholics, and twenty Jews—to a Nazi camp in southern Poland, in the town of Auschwitz.

The following day, Eve wrote a hurried postcard from Biarritz, in southwestern France, responding in English to a letter from her brother Yerachmiel. Eve was in motion: she had received her brother's letter in Nice, she'd lived in Cannes for six weeks, in Biarritz for ten days, and she didn't know how long she'd stay there.

"I would like very much to come to your country," Eve said, "but rather difficult traveling now—and much funds are needed." Without

cash for passports, visas, and transportation, Jews without money, especially foreign Jews like Eve, were forced to stay in France, out of sight,
and hope. Eve asked Yerachmiel to "embrace your wife and the dear
children for me," and to write at once. Though Eve did not mention
Hella to her brother, her companion was traveling with her, further
complicating travel plans.

> JUNE 22, 1940: French officials signed an armistice with Nazi Germany.
> France was divided into a northern, German-ruled zone, and a
> southern, French-ruled zone. Marshal Philippe Pétain headed the
> French government based in the town of Vichy.
> JUNE 24, 1940: Pétain's officials signed an armistice with Italy's Fas-
> cist leaders. Italian Fascists occupied a small zone in southeastern
> France in which Nice was the largest city, with Cannes sixteen miles
> away.

On July 21, 1940, Hella Olstein wrote to her brother André, a young
lawyer, in Switzerland. Her singing work in Cannes had ceased suddenly, one day, when her bosses took the train west for Bordeaux. So

Yerachmiel Zahavy, 1948.

she and Eve had also left. People were "packed like sardines" on the train," Olstein said, "even people in the toilets and standing the whole night." Having stopped in Biarritz, then in Toulouse, and not finding permanent rooms, they had retreated back to Nice.

Eve added a page in English, her words guarded: André's letter had calmed Hella's anxiety. "We went through some anxious times lately and your sister was a brave & courageous girl—How we managed to get to places & get away from places I cannot tell you in detail now. But I can tell she is a great kid and wonderful in difficult moments."

Back in Nice, Eve reported, Hella was tan and looked like "a little mulatto and has her hair up beautifully & looks a picture of the lady aristocrat of the 18th century." Eve added, "Only one thing is lacking." Eve hoped they would soon find jobs.

Two months later, on September 13, Hella Olstein's postcard to André included a note from Eve thanking him for his "help"—money he had sent—which allowed them to enjoy a restaurant lunch and toast to his health.

OCTOBER 3, 1940: French officials passed their first law excluding Jewish citizens from jobs in public service. On their own initiative, they also passed a law allowing the immediate arrest of foreign Jews.

On August 4, 1941, a "very worried" Eve had not heard from Hella Olstein for eight days. Her postcard to André Olstein in Switzerland asked, "What happened to the child?" Eve asked him to write at once if he had any news of his sister and her current address. Nine days later Eve's postcard told Olstein she had heard from Hella.

AUGUST 18, 1941: French police arrested Jews, sending them to a camp in Drancy, a Paris suburb, prior to their deportation to concentration camps.

Writing from Nice, in Italian Fascist–occupied southern France, Eve came right to the point in a letter to Reitman on September 1, 1941: "I need not tell you what life has become here in Europe—and I want to desperately come back to the States. I must! And I need your help

Ben in every way." She explained, "Everyone wanting to enter the USA now must have 2 sponsors in the USA. So I was thinking of you and Violet Dixon."

A permit for her return, Eve said, could only be secured by someone in the States with influence who went to Washington, DC, and requested the permit directly from a government official. Eve pleaded, "Ben dear you are the only man in the USA I know of who has the will and is capable of turning wheels, so sleep on it and see what you can do for me."

Eve enclosed two copies of a signed passport photo, adding, "I just turned 50 (a good age) and photos taken only a few days ago." (Eve's 1941 photo precedes p. 1 of the text.) She listed the attributes that would made her a good American: "I am in excellent health. Speak 5 European languages besides English and can be useful in many ways. A very conscientious worker when in an office."

She had a Polish passport, she wrote. She had received her first American citizenship papers and a permit to reenter the United States in 1925. She had left the United States in 1927. Desperate to return, Eve failed to mention her US trials, convictions, prison terms, and deportation. These made it inconceivable that US officials would permit her return.

Eve might have heard that Emma Goldman, also a convicted and deported radical immigrant, had received a temporary US return permit in 1934, but Goldman was then considered a defanged, harmless sixty-five-year-old celebrity, lecturing for three months on nonpolitical subjects. Eve was an obscure, convicted undesirable.

Passage by boat from France to Lisbon cost $100, Eve said, and from Lisbon to the United States cost $400, and that money had to be secured in the United States. A "good friend," Watson White, could be approached to fund her return trip. She called White a "sculptor, writer, millionaire," and "Harvard man," whose address was the New York City Harvard Club. White, a Harvard graduate in 1910, was a lifelong bachelor who worked briefly as a journalist and then pursued an acting career. On TV, he played the defense attorney in a 1951 science fiction series, *Tales of Tomorrow*.

Eve's uncle in Brooklyn, Isidor Meegdall, couldn't help, said Eve, but she could, upon return, "certainly put up with the family for a while," though she hoped to live in Chicago. (Eve's businessman uncle, Alexander Migdall, who had once promised to pay her bond, had died in 1935.) Eve told Reitman she had "no savings whatsoever" to pay her fare, for "I am still making a living selling English books," but with English-speaking tourists gone from France "it is a great struggle."

If Reitman succeeded in getting Eve a return permit, and in raising the money for her US trip, she promised to "certainly make it up as I always did. I am a good saleswoman. Can promote business." She was an "excellent cook, housekeeper—and never shirk any work."

Eve asked about Reitman's son Brutus: "He surely will remember his visit to us here in Nice and will want to know news of Hella." Eve casually reported that Hella Olstein was "happily married to a poor artist" and was singing "on the stage and cabarets." Hella had married a man named Gaston Soldner, but her life and Eve's remained closely intertwined.

Eve would "appreciate it greatly" if Brutus wrote to her, for "I am all alone here. Father mother both died recently." Eve's father had actually died eight years earlier, in 1933; perhaps Eve misspoke to win Reitman's sympathy. All members of the Zloczewer family living in Mława during World War II were reportedly murdered by the Nazis.

Eve pleaded again: "Dear Ben, I know you will come to my aid after you think it over. It is not a little request I make! And you are the only one I can turn to. . . ." Once she was back in the United States, "no matter in which capacity I am put to work there I shall make good. That is faithfully promised, for I know myself. Once I undertake a thing I carry it out."

Eve asked Reitman to excuse her letter's blotches, for the available ink was bad and difficult to find—"just as everything else. You will understand." Bad ink was the least of Eve's problems. Her anxiety about living as a foreign Jew in Nazi- and Fascist-occupied France is palpable in her letter.

In Reitman's 1933 essay "Homosexuality," he summarized Eve's life and commented on the notes he received from her: she "writes me pathetic letters begging me to find a way for her to come back." But by September 1941, when Eve wrote to Reitman from southern France, the Nazis were tightening their grip on the country's north. Eve's plea to Reitman for help recognized her grave danger as Jew and alien. Eve was delusional in imagining that US government bureaucrats would permit her return. But her fantasy of a return expressed her fierce, ardent desire to live. Given Eve's situation, her desire to return to the US was not "pathetic."

On September 18, 1941, Reitman wrote a short, rambling letter to anarchist Harry Kelly, an education reform activist: "Had a letter from Eve Adams who is now in Nice France asking for help to get her back to America." Changing subjects, Reitman said he did not share Emma Goldman's and "the other Anarchists' hatred of the Communists. I don't hate anybody not even Hitler."

On September 29, Swiss immigration officials denied Hella Olstein Soldner's request to escape Nazi- and Fascist-occupied France and join her family in Switzerland.

> OCTOBER 1941: The Nazis began construction of a second concentration camp in the Auschwitz complex, Auschwitz-Birkenau. The new camp contained a killing center to facilitate the Nazis' plan to exterminate all of Europe's Jews. Zyklon B gas was to be the means of mass murder in all the gas chambers in the Auschwitz complex.

In a postcard to Reitman from Nice on October 31, Eve thanked him for his card about him and his family, wished she could attend his children's birthday parties, and added, "But let us hope dear Ben that you will succeed and I can look again at old Chicago in the near future." Eve had on her wall a "splendid" framed photo of Emma Goldman, "taken by a friend of mine in Paris, Mrs. Dolly Stamm." Eve said, "Yes I know of poor Emma." Goldman had died in 1940 and been allowed one last, silent return to the United States, to the German Waldheim Cemetery (now Forest Home Cemetery) in a Chicago suburb.

Eve said she missed Alexander Berkman and his partner Emmy Eckstein: "They were such dear friends. Life was different when they were here among us." Berkman had died in 1936, Eckstein in 1939. If Reitman saw Ruth Norlander or Eulalia Burke, Eve said, "give them my love."

"Let me hear from you again soon," Eve ended. "A bientot"—see you soon.

JANUARY 20, 1942: Nazi officials gathered in the Berlin suburb of Wannsee to implement what they privately called the "Final Solution of
the Jewish Question," the mass murder of all Europe's Jews.

MARCH 27, 1942: In Paris, the French police helped the Nazis arrest
Jews.

Employing highly formal German, Eve wrote to Hella Soldner's
brother André in Switzerland on May 26, 1942: "Honorable Mr. André,
would you be so kind (if it is possible)" to send "two samples of the
journal 'Swiss Illustré No 6'"? The stilted German, the fact that Eve
wrote many times to André Olstein in casual French and English, and
the odd journal request, suggest that Eve was making a coded request
for money.

JUNE 1942: Rumors began to spread: Jews were being deported to camps
and murdered.

JUNE 5, 1942: In Paris, the French police helped Nazis arrest Jews.

JUNE 16, 1942: In Nice, right-wing French militants and German Nazis
pillaged the city's synagogue.

JUNE 22, 1942: In Paris, the French police helped the Nazis arrest
Jews.

JULY 16 & 17, 1942: The French police arrested 12,884 men, women, and
children and held them in the Vélodrome d'Hiver sports stadium
with little food or water, and few toilets, the single biggest roundup
of Paris Jews.

AUGUST 26, 1942: Five hundred Jews, arrested in Nice, were sent to the
Drancy internment camp.

AUGUST 26–28, 1942: Roundups in the French zone netted over 6,500
Jews.

OCTOBER 1942: The French resistance newspaper *J'Accuse* warned that
gas was being used to execute Jews.

On October 15, 1942, a major Jewish relief organization reported
the reimbursement of twenty-nine francs to "the Misses Zloczower and
Weiss" for postage expenses dating back to May 29. Zloczower was
almost certainly Eve.

The reimbursement was reported at a meeting in Marseille of the administrative council for the southern branch of l'Union générale des Israélites de France (the UGIF-South). Participants, perhaps including Eve, discussed the arrests and deportations of foreign Jews and Jewish veterans. They feared seeing their organization's personnel arrested and hoped to receive safe-conduct cards. They talked of caring for children, ages five to fifteen, separated from deported parents. They spoke of supporting the French Red Cross's assistance to Jews in French internment camps. They mentioned the provisional budget requested by the Commissariat-General for Jewish Affairs (established by the Vichy government, in collaboration with the Nazis, to introduce anti-Jewish laws). They considered the salaries of the organization's employees and the expense invoices they'd submitted.

The UGIF had been created by Jewish leaders at Nazi request, so its northern branch remained strictly bound to legality. But the relative autonomy of the UGIF-South allowed some associated groups to undertake secret, illegal rescue work.

Eve was at special risk of arrest as a foreign Jew, but, given her earlier participation in the US activist left, it would not be surprising if she had joined some resistance effort. That Hella Olstein Soldner, also a foreign Jew, played some part in the resistance was a tale passed along orally in the Olstein family. Documentation is lacking; resistance groups under fascist regimes do not often keep careful records of members' names and acts.

NOVEMBER 11, 1942: Nazi troops invaded the area of France ruled by Philippe Pétain's government in Vichy. German Nazis and Italian Fascists extended their rule over all of France. A large new group of Jews flocked to Nice, located in the small, southern Italian zone. Italian Fascists' policies toward Jews were known to be less harsh than the Nazis' policies.

On February 8, 1943, Hella Olstein Soldner sent a postcard to her father, Jacques, in Switzerland, begging for family news. On the postcard's other side Eve stressed in French how "anxious" Hella was for news. The logo of the Nazi military "High Command," stamped on the card, includes a swastika.

Postcard from Hella Olstein Soldner and Eve Adams to Jacques Olstein, February 8, 1943.

On February 22, Hella wrote from Nice to her brother André in Basel, Switzerland, asking about friends and family. Her brother had found her photos sad, she indicated, responding that they publicized her as a singer and her songs were sad. Some French newspaper ads billed her as a réaliste singer—a performer of tough, down-to-earth tales of Paris's poor working class.

She reported, "At home all goes well, Eve does the housework in my little apartment and my stomach is completely in order." Soldner was probably now the only breadwinner and Eve the homemaker. Hella added casually after further small talk, "You know my husband has disappeared." She elaborated: "It's the Geneva Red Cross that gave me this news which is not very jolly. But I hope all the same that he is still alive, he was so nice" ("*gentil*," in French). She added, "One could only wait." The odd language may be explained by Soldner's fear that her letter would be read by postal inspectors. A line through its two pages marks it as inspected.

APRIL 27, 1943: In Nice, antifascists shot three Italian Fascist officers eating in a restaurant, killing one.

MAY 6, 1943: In Nice, Cannes, and Marseille antifascists bombed Italian Fascist soldiers.

MAY 11 & 16, 1943: In Nice, Italian Fascists arrested civilians considered unsupportive of the regime.

MAY 19, 1943: In Nice, Italian civil authorities arrested a German Jew, Theodor Wolff, the former editor of the influential left-liberal paper the *Berliner Tageblatt* and a founder of the German Democratic Party. Wolff was sent to a concentration camp in Germany, then to a hospital, where he died. Despite Nice's location in the relatively safe Italian occupation zone, anti-Jewish incidents were frequent in the city.

JULY 10, 1943: US and British troops began to occupy the Italian island of Sicily, suggesting to many that the Italian Fascists were losing the war.

JULY 25, 1943: Italian government officials voted no confidence in Prime Minister Benito Mussolini, and his fall ended the Italian Fascist government.

On August 10, 1943, Hella Soldner wrote again from Nice to her father and brothers, apologizing for not writing sooner and begging for word of them. All was well with her; she had a little work. She had sung on Radio Monte-Carlo a week earlier but could not let them know in time "because by telegram we cannot," and a letter would have arrived too late. Her failure to write was not laziness: "A friend of mine who is very dear to me had troubles, so I have taken care of him a bit," but "now everything is going fine for him so I am also more relaxed."

"Eve still lives with me," Soldner said, and "does my housework." Hella had a small dog, and if she came to Switzerland she hoped to bring him. "I will most likely not come alone, but not with Eve, but with him." She censored her husband's name, then described him: "He is a great artist, but for the moment he can't work in his profession, because he is an Israelite [a more polite term than "*juif*," Jewish]. He is a brave young man," and it pained her to think of him. A postal inspector stamped the number 4098 over Hella's words. Defiant, dangerous assertion fought nervous caution in Soldner's letter. Like Eve, the desperate Hella Soldner fantasied returning to a country that had officially rejected her.

SEPTEMBER 8, 1943: An armistice between Italian Fascists and antifascist Allies was publicly announced by US officials. The Italian military began an immediate retreat from southern France. The German military began an immediate occupation.

SEPTEMBER 10, 1943: The "violently sadistic" Alois Brunner, Adolf Eichmann's assistant and a senior officer in the Nazi SS, arrived in Nice with a highly trained team, eager to find, deport, and destroy Jews.

SEPTEMBER 26, 1943: A "Confidential" memo from Heinz Röthke, chief of the Nazis' French Department of Jewish Affairs, was titled "Final Solution of the Jewish Question in France."

SEPTEMBER 30, 1943: At midnight, in Nice, the terrified eight-year-old Serge Klarsfeld hid behind the false back of a closet with his sister, Georgette, and his mother, Raissa, as the Germans pounded on the family's door. The Nazis took Klarsfeld's father, and Serge never saw him again.

OCTOBER 20, 1943: at Eve and Hella Olstein's address in Nice, the Nazis arrested Samuel Straussman, age thirty-nine, a Polish-born dentist. Sent first to the Drancy camp, eight days later he was transported to Auschwitz-Birkenau.

On Tuesday, December 7, 1943, Eve Adams, fifty-two, living at 10 rue Alphonse Karr in Nazi-occupied Nice, and Hella Olstein Soldner, thirty-eight, were arrested. They had managed to escape arrest for three years of the German Nazi and Italian Fascist occupation. Then their luck ran out.

Soldner's arrest was described to her brother André by a friend, Lillian, who passed on an account from her cousin in Nice. Hella "was not in hiding, but had the wrong papers [perhaps meaning forged papers]. When she came home from work . . . one evening a 'car' was already waiting in front of the house and she was not allowed to go upstairs to take something with her." A man in the house met the same fate. (After the Germans occupied the Italian zone, one Holocaust survivor recalled, "official black Citroëns cruised the streets of Nice" picking up men who looked like Jews, examining them, and if they were circumcised, sending them to the Drancy camp, then to deportation.) The cousin added: After arrestees were sent from the Drancy internment camp, "there's no way of knowing where people are being deported to."

Lillian added, "It hurts me a lot to give you such a horrible message," but after not hearing from his "beloved sister" for so long, it must have been clear to Olstein that his sister had "disappeared in this way." Lillian hoped that Olstein's sister was "still alive" and would one day reappear. Lillian realized that her "banal words" would bring Olstein "little comfort," but "be sure that I feel for you." Lillian had learned in the same letter from her cousin that six close relatives had been transported from Holland to Nazi-occupied Belgium.

The day of Eve's arrest, a French police official wrote her a receipt for cash confiscated: 365 francs (about $7.82 in 1943, about $117 today). The fraudulence of this receipt-writing ritual was no doubt clear to the official and, probably, to Eve. Rumors were circulating about Nazis murdering Jews in extermination camps. Surely, the receipt writer knew that he or she was playing a ghoulish game.

Sent to the Drancy internment camp in a Paris suburb, Eve arrived five days after her arrest, on Monday, December 12. She was assigned number 9765 and listed on one document as a "governess." Eve probably hoped to work with the camp's children. Hella Soldner was also sent to the Drancy camp.

Eve and Hella briefly experienced the regime of Drancy's new director, SS leader Alois Brunner, sent by Adolf Eichmann to speed up deportations from the camp. They were imprisoned in the camp for about five days, sharing with other inmates the crowding, unsanitary conditions, and food shortage that made Drancy notorious.

Earlier in December, Heinz Röthke, head of the Nazis' Department of Jewish Affairs in France, had asked Adolf Eichmann in Berlin for permission to send 800 to 1,000 Jews on a new "Juden transport." On December 15, Röthke received permission to deport 850 Jews.

On Friday, December 17, Eve, Hella Soldner, and about 848 other deportees were loaded on transport 63. Eve was number 847 and her occupation was listed as "*Lerherin*"—a typo for "*Lehrerin*," teacher. Soldner was number 715 and her occupation was listed as "*Schauspielerin*," actress. A list signed by Alois Brunner asked that "high-grade" food carried in one car not be used for concentration camp prisoners."

The freight cars were sent about 930 miles—a trip, with stops, of three days and three nights. The prisoners' destination, though they did not know it, was Auschwitz-Birkenau, the work and extermination camp.

Camille Touboul, twenty-two, a Moroccan-born Jew, another a passenger on transport 63, recalled leaving Drancy ten days after her incarceration:

> The operation began with a brutal and noisy assembly, accompanied by blows and shouts, in the courtyard of the Drancy camp. We knew that this time it was a major departure, that we were going to leave French soil, and our hearts clenched. We were piled into trucks that took us to the station. On the way, to overcome our sorrow a little, we all sang the Marseillaise.
>
> At the station, we were literally assaulted by SS men armed with billy clubs, who were waiting for us and made us topple off the platforms. Blows rained down from all sides, amidst screams of agony, groans, and the cries of pain from the herd of victims. We wound up in a heap, tossed on to the bare boards of cattle cars. The mutation was complete this time: animals, that's what we had become.

When transport 63 departed it was carrying 848 to 850 deportees (the total is uncertain). The cars included French Jewish citizens and foreign-born Jews from Algeria, Austria, Belgium, Bulgaria, Czechoslovakia, Germany, Greece, Hungary, Italy, Latvia, Lithuania, Luxembourg, the Netherlands, Poland, Romania, Russia, Spain, Tunisia, Turkey, Ukraine, and Yugoslavia. One deportee, Gustave Bloch, came from Brooklyn, New York. The Nazis were efficient bookkeepers.

When transport 63 reached its first stop, the Bobigny station, the deportees were ordered to disembark and another passenger, Serge Smulevic, then twenty-two, born in Warsaw, recalled that Alois Brunner talked to the assembled captives. Brunner warned that if anyone tried to escape,

> all the other occupants of the car would be executed. He also warned us that it was forbidden to carry in our luggage any knife or other sharp object made of metal, to possibly attack the floor of the car, and that there was still time to spontaneously turn in such objects. And he began to randomly open luggage

and shopping bags. He stopped in front of my friend François Sandler, leaned over and opened his bag and began to search it, and took out a small knife to peel potatoes. Brunner got up, a sarcastic smile on his lips, and brought the little knife to my friend François's eyes, going at full speed from one eye to the other, as if he were going to kill him. And suddenly, with a precise and rapid gesture, cut off more than half of François's left ear, and handed the knife to one of the two henchmen who accompanied him. The blood dripped profusely down François's left side, but no one dared to move, and a few moments later we got into the car. Of course, as soon as the train left, we wrapped François's ear in a piece of shirt. The image of this hanging ear, I never managed to forget.

A third deportee on transport 63, Léon Arditti, twenty-seven, born in Bulgaria, recalled the train's halting movement:

> From time to time, a stop. Opening doors, orders shouted . . . we must give our watches, the one who will keep his will be shot, . . . then it is the turn of our pens . . . our portfolios . . . . These successive confiscations, these threats, appear as part of a well-orchestrated conditioning, intended to terrify us, make us bend, break us.

Approximately 501 of the deportees on transport 63 were male, 345 female (in a few cases, the person's sex was unlisted). About 99 of the deportees were children under eighteen. Among those on transport 63 were André Bauer, a former leader of l'Union générale des Israélites de France, his wife Odette, and their four children, Pierre (ten), Myriam (nine), Antoine (six), and Francine (three).

Camille Touboul continued her recollection of transport 63:

> We were too many in each car to find ourselves a place. Standing, pressed against each other, we were incapable of any movement. We became irritable in this untenable position, we called out, we shouted our rage at our torturers, we banged our fists and our feet against the walls. In the midst of this hellish racket, we could

hear the doors of the cars bolted and, with a shake that crushed us all the more, we headed for the unknown. Our impotence could not prevent tension from mounting: we lacked air in this car whose only opening, a mere small latticed window-slit, was located in an upper corner that everyone tried to draw near. We also discovered that no food had been distributed to us on leaving Drancy. How long would we be dragged about in conditions worse than those imposed on animals?

Even today I think, whenever I might want to free myself from this horror and emerge from this nightmare, of all those who took part in this transport, those children, innocents among the innocent, suffering thirst, hunger, and who, throughout the journey, never stopped whining, crying, screaming; I think of that wretched man who, for not having jumped into our car fast enough, had been beaten by one of the SS and lost his glasses; he made the trip as a blind man, in the heap that we were, and, shortly before we arrived, we noticed that he had lost his mind.

Touboul recalled two brothers on transport 63, Edmond and Léon Lachkar, who

set about helping the most disoriented of us, the elderly and children, opening for them a way to the window-slit, making a blanket into a sort of screen when it was no longer possible to resist the need to use the only "potty," placed in a corner of the car. Ah! those frightful bodily necessities! The smell, in that confined air, rarefied, became intolerable; people fought, without thought of everyone else's unhappiness, to get away from it.

Touboul abstained from relieving herself during the whole three-day trip and became ill. "Other nauseating smells," she remembered, "contributed to stinking up the car: the dead were already among us."

On February 14, 1944, four years after Eve's last communication with her brother, Yerachmiel Zahavy wrote two letters to Jewish relief organizations in Spain and Portugal. He asked for word of his sister "Eve Zloczower (Adams)" and requested a "quick answer," clearly yearning to hear that his sister had escaped Nazi-occupied France and was alive

826	WOLFF Léonie	8. 8.00	Ohne	2287
827	WOLFF Margot	21.12.01	Ohne	10214
828	WOLFF Maurice	21. 1.96	Kaufmann	2286
829	WOLFSDORF Abraham	30. 8.94	Päcker	9927
830	WOLLMAN Elisabeth	15. 8.88	Ohne	9942
831	WOLLMANN Eugène	26. 5.83	Arzt	9930
832	WULFOWITCH Henri	11.12.27	Mechaniker	9822
833	WULFOWITCH Joseph	4. 5.94	Elektriker	9820
834	WULFOWITCH Mindla	26.10.00	Arbeiterin	9821
835	ZABLOTZKI Ari	17.12.81	Friseur	9686
836	ZABLOTZKI Esther	15. 1.91	Ohne	9687
837	ZABOURI Roger	25. 2.23	Arbeiter	10180
838	ZELASNY Smil	4. 8.91	Stricker	10080
839	ZERMATI Claire	29.11.66	Ohne	10134
840	ZINGER Livia	2. 8.28	Ohne	9011
841	ZINGER Olga	26. 8.97	Ohne	9010
842	ZILBERMANN Bernard	19. 4.15	Pelzarbeiter	2283
843	ZILBERMANN Claudine	11. 4.43	Ohne	7951
844	ZILBERMANN Esther	1889	Hausfrau	2284
845	ZILBERMANN Fortunée	10.12.22	Ohne	7950
846	ZIMMERMANN Aron	4.91	Schneider	10078
847	ZLOCZOWER Eva	15. 6.91	Lehrerin	9765
848	ZONLIGT Moses	11. 9.77	Vertreter	9912
849	ZYLBERSTEIN Laja	1867	Ohne	9648

"Eva Chawa Zloczower" listed in the German binder of persons deported to Auschwitz on transport 63, December 17, 1943.

somewhere. Zahavy's letters were returned to him by the British censorship office, which said he was not allowed to send such letters under the terms of the British Mandate for Palestine. In 1945, André Olstein, in Switzerland, wrote to several organizations seeking word of his sister Hella Soldner and her friend Eve.

When transport 63 arrived at Auschwitz-Birkenau in German-occupied Poland, about 233 men and 112 women were selected to work. About 505 men and women were gassed. At the liberation, in 1945, of 31 survivors of transport 63, 6 were women. Eve Adams and Hella Olstein Soldner were not among them.

Epilogue

Eve Then, Us Now

IT'S DAUNTING TO FOLLOW ATROCITY WITH WORDS. No language is adequate to Eve's cruel murder, and the executions of millions. Silence seems more fitting; it gives us time to catch our breath. But after silence words are called for—emotions are not enough. Intellect is needed to contemplate what Eve's life might mean to each of us.

First, it seems important to affirm that my writing this book and your reading it are not redemptive. Nothing can undo the barbaric crime that ended Eve's and so many others' days on earth.

Second, Eve would want us to remember, I believe, her resistant spirit and acts, and her human complexities of character, as well as her cruel end. Eve's active life and involuntary death made me consider the relative weight each should play in my account of her. Certainly, justice required my fully reckoning with the Nazi monsters who had made her their prey. But would Eve have wanted her murder and murderers to define her life? She was a Holocaust victim, yes. But she was not only a Holocaust victim. She was also the complex, contradictory creator of herself. Without denying the barbarity of her death, I concluded that the focus of this history should be on Eve's acting in her world.

Third, it's time that Eve got her due, her story told and her killers named. She was murdered because she was Jewish. But she fell into the path of the destroyers because she was a lesbian who dared to speak publicly in the United States for a love that was supposed to shut up. She fell into the killers' path because she associated with famous, anarchist, radical leftist activists, and became the target of small-minded, cruel men—moralistic, powerful state employees. She was killed because she was a Jewish, lesbian, gender-bending, alien immigrant leftist radical of a class too poor to escape the Nazi juggernaut. Multiple intersecting human judgments, acted on finally by powerful Nazis, led to her murder.

The serious Eve and the witty Oscar Wilde seem an odd couple. But on April 5, 1895, a warrant for the arrest of Wilde set him on the path to prison and martyrdom. Just thirty years later, on June 17, 1925, the arrest of Eve Adams set her on the path to Auschwitz and death. As Wilde predicted in 1897 to George Ives, an early activist for "the Cause" (homosexual emancipation): "I have no doubt we shall win, but the road is long, and red with monstrous martyrdoms."

Perhaps, I hope, this biography's publication will lead us to a bit more evidence about Eve's time on earth. This possibility is suggested by the discovery, late in my research, in Israel, in a Zahavy family closet, of a file left by Eve's brother Yerachmiel. The evidence includes a letter dating, probably, to 1972, from Zecharia "Zachy" Zloczewer, a book-adoring, poetry-writing cousin in New York to whom Eve had provided "a little help" immigrating to the United States several years after her, when he was twenty-three.

Affectionately calling Eve "Khavtshe" and "Evelyn Adams" (a variation on her *Lesbian Love* pseudonym), Zloczewer remembered her as "a mercurial girl, red curly hair, actually wearing pants. Short hair, aggressive, learned English very quickly."

Like "so many other youths," Eve had torn herself "away from the ghetto in antisemitic Poland." Zloczewer called Eve "a suffragist, a bit of an anarchist, a bohemian," who "was close to a lot of social leaders." She had not become a citizen, he noted: "What does an anarchist need citizenship for?"

Eve was expelled from the United States, he stated, "because she had opened a sort of teahouse in a bohemian hub, where homosexuals used to gather . . . and she herself had actually written a pamphlet in English about lesbian love."

After Eve's deportation, Zloczewer had seen her in Poland in 1929 and had given her "a little money." He thought, falsely, that Eve had "deteriorated" and died at the start of World War II.

He ended: "So lived and died a creative person, a very interesting person who believed in a better life and was herself corrupted." Shifting judgments (as in Reitman's comments) reveal cousin Zloczewer's conflicted feelings about Eve's sexuality. Zloczewer's negative judgment should be "replaced with a positive phrase," suggested the friend who forwarded his letter to Eve's brother.

Each of us will certainly respond differently to Eve's history depending on our singular life experiences. Our personal stories will clearly color the emotions and thoughts that Eve's life evokes. A young, African American, gender-bending lesbian, born in 1990, who grew up in South Carolina, will have different insights into Eve's life than I have had, a White, gender-boring gay man, born in 1938 and bred in New York City.

Growing up, I had long heard that six million Jews had been murdered by the Nazis, and I had later learned of other groups marked by the Nazis for arrest, internment, and, often, extinction: anti-Nazi activists of all varieties, Communists, Socialists, Social Democrats, anarchists, Roman Catholics, Jehovah's Witnesses, Romanies, the physically and mentally disabled, male homosexuals, Soviet prisoners of war—the list goes on. Documentaries like Marcel Ophüls's *The Sorrow and the Pity* and Claude Lanzmann's nine-hour *Shoah*, while both praised and criticized, had years ago provided me an introduction to the Nazis' institutionalized horror. The Hollywood inventions *Judgment at Nuremberg*, *Sophie's Choice*, and *Schindler's List* provided shards of Holocaust history. But no one in my family had died at the hands of German Nazis or been interned by Italian Fascists, and the deaths of Holocaust victims had remained abstract. Until my research on Eve. Her last journey on that transport 63 freight car made the Holocaust concrete—that horror happened to someone about whom I had learned to care.

The Holocaust had begun to come into focus for me years earlier in the person of a survivor. As a resistant Jewish teenager in Frankfurt, Herbert J. Freudenberger had fought with a gang of Nazi youths and poked out the eye of one antagonist. That night his parents, fearing the Nazi gang's violent retaliation, put their son on a train alone, with false identification papers, on his way out of Germany forever. Somehow that terrified boy—"Herb," as I learned to call him—made his way from Zurich to Amsterdam to Paris and, finally, by ship to the US, I assume with the help of a resistance network alerted by his parents, though he recalled none of that. After many tribulations that boy grew up to become—almost accidentally but fittingly—a psychologist dedicated to helping victims of life's traumas discover the best in themselves and thrive.

I got to know Herb around 1960 as the astute and empathetic but challenging therapist who, after about a year of private sessions, announced to me one day, "Your problem isn't that you're gay. It's that you don't relate to anybody." I blanched, of course, at his unadorned words, but had to agree: I didn't relate to anybody. I trusted Herb by then, so when he declared, "I'm starting a new therapy group and you're in it," I gulped in fear and anxiously complied. Joining Herb's group helped this longtime isolate make a break out of the protective prison to which I had sentenced myself since childhood. Herb helped me join the human world.

In that group, and in private sessions with me and other group members, Herb sometimes offered relevant bits of his own childhood experience. Group members and I sometimes compared notes on the different bits of Herb's story revealed to each of us. One account that I recall was that Herb, as a boy, watched his synagogue in Frankfurt get set on fire, burning as a lone watchman waved frantically for help from an upper window.

One incident that I heard directly from Herb concerned his terrifying childhood escape from the Nazis. On that night train out of Germany, at just the slightest nod of a cooperative conductor's head, the boy knew he had to jump quickly off the back of the slowly moving train into the darkness. An image of that frightened boy jumping into the unknown haunts me still.

Another incident that Herb recounted was of waiting, fearfully, with false identification papers, to finally cross out of Germany. Ahead of him he watched a grand, aristocratic woman confront Nazi officers with the imperious demand for a chair, and their scrambling to oblige. After she received her papers and was walking passed Herb, she suddenly winked, giving the anxious boy courage to face the same officers with his forged papers.

When I first heard that Steven Spielberg's newly founded Shoah Foundation was recording video interviews with Holocaust survivors, I urged Herb to tell his story. A number of years later, when Herb was already ill with the kidney disease that killed him, he did sit for an interview. Watching that video many years after Herb's death, I learned details of his desperate escape and troubled youth that he had not been free to reveal to clients.

By the end of the 1960s, Herb's group, and Herb himself, had helped me feel good enough about myself to start exploring the gay liberation groups that had started up in New York City after the 1969 Stonewall Rebellion. In the winter of 1971, I nervously attended my first meeting of New York City's Gay Activists Alliance. By June 1972, GAA was producing my documentary play *Coming Out!* based on my first foraging for our lost history. That play led to a first book on US homosexual history, a collection of documents, and, over the next forty years, to three more sexual history books and a career as a historian of sexuality and gender. So I owe Herbert J. Freudenberger a loud, public, heartfelt thank-you for helping me affirm a deep, good part of myself and become a historian.

Herb is certainly one of the reasons I set out to research and tell Eve's story. During my talks with him I had come to understand how important he considered his own active link to a Jewish heritage so early and so violently attacked. As I struggled for my own new links to other humans, I knew Herb would have liked to hear of my exploring my almost nonexistent relation to Jewish culture. As I began researching Eve's history, I knew Herb was looking over my shoulder, proud to see me become a tracer of this missing Jewish woman.

As I worked on this book from 2017 through 2019, every major investigative agency of the US government had found that Vladimir Putin's techno-spies had intervened in the 2016 US presidential election with the aim of electing Republican Donald Trump. As I researched Eve's life, I rooted for Robert Mueller, a Republican former head of the Federal Bureau of Investigation, and the career officers at the US Department of Justice who were investigating whether Trump and Trump's team had colluded with Putin's effort and then obstructed US government investigators' efforts to document it.

As a child and teenager in the 1940s and '50s, during that era's Red scare, I well recall the anxiety fanned by newspaper headlines and US politicians' warnings that Russian, Commie, pinko perverts were conspiring to overthrow our government. So, I found it remarkable to experience, in my eightieth year, a historical moment in which a US president was denouncing as a "witch hunt" the efforts of the FBI and US Justice Department investigators to discover how a Russian authoritarian leader had compromised a democratic US election.

My rooting in my old age for the FBI and the Justice Department caused me to contemplate the strange political fluctuations of history. Years earlier, I'd been horrified to open the file that FBI agents had kept on me. Their surveillance started in 1956 after this eighteen-year-old had, I'm ashamed to say, done nothing more subversive than attend a meeting of the Antioch College "Socialist Discussion Club."

When I dropped out of Antioch after a year and returned to my family's New York City home, the file showed that FBI agents had continued their spying on this teenager. One file entry quoted a sign on the door under the front stairs of my family's home: RING TWICE FOR JONATHAN KATZ—obviously a coded message to my Soviet handlers. I was further disgusted to read what a busybody informer neighbor had told the FBI: "Jonathan Katz leaves the house early every morning with what appear to be school books." I was indeed traipsing off to City College with apparent schoolbooks.

I was later unpleasantly surprised to find myself among the victims of a notorious, illegal CIA project that had agents opening and copying letters that US citizens wrote to Soviet bloc countries. I'd written several innocuous letters to citizens of Poland and the Soviet Union whom I, in my early twenties, had met on a European tour.

As I was writing one day about Eve's surveillance by US Bureau of Investigation agents, I realized that my office occupied the room in which, during my childhood, my father, Bernard, had been asked by two FBI agents if he was ever a "card-carrying Communist." "No," he told them, explaining to me later, with a triumphant laugh, "We didn't have membership cards."

Yes, my father was a Communist Party member who in the 1940s idealized the Soviet Union and completely denied its rulers' monstrous crimes. But in everyday practice, my father's (small-c) communism meant that he was deeply, personally offended by the discriminatory acts suffered by African Americans and did his pioneering bit as a White guy to combat it. As a member of the Committee for the Negro in the Arts (a "subversive" organization according to the US attorney general), and as a self-taught student of African American history and early jazz and blues, my father gave lectures on those subjects and organized concerts at New York City's Town Hall. After my father's death, I requested his FBI file and learned that, among other illegal breaches of his and my mother's civil liberties, it documented government agents reporting who my parents voted for in the 1948 presidential election (Henry Wallace, the Progressive Party candidate, supported by the American Labor Party). The outcome of Eve's surveillance by servants of the US state was deportation and death. The outcome of my own and my family's surveillance made me a rebel historian.

Eve's murder by the Nazis, and their killing of millions, makes it clear once again that, given free reign, the cruelty of human to human sometimes knows no bounds. Closer to home, unfortunately, two examples make that point: the abduction of Africans and the institution of slavery in the southern United States, with the complicity of northern businessmen in maintaining the slave labor system; and the bombing of Hiroshima and Nagasaki with atomic weapons, which, however you judge the utilitarian rationales, was explicitly and purposely an act of terror inflicted on a civilian population by agents of the US state.

It would be remiss of me not to suggest that there is an alternative to institutionalized hate and unlimited personal power. It's that utterly subversive system: a fully realized democracy. That's a system in which all those with power hold it provisionally and must use it transparently, a system in which those with power are subject to daily scrutiny by those with equal power and are replaced if their actions harm the public good. That's a system in which those with power may be voted out if they use their power for cruel ends, and money doesn't buy some people extra votes, a system in which freedom of the press is guaranteed by the public ownership of the press, and journalist and historian sleuths are paid to freely follow clues wherever they may lead and support all truth claims by evidence.

It's a system in which the hunt for private profit does not annihilate all other values, a system in which the great means of power are held in common and used to ensure the public welfare, a system in which democracy is extended to the way we make the whole social world.

In Eve's 1941 passport photo she's dressed casually and has a familiar look—she could be one of my arty, brainy, political pals. People who knew Eve passed away fairly recently. Eve's actor friend Watson White died in 1968, and poet Kenneth Rexroth died in 1982. Eve lived "not long ago," and "not far away," as the subtitle of the Auschwitz exhibit at New York's Museum of Jewish Heritage pointedly stressed. Eve Adams is our contemporary.

I was thinking about Eve's death and life as I celebrated my eightieth birthday in 2018 and contemplated my own mortality. A longtime woman friend my age was facing a disease that made her wish she had the power, when the pain of living outweighed the pleasure, to call it quits. I was in good health but knew that, realistically, most of my life was behind me. If my luck held out, I had at most ten or maybe fifteen more years to complete a few more historical and creative projects. I wasn't dwelling morbidly or fearfully on my death; I was confronting a scheduling problem. My calculations put me on alert: if I wanted to finish a few more projects, I'd better get on with Eve's story. My sense of time passing more quickly each day kept me busy searching, and then searching again, for some elusive document, typing and then retyping each draft of Eve's story.

I can't end without mentioning my own, direct, personal family link to Eve's friend Emma Goldman and, thus, indirectly, to Eve. According to my late mother, Phyllis Brownstone, in the winter of 1927 she and her Jewish sorority sisters (Kappa Chapter, Delta Phi Epsilon) in Winnipeg, at the University of Manitoba, invited Goldman to speak to them at my mother's family home at 83 Yale Avenue, in that midwestern Canadian city.

It's hard to imagine what the world-weary, fifty-eight-year-old anarchist jailbird Goldman made of those earnest, respectable middle-class young college women. All my mother remembered and appreciated was that Goldman was warm and "motherly"—a trait she missed in her own mother.

I still have the Victorian silver tea set out of which my mother poured tea for Emma Goldman. I myself plan, in the not too distant future, to join a group of dear departed friends and family and pour tea for Emma Goldman. And, of course, I've invited Eve to join us. What stories those two will tell.

Wait a minute! I see a small figure way, way off in the distance. I can't make out who it is. Oh, now I see, it's Eve. She jumping up and down, waving her arms frantically, trying to get our attention. She's yelling something. I can't quite make it out. Oh, now I hear. She's shouting, "Don't mourn. Organize!"

Acknowledgments

I'VE SAID IN MY INTRODUCTION how much I owe Barbara Kahn and her collaborator the late Steven Siegel, Eran Zahavy, Daniel Olstein, Martha Reis's thesis and research, and Nina Alvarez.

For their belief in this book I am grateful to my literary agent Robert Guinsler and my editor Jerome Pohlen. At Chicago Review Press, I'm also thankful for an intrepid fact-checker, continuity supervisor, and copyeditor, developmental editor Devon Freeny, and for everyone else on CRP's team, including Andrea Baird, Hailey Peterson, and Sadie Teper.

For her early support I recall and thank the late Andrée Abecassis. For early support I'm also grateful to John D'Emilio, Jack Dowling, Lillian Faderman, David Gibson, Bert Hansen, Philip Harrison, Edward Jackson, Laurie Marhoefer, Tim McCaskell, and Arlene Stein.

For great editorial advice, thank you, Michelle Memran.

For discovering important, amazing, fabulous documents, thank you to Elizabeth Evens, Brian Joseph Ferree, Channing Joseph, Keava McMillan, and Dale Sheldon.

For valuable research assistance, thanks to Sukie de la Croix, Sara Dorfman, J. D. Doyle, Candace Falk, Malka Gross, Chad Heap, Paul Herron, Jarek Janiszewski, Jamey Jesperson, Serge Klarsfeld, Josh Lambert, Marie K. Rowley, Clifford Scheiner, Laurence Senelick, Noam Sienna, Doug Skinner, and Karl Sokalski.

For translation help and discussions of language I thank Naomi Cohen, Mimi Segal Daitz, John C. DeSantis, Melanie C. Hawthorne, Keanu Heydari, Hannah Leffingwell, Lauren Shulsky Orenstein, Liliana Ossowski, Victoria Pass, James Steakley, and Ri J. Turner.

I've been privileged to have known and been inspired by a number of extraordinary women no longer with us: Lois Adler, Cecily Brownstone, Becky Johnston, Carol Joyce, Mimi Kley, Margot Lewitin, Ann Snitow, Elly Weiss, and Connie Zoff. My beloved friend the late Allan Bérubé still guides me.

So many other people helped me in so many profound ways, material and psychological, objective and subjective. Thanks to each of the following for their assistance and enthusiasm for this project and others.

- Peggy Brady
- Kate Conroy
- Marty Correia
- Laurie A. Duncan
- David W. Dunlap
- Deborah Edel
- Carolyn Feigelson
- Luca Fenoglio
- Kathy Ferguson
- Ed Field
- Miriam Frank
- Richard Fung
- Thomas Glave
- Daniel Goode
- Edna Haber
- Kim Harris
- Elizabeth Heard
- Michael Hildebrand
- Wayne Hoffman
- Rebecca Jordan-Young
- Dan Kao
- Kimon Keramidas
- Larry Krasnoff
- Terry Lemke
- Judith Levine
- Liz Lindsey
- Bennet Marks
- Daniel Marshall
- Sandra Masur
- Caitlin McCarthy
- Don McLeod
- Janet Miller
- Joan Nestle
- Jake Newsome
- Livia Parnes
- Avivah Zuchman Pinski
- Joey Plaster
- Claire Bond Potter
- Harvey Redding
- Sheila Rowbotham
- Hugh Ryan
- Judith Schwarz
- Randall Sell
- Nikita Shepard
- Jay Shockley
- Dara Williams Smith
- Frank Stark
- Marc Robert Stein
- David Thomas
- Carole S. Vance
- Philip J. Virta
- Richard Wein
- Emily Weiner
- Alice Wexler
- Richard Wilcox
- Mary W. Wright

People at the following institutions provided valuable help:

- Arolsen Archives, International Center on Nazi Persecution, Bad Arolsen, Germany: Elfi Pohlmann, Reference Service
- Barnes Foundation, Honickman Art Library, Archives and Special Collections, Philadelphia, Pennsylvania: Amanda McKnight, Associate Archivist and Librarian
- Beinecke Rare Book & Manuscript Library, Yale University: Timothy Young, Curator of Modern Books & Manuscripts
- Center for Jewish History, New York City: Melanie Meyers, Senior Manager for Reference and Outreach
- Emanuel Ringelblum Jewish Historical Institute, Jewish Genealogy & Family Heritage Center, Warsaw: Anna Przybyszewska-Drozd
- FDR Presidential Library & Museum, Hyde Park, New York: Dara A. Baker, Archivist
- Ghetto Fighters' House (Beit Lohamei Haghetaot; full name Itzhak Katzenelson Holocaust and Jewish Resistance Heritage Museum), Documentation and Study Center, Western Galilee, Israel: Nadav Heidecker
- Illinois Historical Art Project: Joel Dryer, Director
- International Institute of Social History, Amsterdam, the Netherlands: Joppe Schaaper, Reading Room / Public Services
- Jüdisches Museum Berlin, Germany: Inka Bertz, Head of Collections / Curator of Art
- Mémorial de la Shoah, Paris, France: Cécile Lauvergeon, Documentaliste, Service Archives; Ariel Sion, Responsable du Service Bibliothèque; Dorothée Boichard, Documentaliste, Service Photothèque
- Michigan State University Libraries: Sharon Ladenson, Gender Studies and Communications Bibliographer Reference Librarian
- Minneapolis College of Art and Design: Eva Hyvarinen, Visual Resource Assistant
- Musée de la Résistance azuréenne, Nice, France: Jean-Louis Panicacci, Professeur honoraire d'histoire contemporaine à l'Université de Nice et Président des Amis du musée de la Résistance azuréenne
- National Archives, Chicago, Illinois: Glenn Longacre, Archivist
- National Archives, College Park, Maryland: Onaona Guay, Supervisory Archivist; Haley J. Maynard, Archivist, Textual Reference Operations

- National Archives, Washington, DC: William Creech, Archivist
- New York City Municipal Archives: Kenneth R. Cobb, Assistant Commissioner; Katie Ehrlich, Records
- New York County Clerk's Office, Division of Old Records: Joseph Van Nostrand, Archivist in Charge
- SteveMorse.org: Jean-Pierre Stroweis
- Strassler Center for Holocaust and Genocide Studies, Clark University: Robyn Conroy, Program Manager / Rose Librarian
- Syracuse University Art Galleries: Laura J. Wellner, Registrar
- United States Holocaust Memorial Museum, Holocaust Survivors and Victims Resource Center, Washington, DC: William Connelly
- University of Illinois at Chicago Library: Marilyn Bergante, Senior Library Specialist, Special Collections; Kellee E. Warren, Assistant Professor and Special Collections Librarian, Public Services and Rare Books
- University of Pennsylvania Libraries: David McKnight, Director, Rare Book and Manuscript Library; Eri Mizukane, Administrative and Reprographic Services Coordinator, Kislak Center for Special Collection, Rare Books and Manuscripts
- Wiener Holocaust Library, London, England: Mary Vrabecz, Senior International Tracing Service Archive Researcher
- Yad Vashem, Jerusalem, Israel: Yael Robinson, Reference and Information Services

Appendix

Lesbian Love

NOTE FROM THE AUTHOR: *Eve Adams's* Lesbian Love *is reprinted here with its original misspellings and style errors, because they are evidence that no one edited Eve's book for her. It represents her own voice and hints at more about her situation.*

LESBIAN LOVE

by
Evelyn Addams

Printed for private circulation only
Limited to 150 copies

Dedicated to my last love
Rosalie O. N.

CONTENTS

INTRODUCTION

Poem by Swinburne, from Sapphics

"Turn to me, O my Sappho";
Yet she turned her face from the Loves,
    she saw not:
Tears or laughter darken immortal eyelids,
    Heard not about her.

Fearful fitful wings of the doves departing,
Saw not how the bosom of Aphrodite
Shook with weeping, saw not her shaken rainment,
    Saw not her hands wrung;

Saw the Lesbians kissing across their smitten
Lutes, with lips more sweet than the sound of
    lute-strings,
Mouth to mouth and hand upon hand, her chosen,
    Fairer than all men.

GLIMPSES

JONNIE—tall, broad-shouldered, an oval face, strictly tailored clothes. A drink or two in her. Tenderly she embraces the little blond with Madonna eyes, and whispers: "Why Gretchen! You are not angry with me? You seem sad. I did not mean to run off last night and leave you. . . . Why child, you may have anything I have." Gretchen looked pitiful. It was rumored that at one time Jonnie kept six women in her apartment and treated them all royally!!!!

ANN—Came to our midst not long ago, all the way from the West Coast—left her past behind, and brought all the fire with her. She has striking yellow curls, big brown eyes, a figure that one cannot pass up, and most of all—she has a charming deep voice, almost masculine, but is able to impersonate a hundred other voices. Ann is the magnet, the fire, and wherever she appears she always leaves behind some victim. She is like a butterfly and is only attracted to virgins.

For a short time she fondles and caresses them, soon tired she exits, looking for someone new.

SARA—Just a slip of a girl; Ann's first love here. When Sara would sit at the piano and play jazz, her thin body would sway to and fro. She always appeared to me like a little rooster with a stretched neck. Sara loved Ann, loved her passionately, but she had a hard task. "There are so many rivals", she once complained bitterly. Sara loved her so deeply and her constant fear of losing Ann was so great that she became ill.

There was a scene in a little rendezvous tearoom, late after dinner hour, where six or seven girls had gathered. One lone man sat silent in a corner. Whispers and love sonatas could be heard among the group of girls—occasionally laughter. The atmosphere felt heavy—the man was intruding. . . . At closing hours he finally left.

They all, as one, threw up their hands: "Thank God, he has gone!"

May, the proprietress, known as Jim, suggested that Sara play the song she had composed for Ann. They all joined in the request.

With the windows shut tight, a dim candle light flickering, and, here goes the song:

"I love to have parties with you,

I know it's not right, but I do!

Day and night, night and day, etc. etc.

They all joined in the chorus—the song went on.

Jim smiled and the girls roared. She got a kick out of the song. It appealed to her greatly.

The song is full of passion and pictures before you, two nude girls, in ecstacy of love, fondling and kissing each others breasts, murmuring words of love.

Sara is gone—the scene shifts.

Dick is attempting suicide by trying to cut the veins in her wrists; Fritzie is threatening Ann with a revolver and finally attempting suicide because Ann trifles with them all.

It is all forgotten: Ann is triumphant. She laughs that big laugh of hers. . . . There appears a Goddess in their midst. Sulamith is her name. Sol they call her for short.

SOL—Slender, stately. Eyes deep and black as the sea. Hair of the blackest black and soft as velvet. Little lips, sensual lips of the deepest red, white pearly teeth.

A body perfect in statute, a body made carefully by the hand of God. A model of His great heavenly work. God's choicest child, God's pride—a perfect woman; but—

Sol has a hand of a man, a hand broad, big, strong, powerful, masculine, and Sol loves her own sex.

And when she first saw Ann she trembled and asked, "Who is this woman?" "I must meet her."

And she did!!!!

A few weeks pass by, Sol and Ann are seen together at dinner and in tea rooms.

"I wonder how long they'll last together?" everyone asks, for Ann is so fickle . . .

DAWN—A little Jewish girl with a mass of golden hair, wistful eyes, who has suffered and struggled way back in old and new Russia. Life is serious and a finer thing to her. She loves art and music above everything.

Dawn has worshiped Sol, now she looks on, and is sad. Fate had brought them together one day in one of those popular restaurants, when Dawn was having a gay dinner party, which was an unusual thing for her and at the next table Sol appeared among a group of her own.

As Dawn looked at Sol, their eyes met. Vino rosso was passed and they drank together, to their next meeting, and since then a beautiful friendship formed between them, which had grown later into a deep love.

Dawn is quiet now; looks on at life with a sad smile and hopes that Sol may come back to her, some day.

Weeks have passed—Sol and Ann's friendship has grown stronger and stronger—they are inseparable. Dawn realizes the situation. She has a tender heart, caused by much suffering and disappointments, and she yields to fate.

Both Sol and Ann love Dawn for her human understanding, and now Dawn is often seen with both of them—either at dinner, or a quiet visit to Sol and Ann's little home, chatting happily over a "million" trifles.

What a bad cook the "husband", Sol, makes; and what an untidy wife Ann is, they both smilingly complain. Sol says "it took her all afternoon to put things in order after her wife's toilette."

The three of them eat the burned spaghetti that Sol cooks, followed by fruit, coffee and cigarettes for desert.

Dawn has a delightful smile over it all—rejoices earnestly over their happiness.

WILLIE AND JACKIE

These two are a tiny world by themselves; outstanding so beautifully from the rest of them, with their charming innocence and youth.

Willie is about eighteen. "Oi!" once exclaimed Sasha, in her foreign accent, on seeing Willie for the first time, "Oi! how beautiful she is!"

Willie has a round face, pink cheeks and sensual lips, which remind one of a fresh apple just picked from the tree. She is a bit stout, loves to wear knickers, collar and tie, rolls her shirt sleeves up with a pair of garters, and is so proud when Jackie tells her that she is masculine.

Jackie is about the same age as Willie—a very refined type of Oriental—soft features, tender little body. She is all feminine.

Following is a description of a little scene which actually happened:

"Early one spring morning I walked into their private chamber. Willie and Jackie were wide awake with the sun-rise. I found them tightly clasped in each other's arms. Willie looked affectionately into Jackie's eyes, saying the following prayer:

"God bless Jackie and make her love me, because I idolize her" . . . and Jackie said a similar prayer in return.

Here, one may run into Willie and Jackie, standing in front of a furniture store window, admiring a day couch, a Morris chair, and you should see the smile and the glamour in their eyes when they look at a baby carriage. They really believe they can have a baby, and talk of getting married to each other—all so innocently and beautifully.

"Look at the birthday present Jackie gave me," says Willie, producing a silver piece of mechanism to light cigars and cigarettes, with her initials engraved upon it. She looks up with a smile and continues: "It was so sweet and thoughtful of Jackie to give me such a mannish present."

Jackie tells the following story—looking innocent and with much confidence: "One night Willie felt so tender and affectionate toward me—you know, she always takes the aggressive part, just like a man—I was so tired and wanted to sleep. I asked Willie to let me sleep awhile; then awaken me, and I'd let her love me. So I went to sleep, all the while I could feel her arms about me. I could feel her lips gently pressing to my forehead, to my eyes, to my lips—it was all like a beautiful dream.

"When I awoke in the morning Willie was still awake. She had kept vigil all night, too gentle to really awaken me when she thought I was fast asleep."

Greatly impressed with her story I asked, "And then . . . ?" Her face brightened up, and she added, with a smile:

"I want you to know, I was 'good' to Willie, too."

JUST A SNATCH

Otto and Juliet, both Lesbians, sat in a cafe, at opposite tables; their glances met.

Otto is a very energetic and fearless type. She secretly passed a little note to Juliet telling her how she admired her beautiful brown silken hair and blue eyes, in spite of the fact that there was a man and several women at her table. Juliet sent a note in return giving her name and telephone number.

The next afternoon Otto silently sat in her studio, looking out into the little park, watching the fresh young buds breaking. It was early in the spring. She was full of thoughts . . .

Suddenly, she jumped as from a long dream, picked up the receiver and called that number. The sweetest voice of a man answered: "Why, Juliet's not at home. She's at her office." Otto thought for a moment, and said: "Were you the gentleman in her party yesterday?"

A still sweeter echo rang in reply: "Why, I'm only her father!"

Otto felt bewildered, and just left a message.

Not more than ten minutes passed. Otto's phone rang. "Hello, beloved. This is Julius." and continued in the same breath, "I just rang home—something told me to do so, and received a message from father. How sweet and lovely of you to call. I thought you had forgotten all about yesterday."

Otto was still bewildered, and could think of nothing to say but, "No, I did not forget." Juliet's voice rang with laughter: "I bet you will not know me when you see me."

"Let's convince ourselves."

"What are you doing this evening, dearest?"

"I am at liberty to see you this evening, and all other evenings to come. Nothing will make me happier than to see you. Will you come, love?"

Otto said all this in one breath. She really was not certain of all she was saying. She merely pictured a beautiful adventure, and loved flirtations which often turned out to be serious, to her misfortune.

Juliet promised to come to her studio as soon as possible, and hung up.

When everything was silent again, Otto thought: "I really don't remember what she looks like. I wonder if I will know her. . . . Funny for Julius to think of that." And she tried to recollect that mysterious face.

In a few moments a knock at the door. Otto jumped up. "Oh yes, George! Is it you?" And she wakes as from a dream. "I am expecting a friend to dinner. Will you have some real Italian spaghetti, mushrooms on toast, asparagus, some fruit and wine?"

"Yes, madam," George replied with a bow and smile. "At what time is your lady friend expected?" "Oh, come back in an hour," Otto said, bored, sinking in a deep, soft chair and looking at the clock. "How slowly it moves!" In deep thought again—she picked up a book, glanced thru its pages, but could not understand a word. She walked softly up and down her room. It was twilight. She kept looking out of the window. "I wonder if she got lost? . . . The numbers on this square run so carelessly, and I forgot to mention South." And again she remained in deep thought.

Finally, a strange slight knock was heard. She got up and quietly opened the door.

"Here I am! Did you expect me?"

"Of course I did," Otto answered calmly, but inwardly trembling. "But why did you let me wait so many, many endless hours?"

"Why dear, it is not quite two hours since I called you, and I hurried here. Are you glad, dear?"

Otto seated her, took her face in both hands, looked at her for a moment, and said: "Of course I know you. And for that, will you allow me a kiss?" And she gently pressed her lips to Juliet's.

A slight knock. They both got up with a start. "Dinner!" George's voice. And he brought in an elaborate tray, covered with all sorts of fine things to eat. Otto saw some new cups she had not seen before, looked at them, and smiled. George nodded—meaning that they were for the special occasion, and said: "I did not forget the wine glasses this time, madam," and disappeared with a bow.

Otto and Juliet tenderly embraced each other.

"Now Julius, sweet angel, you must have a little dinner."

"Oh, how can I eat, beloved? Food? Who can think of food?" and she looked at Otto, full of longing. "But you must, dear," Otto replied. "You have not eaten, and worked hard all day, I believe."

"Now come, dearest, just a little taste of this excellent spaghetti that George prepared, and this beautiful fruit. And how about some wine?"

"If I must," Juliet sighed. They both smiled and endeavored to eat.

"I refuse to drink any wine tonight," Juliet announced.

"Why?"

"Because I am drunk already."

"Drunk with what?"

"Why, don't you know, dear?"

And of course Otto knew!!! One dimly shaded light while they both were trying hard to indulge in some sort of conversation.

"Oh, why talk? Ottilia dear? Now you must be silent!" She suddenly embraced her, and with so much strength and intimacy!!! "How beautiful you are! How I was looking forward to this! I never thought of this happiness tonight! Let me just love you, Otto, tonight. You must not even kiss me. This is going to be all my party! How lovely you are! What arms! Now let me undress you. I want to see you entirely nude in this light." . . . "What lovely breasts! One would never believe that of you, in your boyish clothes, the way you appeared yesterday. Now I shall kiss each part of your body separately, and you must let me!" Otto responded to all this, like an innocent child, with strange surprise, ecstacy and forgetfulness.

And so the evening drew into night. . . . Such silent melodies of love and joy, lasting moments of eternity . . .

Suddenly, Juliet wakes. "Oh! it is after midnight. My father will be sitting up, waiting for me. I must go!" It sounded like an ill-omen to Otto. Her heart sank. Never had anyone loved her so before. She sadly awakened to reality, and whispered: "If you must go, Juliet dear, I dare not keep you."

"We shall see each other again, Otto love—tomorrow, eh!!!"

"Till tomorrow, then." Julius kissed her and quickly disappeared.

Julius phoned Otto the next day, telling her that she could not see her, for little Jeanette the girl she has been living with for two years, or rather her wife, and found out where she was the night before. Father thoughtlessly mentioned the message left by Otto. . . . Poor little Jeanette had threatened suicide, and to calm her, she promised her never to see Otto again.

"Therefore we must not see each other for a while," Julius added and hung up.

Otto did not see Julius again. She was sad for days and weeks to come. That mysterious and lovely face of Julius haunted her. She could not forget. She grew sadder and sadder, and was waiting . . .

One gloomy morning, as she arose, her thoughts were of Julius, as they had been since that fateful day, and this particular morning she decided that she must see her, if only for one moment.

She did not know exactly where Julius might be found, and after many unsuccessful efforts finally located the office where she was employed, much to Julius' surprise, and whispered:

"Sorry to disturb you, Julius, but I had forgotten how your face looked, and just had to see it once more.

"Now I am happier," Otto quietly added, "and hope you are happy, Julius." And with that she disappeared.

Another page of sorrow was added to Otto's life.

SAMMIE AND DOTTIE

Sammie and Dottie got tired of back stage life and applause and decided to go into business. They came down to a famous neighborhood of the metropolis, looked around, got acquainted, and with the little savings they had put aside, rented a basement, and named it the "Flowery Tea Pot."

Soon the two personalities attracted wide attention:

Sammie is so masculine that even in her skirts she is a puzzle to everyone.

"Impossible," strangers say, "you can't tell me that this is a woman."

Sammie, with straight boyish figure, clean country lad's face, and a mass of flaxen hair, vaselined and tightly brushed back, is magnetic.

Dottie is pretty and stout, with long, fluffy black hair, black eyes. She always wears sleeveless gowns, while Sammie "struts" her tightly fitting tailored suit, and the inevitable attached collar and tie, which means so much in the life of a Lesbian. The two often get publicity in current periodicals and are generally called "husband and wife."

Sammie smiles when she reads these articles, while Dottie silently blushes.

This "Flowery Tea Pot" has become a very popular and interesting rendezvous for loving couples of the same sex, mostly the fair sex . . . where over a cup of tea lovers meet and wistfully look into each other's eyes . . . where new ones and lonely ones get acquainted and embrace each other, swaying to the melody of a dreamy waltz.

AN ADVENTURE

Little Jimmie was a working girl, of the Russian Inteligentzia, foreign in this country. She found employment in a ladies waist shop. The waist union was not only interested in dollars, but also in recreation.

When spring came the organization rented a hotel in a picturesque vicinity in Pennsylvania, surrounded by a lake, forests, and beautiful scenery, a lovely resort for their workers. Early in the summer illustrated circulars of the hotel were distributed in the shops, telling the girls of the country life, games and plays, and how they could enjoy their vacation away from the sweat-shop. One of these circulars reached Jimmie, and as she loved nature and the out-of-door life, she made it a point to spend her vacation there.

Mid-summer came and little Jimmie left the city, with its depressing atmosphere, for that country place. She found the people there just to her fancy—they were all radicals, and were free and unconventional in their attire and speech.

Little did Jimmie know of herself; little she knew of the masculine spark within her—all she did know was that she felt far more comfortable in boyish clothes. She could run better, climb trees better, and feel unhampered in every action and move in that free out-of-door place. Although she was the only girl there enjoying this boyish freedom no one seemed to take it amiss and she was therefore perfectly at ease.

One Saturday evening an entertainment was arranged by the workers. A play directed by the workers themselves was produced—famous singers and actors were brought from the city, pageants were arranged, and later on social dancing for every one. It was a very beautiful evening.

Jimmie was a very good ball-room dancer, and was therefore popular with both the girls and the boys. When dancing with a girl she always took the lead. She liked being the leader, somehow, and found that she took a keen delight in dancing with a girl rather than with a man.

While she was resting and observing the couples dancing, the idea occurred to her to choose a girl and request a dance. When the music stopped she quietly approached a little girl, with a youthful, eternal spring-like form, beautiful face and black, penetrating eyes. Jimmie asked her for a dance. The girl looked up with a smile and asked: "Can you lead?"

"Yes," Jimmie replied quickly.

As they were waltzing, Jimmie turned to her partner with a great deal of surprise, and remarked: "Why, you are not a working girl, you are a dancer—how do you happen to be here?"

"I am not a working girl—I am a dancer," she timidly replied.

"I am with the Metropolitan Ballet in Philadelphia. I heard of this place, and as it is near my home, I managed to come out here for a few days thru the privilege of my Union friends."

Jimmie looked at the girl and had a great desire to know more of this new acquaintance. As if in response to her thought, the girl informed her of the sad news of her departure the very next day. Jimmie felt much depressed for a moment, but as the music played on they continued to dance, and talk together until the very end of the evening.

Early next morning, they took a long hike together, and faithfully promised each other to continue their friendship, and as a result of that Bellina extended an invitation to Jimmie to visit her home as soon as possible. Jimmie was greatly elated with the invitation, and after a few moments pause, convincingly promised to visit her within three weeks time.

The same afternoon, the buses arrived, suitcases were loaded, people were bidding each other good-bye, and the atmosphere was filled with commotion and excitement. Bellina was among the people leaving. Jimmie had kissed the girl good-bye, but stood there silently, as if in a stupor, in the midst of all the noise. As the last bus left she suddenly made one dashing leap and was in the bus riding away with the departing guests.

The distance to the railroad station was about three or four miles, which gave Jimmie ample time to be close to Bellina and, oblivious of every one around them, they were both happy and rejoicing to be in each others company. When the train arrived, Jimmie entered it unaware of her boyish clothes. The train was not going to pull out for fully twenty minutes. They both sat down at ease on one of the seats, and Bellina childishly fondled one of Jimmie's curls. They did not say much—they were too over-joyed. Suddenly, Jimmie said: "Do you like that curl? You may have it." "Yes," Bellina replied, with much childish enthusiasm. Jimmie immediately jumped up, made a round among the passengers, and found a pair of shears. Bellina cut the curl, and by the time she had accomplished her task, the last whistle blew and Jimmie had to leave the train. Dazed, she walked slowly in the twilight of the winding country road to the hotel.

Precisely, three weeks later, Jimmie arrived at Philadelphia and was met at the station by her friend, Bellina. She announced to her that she had left New York for good and was going out West.

"How?" Bellina asked, "and how much money have you?"

"Just now I have seventy cents, but wait until to-morrow," Jimmie replied, with much enthusiasm. "I'll have more then."

"How?" Bellina asked again, questionably.

"I am going to work my way circulating for a publication," Jimmie replied.

Bellina took Jimmie's little bag and checked it, intimating that her mother was not well, which prevented her from inviting her home, and asked Jimmie where she was going to put up for the night. "I don't know and I don't care," Jimmie answered with a carefree smile on her face, "but won't you meet me at 8 o'clock tonight at the workers' library?"

At the appointed time they met, and Bellina asked Jimmie home.

Jimmie made a favorable impression upon mother and the rest of the family—and everyone seemed to be happy.

At bed time Bellina asked Jimmie up to her room, which she shared with her sister, and started to make preparations for retiring. She found a pair of pajamas for Jimmie. Jimmie felt strange, and said she always slept nude, but if she insisted she would wear them. "You must," said Bellina, "mother is very strict about it, and besides they are very comfortable, and were made by mother." Jimmie put them on and felt very much at home with them, and started to dance around. "Time to go to bed," Bellina said, in a commanding voice.

"Where?" Jimmie joyfully asked. "On this one," she said, pointing to the couch towards the window. "I want you to be comfortable, you are our guest, and I'll sleep with sister."

"Oh, no!" Jimmie replied. "I never sleep alone; I can't." (Jimmie was fibbing, for she always slept alone.) She added: "I'll sleep with you or sister—now it's for you to decide." Of course, Bellina decided to sleep with Jimmie. . . .

When they were assured by the soft breathing of sister that she was asleep, they nestled closer, silently kissing each other, and finally discarded their night clothes, against the rules of mother.

Neither of them knew what it was all about. All they felt was that they were happy, and lay awake until dawn in each others embrace. They were quite sure that the secret was theirs only, for sister was fast asleep.

At breakfast table, when the family gathered, each with due respect to mother and respectful courtesy to each other, sister suddenly blurted out: "What were you two talking about all night long? Was it a new Rome you discovered, or what?"

They both blushed and silence prevailed. . . .

SORINE AND IRENE

Out in the Middle-West, among the Norwegian folk, grew up a girl—Sorine.

At twenty-four she became a mother, giving birth to a girl—a child of passion.

Sorine became a promising artist, perhaps a genius to be. Stern, serious and indifferent she appeared to those who did not know her. Aside from her art she devoted her life to music and books.

To a chosen, unhappy few, she became a great teacher, and they her disciples. She taught that life does not mean merely personal happiness and existence, but we must love all people and things on earth, and give, give and never cease giving, and while talking her face would look so strange, her eyes so convincing.

One could see that she had suffered. Some hidden secret lay behind all that. The body meant nothing. She tried to awaken a good and beautiful soul in each one that crossed her path.

But her teachings were not in vain. Scattered over the world there are those, who once were full of life and passion, full of hope and desires, and earthly love, but who now have become silent, have struggled to suppress all earthly desires, and see things everywhere beautiful, all in the image of God.

Men and women they are, and are commonly called fools.

Sorine was a beautiful mother, one of her unhappy disciples once thought. A mother whom God could only create by his own hand, for her child of five proved it so by its beauty of mind and body. Now the page turns.

On one of those mysterious nights in the city of Chicago a party was given in the artists quarters, called the "Arabian Nights Ball."

We don't know how it happened, but Sorine was there, clad in costume. She was never seen at a ball before, for all knew she did not dance, and parties like that did not exist in her life.

But there she was, and when the party was at its gayest, a dancer appeared, a girl dressed in a tramp's outfit, half under the influence of liquor. She began to entertain the crowd by exhibiting a negro dance with all the life and passion there is in the black race. It was Irene, a girl of twenty-three—tall and boyish, with big, penetrating grey-green eyes.

She danced well, we must say, and Sorine, who was silently sitting watching the dancer was taken aback, and her face changed.

Irene was brought up in an orphanage and the moment she was let out she took to the freedom of the road. She traveled from coast to coast on the highways, back and forth, took jobs here and there and was always independent. She had learned a lot of life, and learned it not alone from books. Her knowledge of the English language fascinated one, and her boisterous character the more so. When she hated she hated, and when she loved she loved—no doubt about that.

When she wanted something she got it, and when anything or anybody was in her way, she brushed them aside with ease. Nothing will stop her when it comes to real fighting, not even a bullet. She has fought men and can prove it by several scars on her body. No one can dominate her.

Sorine was always the dominating type, the master. One look into her eyes, and you knew her great will, and had to obey. She was master at all times, and never obeyed anyone. . . .

Now in a little cottage far away in the North-West, by a lake, Sorine and Irene live, where once was the dwelling of her child and its father, and later on her disciples whom she taught love, and loved.

Sorine is not the same. She no more dominates, she no more rules. That mystic power of hers is gone. She is silent and obeys Irene. She no more preaches love for all humanity, and even expresses hate to a few, for Irene has influenced her.

At moments you may see that her soul is tortured by some thought of the beautiful past, but soon it is forgotten.

You may see her in Irene's arms, sitting by the lake, in the bright sunlight, kissing and caressing her, regardless of an occasional passerby, exposing the feelings that were always sacred to her, and kept a secret.

Referring to passion she would say: "It's sacred and should be kept to oneself and seldom practiced for it interfers with real love. Now passion occupies every moment of her existence. Even at their meals there were kisses and caresses.

"Honey," Sorine will say. "Yes, my love," is the reply. There may be thunder and storm outside, and there may be the banners of revolution storm, the world may change its whole appearance, but nothing matters to Sorine anymore.

I wonder! I wonder!

A RENDEZVOUS REVIVAL

It was toward the end of the Summer vacation, around Labor Day, when crowds of the city folk came out to the country to enjoy their weekend holiday. Miki was there too, a dark-haired girl unconscious of her feelings toward her own sex. She only knew she liked boy's clothes best, therefor she took advantage of being away from the city with its conventionalities. She dressed herself in a Palm Beach suit, which she had borrowed from a boy-friend before leaving the city, white silk sport shirt, windsor tie, tan silk stockings, and white canvas oxfords. In that manner she paraded around in the country, unconscious of herself.

At the end of a particular strenuous and rather exciting day, as the sun was setting, groups of people sat peacefully around everywhere, leisurely gossiping and enjoying the silence of the reclining day.

Miki moved restlessly from place to place. Notwithstanding the silence around her, and the subdued mood that all the people were brought into by the end of the summer's day, she still kept aimlessly wandering—perhaps she did have an aim—who knows?

She was about to decide whether she was to retire for the night when she over-heard a woman remark to a group of people, "Who is this undecided person?" pointing to Miki. Miki took advantage of the remark, approached the group without any ceremony, and looked at the stranger in a quizzical way.

She noticed a woman whose attire was in great contrast to her rather charming and feminine appearance. She wore a tailored blouse with a white turn-over collar, a blue silk windsor tie. She was about forty, but appeared much younger, due to her clear complexion and child-like trusting face, mass of brown silken hair, and guilless eyes.

Miki's interest was greatly aroused. Not much was spoken for there were people around. Miki just found out that this woman was a doctor, the city she came from, and her name. Miki did not know why, but she was curious about all, and as she was leaving the party (for she never had patience to remain long in one spot) the doctor playfully remarked: "Come to see me, Miki, if you happen to pass my city, without giving Miki her address of her home or office. Miki just walked off and thought nothing of it.

One year later, on one hot Summer day, Miki landed in a big city. She was aimlessly wandering from town to town for pastime or perhaps, adventure. To this city she arrived by train, which was not always the case in her travels, sometimes she would land by foot or in some one's automobile from which she had gotten a lift. She slowly walked out of the big central station and landed in the heart of the city to face a busy afternoon. She was a bit dazed, she was hot, she stopped and wondered where to go. She had a sum of money with her, an unusually large sum for her, $16. She was uncomfortable and felt the need of a lake or a mountain brook, where she could just throw her clothes off and plunge into the cool, refreshing water. But this was a city—a busy city. She thought for a while, and started for a hotel. The first hotel she reached she inquired about the rates and was told $6 per day. She was angry and started towards the next—there the reply was five and at the next four.

Miki evidently had rich taste, for she passed up a number of small hotels and stopped to inquire only at those where there were big lobbies, with palm trees growing in buckets, a lot of busy clerks and bellboys, etc. By this time Miki was very tired and felt very uncomfortable with the heat of the day. She found herself in front of one of Child's large restaurants. She knew of their clean, comfortable rest rooms, and there she walked in. She washed up liberally, used all the soap and water she wanted, put on a clean shirt, combed her hair, and took a deep breath of relief.

"There!" she said to herself almost aloud, "to hell with all the hotels and houses, I am going to get a bite to eat and will start wandering again—the day is young, why worry, and when the night comes I'll find a place to sleep. I have money enough."

Suddenly a thought, like lightning, flashed into her mind: Why, this woman doctor I met a year ago in the country lives in this city, I'll set out to find her. Miki never stopped to look up a city directory or a telephone book, which would have been perhaps a great help to her—it never occurred to her to do that—she simply walked out into the crowded street again, happy and care-free, positive that she would meet with the "adventure."

She saw a crowd heading somewhere. She followed, and found herself in an underground train, not knowing where it was bound for—North, South, East or West.

After a while people were getting off the train; she also arose and followed again—as if she were in a dream. On the platform she took a transfer, as she saw the rest of them do, and landed in the street again.

What a contrast! A big wide street, a few people out, the air was cool and refreshing, evidently near a big park or in a suburb. A street car came along, the train crowd rushed for it; Miki followed, still not knowing where she was bound for—but she was at peace.

Miki remained in the car, standing, leaning against the door, pleasantly recollecting things, hardly seeing anyone about her. Suddenly she felt someone staring at her—she looked up tremblingly and found the observer to be a charming woman, differently dressed. The face of that woman strangely appealed to Miki. She began to think hard, and decided to herself: "I am going over to this woman and tell her I am a stranger in this city, lost and don't know where I am bound for, and ask for her hospitality." As she was still thinking she unconsciously took a step forward, and found herself standing in front of her benefactor. Strange, the woman immediately spoke up with a smile: "Last time I saw you was about a year ago, but you were in boys' clothes; and I wasn't sure it was you, Miki."

Miki was dazed, she felt as if she were drifting in hazy clouds, and had that peculiar feeling that she was about to faint, but she came to and uttered just one word, with an effort: "Why, are you Doctor M.?"

"Yes," the lady replied, and made place beside her.

Miki was still half unconscious of the entire situation and when Doctor M. asked her for where she was bound, Miki replied, "To your house. I started out to find you."

"But how did you happen to come to this part of the city. How did you know?" the doctor asked. "My name is not listed in the phone book; these are my new quarters." Miki merely replied she did not know, she just set out to find her.

"You shall be my guest, then," Dr. M. said, in a way which made Miki happy, and she woke up to the pleasant reality of it all. They both got off the tramcar and Miki was escorted into a private old-fashioned home, facing a beautiful park.

Miki was shown to her room. The doctor remarked, pleasantly: "I am giving you the nicest corner of my house, to rest in, next to my own chamber, where no one ever disturbs me. You are my guest for your short stay in the city, for I know you are a wanderer and will not remain in one place very long.

"There are two girls living upstairs; perhaps you know them—they were in the country that day I saw you for the first time. Be careful. Let us be discreet, for they consider me very aloof, and remote. Now make yourself comfortable child," and with that she kissed Miki. "If you have any baggage at the station, have it sent up here to your temporary home."

Miki felt strange, bewildered, and happy.

At dinner, in the presence of the two other girls, the Doctor acted very reserved and quiet, and Miki did likewise.

At midnight, when the stillness could be "heard," Miki sat up in her bed, "listening" to the strange silence of the night. Her thoughts were wandering; she looked far out into the night watching the stars, and the half-moon, and she wondered why her friend was so strange and quiet when she said good-night to her. Miki wondered, questioningly: Is everyone really asleep?

In the quietness of the night she heard a soft voice: "Miki are you up yet?" "Yes, Doctor." "Come in here!" Miki got up and walked into the Doctor's chamber.

The curtains were raised, and the moonbeams fell all over the large beautiful room. Miki sat down near her and they spoke in whispers. After a while Miki was asked to lie down, so that she might feel more comfortable.

The night was lovely—it was like a heavenly dream . . . Miki was intoxicated . . . she did not know why, she felt strange. . . .

. . . The night lived on . . . a silent, soft ticking of a clock in a distant corner . . . whispers . . . tender, intoxicating soft kisses . . . trembling . . . thrills . . . joy . . . ecstacy . . . sweet pain . . . and the moonbeams slowly fading away . . .

Weary with life and joy, Miki fell into a heavy, and pleasant sleep.

Miki felt strange the next morning, she was ashamed, not knowing why or of what . . . and dared not look into Dr. M.'s eyes. The day brought important calls to the Doctor, and she was off as if nothing really had happened. Nothing was mentioned.

Late in the afternoon, when Miki was putting her few belongings together, Dr. M. walked in.

"What! Miki wandering off?" "Yes," she silently replied. Dr. M. gave her a silent and longing look. She knew well she could not keep Miki. She knew she would wander off just as she had come.

DIANA THORNTON

Beautiful, popular Diana. Penetrating, charming—wicked blue eyes. The perfect woman vampire of women.

Discards her ex-lovers with a grin and movement of her beautiful hands, brushes the unpleasant memories aside with ease and grace: "Can't be annoyed with notes sent by those I once loved they come too often, and in bunches," she says.

"I never read them. My maid reads them first, and if she finds something worth while, I let her read a passage or two for me.

Each new love is Diana's first love. Each new love she meets with childish enthusiasm, powerful passion, and forgetfulness. She honeymoons in fashionable hotels of old New York. If it happens to be a hard winter, it is Miami, a capricious spring, it's Bermuda, and sometimes, Paris.

Her honey-moons last for days, sometimes weeks, all uninterrupted.

"What I want, I take," she says, and she possesses the power and charm of doing so.

"Ice water, more cracked ice," is her popular demand of the bell boy, who stands wistfully in the doorway sometimes to peek at her new lover, for she is well known, it's not her first stop there, but the boy courteously obeys, courteously takes the order, for he knows there is a generous tip coming.

Diana never failed yet to win the affection of the one she wanted. They all yield to her, and they all leave heart-broken, when she commands them to go.

Her present love is perhaps just as beautiful as Diana herself. Gracia is her name, and the name well suits her.

Gracia has been just as fickle as Diana, and there are many with broken hearts that she has left, and left them with an easy conscience.

But the two seem to belong to each other; the honey-moon is lasting quite an unusual while. Is Diana losing her power to lure? Or is this present flame stronger than all the others and therefore powerfully lasting!!!

So girls, your chance is gone!! Look elsewhere for your happiness!!

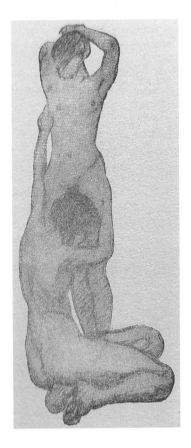

HOW I FOUND MYSELF

As I was traveling around, I landed, one beautiful late summer day, in a little country place occupied by a colony of artists. Tired and weary of my travels, I decided to remain in this colony for awhile and forget my business—rather my mission.

I set out to look around, found a number of summer cottages, all private family dwellings, surrounded by hills and orchards, a swimming pool, lovely avenues, little summer houses. Oh! it looked so different from the rest of the world. . . . I knew I would find peace there. Finally, I was directed to one house, called the "Oak Villa," which was set in shrubberies and oak trees.

I decided to stay there as long as I could. I therefore arranged a plan of my own, suiting my fancy, entirely secluded from the rest, for I was so tired of people and talk with which I had to contend in the business world. I discarded my traveling clothes, put on a pair of overalls and sandals, a cap, and set out for a long walk.

I was 19 then, five feet tall, proportionally built, and appeared very much like a boy of fourteen and as I was entirely to myself, except at meals, the rest of the crowd did not disturb me. My soul was so over-filled with nature and all her beautiful moods that I did not need any diversion from any of the people around me. This is the way my day was spent: A walk in the early afternoon, a dip in the pool in the afternoon, and then lying about in meditative contentment, observing everything about me. I would also occupy my time painting water color sketches, studying Italian for the harmony and the music of Italy was so appealing to my soul. In less reflective moods I would pick up a newspaper or some current periodical and in that manner I felt that my day was complete in every way. After supper I took long walks, far into the night, alone. So the days passed, beautifully, peacefully, harmoniously not a bit of disturbance. I was overwhelmed with happiness, and the joy of living—until one evening . . .

I arrived at a place full of light, gay laughter and music, where people had gathered to dance. I inquired what it was all about and was told the colony had its yearly costume party, given by one of the richer members, and all these people were guests for the evening. I just stopped there for a few moments, curiously observing, and wandered off into the night again.

When I reached the "Oak Villa" the house was dark, and I tried quietly to find my way in, when suddenly I heard a soft woman's voice:

"Hello, little boy." I turned around, saw this woman sitting in one of the rockers on the porch. "Hello," I replied, "but I am not a boy." She chuckled, and said in a sweet voice: "I know you are not a boy, but just a lonely little girl; won't you sit down on my lap?" I did feel a bit lonely that night, and somehow for a long time dreamed of a woman's motherly caresses. I was so tired of my travels, and of men; somehow, I associated with men, principally due to my work, and all I met were men, men, and when I met them socially they all tried to caress me.

I cannot complain and say that they tried to take advantage of me in any way—on the contrary, they were gentle and very comradely in their relationship. They were of a radical type, and sincere men, they admired my work and helped me, but to one thing, even a kiss, I could not respond. I did not know why.

Something was lacking in my life.

So this night I yielded to my stranger. I sat on her lap, looked into her luminous eyes—they were large, and of deepest blue, and what a gentle expression. We sat there and talked for a long while. She held me in her arms as one holds a child—I was happy. I forgot all the worldly injuries and struggles—I felt gentle, tender caresses of a woman's hand about me. "I was happy" . . . .

Later she ask me to her room. In the dim light I could see her young, bright, beautiful face. She seemed thirty, or a little younger. . . . I remained with her. Her body was full of fragrance, soft as the touch of velvet and yet strong, supple, and powerful. When she held me tight and gentle in her arms, it seemed as if our nude bodies melted into one, and a sudden fear came over me that I could never be separated from her body. At that moment the incident of a tragedy of the birth of twins, and their bodies attached to each other, never to be separated, came to my mind, and I, with childish fear, told it to her in a whisper. She only smiled and drowned all my fears with her kisses and ardent caresses. . . .

I didn't know where I was or what happened to me—it was a thing too sublime to give an account of—I still do not know—I often try to think and recollect, but in vain. . . . All that I know is that it was one of the greatest and most significant events of my life, which will never be forgotten, and that the memories are always just beautiful.

Photo Credits

Every effort has been made to contact the copyright holders. The editors would welcome information concerning any inadvertent errors or omissions.

front cover: (center) Portrait of Eva "Eve" Adams (BLRP_0030_0349_012), box 30, folder 394, courtesy of the Ben L. Reitman Papers, Special Collections and University Archives, University of Illinois at Chicago; (clockwise from upper right) Eve Adams's fingerprints, NYPD photo no. 8785, copied February 24, 1927, courtesy of the NYPD Photo Unit Collection, New York City Municipal Archives; *Good Morning* journal illustration excerpt, courtesy of the Marxists Internet Archive; postcard and passport images, courtesy of the Daniel Olstein Collection

p. x: Portrait of Eva "Eve" Adams (BLRP_0030_0349_012), box 30, folder 394, courtesy of the Ben L. Reitman Papers, Special Collections and University Archives, University of Illinois at Chicago.

p. 6: "The 8 Million," *Daily News* (New York, NY), August 8, 1954, via Newspapers.com. © Daily News, L.P. (New York). Used with permission.

p. 11: Courtesy of Wikimedia Commons.

p. 13: DN-0052268, *Chicago Sun-Times / Chicago Daily News* collection, Chicago History Museum.

p. 14 & 47: Courtesy of the Marxists Internet Archive.

p. 15 & 139: Courtesy of the Eran Zahavy Collection.

p. 17: Courtesy of the Ben L. Reitman Papers, Special Collections and University Archives, University of Illinois at Chicago.

p. 29: Courtesy of the Billy Rose Theatre Collection, New York Public Library Digital Collections.

p. 35: Card Index to Names of Persons in General Departmental Files, 1917–1930, entry A1 101, US Department of Justice, courtesy of the US National Archives.

p. 55: New York State Supreme Court, *Declarations of Intention Filed in New York County, 1907–1924*, petition vol. 659, petition 45, courtesy of the Division of Old Records, New York County Clerk's Office, courtesy of the Division of Old Records, New York County Clerk's Office.

p. 61: Collection of the Museum of the City of New York.

p. 63: New York City Municipal Archives, Department of Records & Information Services.

p. 68: NYPD photo no. 8785, copied February 24, 1927, courtesy of the NYPD Photo Unit Collection, New York City Municipal Archives.

p. 72: "Granny Quits the Force: Warred on Dope 19 Yrs.," *Daily News* (New York, NY), September 5, 1954, via Newspapers.com. © Daily News, L.P. (New York). Used with permission.

p. 89: Courtesy of Ancestry.com.

p. 101: © 2020 The Liberty Library Corporation. All Rights Reserved.

p. 118, 125, 134, 135, 136, 137 & 146: Courtesy of the Daniel Olstein Collection.

p. 120: Wambly Bald, La Vie de Bohème (As Lived on the Left Bank), *Chicago Tribune and the Daily News, New York* (Paris), January 3, 1933, 4, via Gallica, https://gallica.bnf.fr/ark:/12148/bpt6k4777547q/f4.item. The illustration is unsigned.

p. 133: Ghetto Fighters' House.

p. 153: Courtesy of Mémorial de la Shoah, Paris (France).

Notes

Introduction: Searching for Eve

"Polish-Jewish immigrant": Maureen O'Connor, review of *The Women Who Made New York* by Julie Scelfo, *New York Times Book Review*, December 1, 2016.

Lesbian Love: Evelyn Addams [Eve Adams], *Lesbian Love* (n.p, "Printed for private circulation only," 1925). Date of publication is per Eve's testimony that the book was published early in February 1925. Published in an edition of 150 copies, 72 pp., four drawn illustrations. Cataloged in the Yale University Library Catalog at http://hdl.handle.net/10079/bibid/5568728. A photocopy of *Lesbian Love* was sent to me by Nina Alvarez, who found a copy in the lobby of her building in Albany, New York, in 1998: Alvarez, e-mail to Barbara Kahn, May 29, 2013. The Alvarez copy is Eve's original edition with four sexually explicit photos of women pasted in to sell the book as porn. While Eve said she published her book in 1925, Dr. Clifford Scheiner, an expert on the history of erotica, identified the four porn photos as dating to the 1930s or later. In addition, having become acquainted with Eve, I am absolutely convinced that she would never have included sexually explicit pornographic photos in her book. The full text of *Lesbian Love* is reprinted in the appendix, and subsequent citations will reference both the original page numbers and, in parentheses, the corresponding page numbers in the appendix.

Claims about Eve: I quote here as many of Eve's and others' expressive words as I can, always distinguishing evidence from my interpretive comments. When the evidence is ambiguous and my interpretation tentative, I hedge with a "perhaps" or "probably." It's important, I think, to support fact claims with evidence and clearly distinguish the probable from the confidently substantiated.

1. Eve Speaks

"show cause why": W[illiam] W[alter] Husband (second assistant secretary of labor, US Department of Labor, Immigration Service), call for hearings, October 16, 1926, Correspondence Case & Policy Files, 1906–1959, RG85, E9, #55588/556–560, 17W3, box 7300, 18/5/6, Tabbed, Archives File. US National Archives, Washington, DC. Husband's is one document in the fifty-nine-page file that constitutes one of the major documents in the Eve Adams archive. This is a file of US government documents associated with Eve's deportation hearings. A copy of this file was discovered by researcher Steven Siegel, who gave it to Barbara Kahn. A copy was sent to me by the National Archives, Washington, DC, in miscellaneous order. I have ordered this file chronologically, numbered each page consecutively, and divided it into numbered sections to make the retrieval of the chronologically arranged sections and pages easier for future researchers. This file is subsequently cited as USDLIS followed by a number sign indicating a section and then a page number. For example, the W. W. Husband citation above is USDLIS #5, 8. Two sections of the fifty-nine-page file—#7 and #11—are themselves paginated. When citing those sections I include the original page number and note the page number of the whole file.

deportation hearing at the women's penitentiary: Transcripts of the first three of Eve's deportation hearings are contained in the twenty-one-page, continuously paginated document that composes USDLIS #7 and is dated, on its last page, April 11, 1927. The text of Eve's fourth deportation hearing, on May 23, 1927, is in USDLIS #11, 1–4 (37–40 of whole file). The texts of the hearing records identify the questioning inspector or lawyer as "Q" and person being questioned as "A." My presentation of these texts replaces "Q" with either "Inspector" or "Lawyer" or the specific questioner's name (for example, "Conry") and "A" with the name of the person being questioned ("Eve" or "Leonard").

"I admit having written a book": Quoted from her second hearing, November 30, 1926, USDLIS #7, 8 (18 of the whole file). During this testimony Eve commented that, of the ten copies of *Lesbian Love* confiscated by the police, four or five were present at her deportation hearing.

Greenwich Village: Caroline F. Ware, *Greenwich Village 1920–1930: A Comment on American Civilization in the Post-War Years* (Houghton Mifflin 1935; rpt. by Octagon Books, 1977), 55, 96 121, 237, 238, 252–253.

"deprave and corrupt": Michael Chabon, "'Ulysses' on Trial," *New York Review of Books*, September 26, 2019, 4–8.

tearoom had occupied the basement: David George Kin locates Eve's tearoom in a "sub-cellar"; David George Kin (pseudonym of David George Plotkin), *Women Without Men: True Stories of Lesbian Love in Greenwich Village* (New York: Brookwood, 1958), 101.

sworn, written testimony of Fitzpatrick: USDLIS #1, 1.

described himself as an "artist": The New York State Census for 1925 lists Fitzpatrick as living in the Bronx with his mother. New York City directories and federal censuses list Fitzpatrick's work variously as "appraiser" (1915–1918, 1920), "real estate broker" (1920), "artist" (1920–1929, 1931), and "Illustrator for art magazine" (1930). New York City directories from 1926 through 1929 list Fitzpatrick's address as 38 Washington Square, the same address at which Eve was living in 1926. Directories and census records via Ancestry.com.

Eve's "landlady": Mrs. Adele Marchesini is listed as "housekeeper" and one of twelve "lodgers" at 38 Washington Square West in the New York State Census dated June 1, 1925, via Ancestry.com. Marchesini, apparently the boardinghouse's concierge, had been born in Italy, was fifty-three, and had been in the United States twenty years. Like Eve, she was an "alien" (not a citizen), which made her susceptible to cooperation with Fitzpatrick and the immigration officials with whom he was probably in touch about Eve. It was from this same board-inghouse, and Mrs. Marchesini's oversight, that the young Eugene O'Neill was forced to flee, lacking rent money, leaving a trunk of his belongings. Robert R. Haslett, "Thirteen Failures of Successful Men," *Brooklyn (NY) Daily Eagle*, December 19, 1926, 86, via Newspapers.com.

"practicing prostitution": Husband, call for hearings, October 16, 1926, USDLIS #5, 8.

"undesirability" of "Eve Zlotchever": Jay Fitzpatrick, "Sworn Statement," June 23, 1925, USDLIS #1, 1.

Eve lived in a first-floor room: An official Immigration Service document dated November 24, 1926, listed Eve's address as "38 Washington Square, 1st floor"; USDLIS #7, 1 (11 of whole file). Eve swore that she lived on the "first floor"; Eve's testimony, November 30, 1926, USDLIS #7, 1, (11 of whole file). Thomas J. Conry, a US immigration inspector, asked Eve where she lived at the time of her arrest and she testified at 38 Washington Square [West], "first floor"; USDLIS #7, 4 (14 of whole file). And Conry asked Eve, "How long did you reside at 38 Washington Square West, first floor?" to which Eve immediately responded without contradicting him, "Off and on for about two years in the house"; Eve's testimony, February 10, 1927, USDLIS #7, 11 (21 of whole file).

"There is not a man rich enough": Eve's testimony, USDLIS #7, 9 (19 of whole file).

describing Eve's alleged attempted sex: Margaret Leonard's testimony, February 10, 1927, USDLIS, #7, 13 (23 of whole file).

"about a little suit": USDLIS #7, 15 (25 of whole file).

Eve listed "Tailoress": List or Manifest of Alien Passengers for the United States Immigration Officer at Port of Arrival, SS *Vaderland*, sailing from Antwerp, Belgium, May 25, 1912, via "Chawe Zlocsewer," *New York, Passenger and Crew Lists (Including Castle Garden and Ellis Island), 1820–1957*, Ancestry. com.

what she was doing the next afternoon: Leonard's sworn testimony suggested that Eve was arrested on June 12, 1926, but all other evidence indicated that Eve was arrested on June 17. USDLIS #7, 12 (22 of whole file).

Love 'Em and Leave 'Em: "Love 'Em and Leave 'Em—Broadway Play—Original," Internet Broadway Database, https://www.ibdb.com/broadway-production /love-em-and-leave-em-9992. According to the *Brooklyn Daily Eagle*, the Times Square Theatre marked its 150th performance of the play the night before Eve and Leonard attended; Goings-On in the Theaters, *Brooklyn Daily Eagle*, June 11, 1926, via Newspapers.com.

contradicted its attempt: Elizabeth Evens, "Plainclothes Policewomen on the Trail: NYPD Undercover Investigations of Abortionists and Queer Women, 1913–1926," *Modern American History*, December 22, 2020, https://www.cambridge .org/core/journals/modern-american-history/article/plainclothes-police women-on-the-trail-nypd-undercover-investigations-of-abortionists-and -queer-women-19131926/BAA8DD80C5B8D33A25194E0690A30C2D.

"lavish presents": Ben Reitman, "Eve," Outcast Narratives, n.d., #61, box 1, folder 15, Ben Lewis Reitman Papers, University of Illinois at Chicago Library (hereafter Reitman Papers).

2. Departure and Arrival

first walked up the gangplank: "List or Manifest of Alien Passengers," SS *Vaderland*. On top of the name "Zlocsewer, Chawe" in the manifest are the handwritten numbers 945/121 and 7/1/25 followed by what looks like two initials of a name, indicating that someone inspected this document on July 1, 1925, probably responding to Eve's application for a return permit to the United States for her planned trip abroad.

twenty-four million or so immigrants: Katherine Benton-Cohen, *Inventing the Immigration Problem: The Dillingham Commission and Its Legacy* (Cambridge, MA: Harvard University Press, 2018). Two years before Chawa's arrival in 1912, the US Census Bureau counted almost 940,000 "foreign born white" American residents born in Russia, Austria, or Germany who spoke Polish as their "mother tongue." This compared with a total population of the United States in 1910 of about ninety-two million. US Census Bureau, "Country of Birth of the Foreign-Born Population (Census: 1850 to 1940)," in *Historical Statistics of the United States, 1789–1945* (Washington, DC: US Government Printing Office, 1949), 32, via US Census Bureau, https://www.census.gov/library/publications/1949/compendia/hist_stats_1789-1945.html.

cost about $52.50: "Lowest Transatlantic Ocean Rates—1910," Gjenvick-Gjønvik Archives, accessed October 13, 2020, https://www.gjenvick.com/Brochures/1910-TravelGuide/LowestTransatlanticOceanRates.html.

about $1,400 today: CPI inflation calculator, US Bureau of Labor Statistics, accessed September 21, 2020, https://data.bls.gov/cgi-bin/cpicalc.pl.

paid for by an uncle: When Eve arrived in 1912 she was asked by an immigration official who paid her passage and she answered "Uncle"; "List or Manifest of Alien Passengers," SS *Vaderland*. Even though young Fannia Cohn's parents were middle class, in 1904 her steamship ticket from Poland was paid for by rich cousins in New York. Annelise Orleck, *Common Sense and a Little Fire: Women and Working-Class Politics in the United States, 1900–1965* (Chapel Hill: University of North Carolina Press, 1995), 23.

Alexander Migdall, an earlier immigrant: Petition for Naturalization, dec. no. 69805, via "Alexander Migdall," *Connecticut, Federal Naturalization Records, 1790–1996*, Ancestry.com. Alexander's birth date was listed as June 7, 1883, his birthplace as "Malava Russia (Poland)," and his spouse as Yetta. He arrived in the United States on April 15, 1904, via New York City.

Mława, Poland: For background on Eve's hometown, see the website of the City of Mława, http://archiwum.mlawa.pl/.

father, mother (Mariem-Ruchla Migdall Zloczewer), and siblings: "Mordka Josif Zlo-czewer" and "Mariem-Ruchla Migdal" married in 1885 per Mława PSA Births, Marriages, Deaths, Jewish Records Indexing, Poland, JewishGen, https://www.jewishgen.org/. A second source, the Central Database of Shoah Victims' Names, Yad Vashem: The World Holocaust Remembrance Center, https://yvng.yadvashem.org/index.html, lists seven names of children from the Zloczewer family of Mława, headed by "Mordekhai Yosef," a "merchant," and "Miryam" or "Miriam" Migdall, including "Ewa" or "Eva" or "Khava," born 1890 [*sic*], "single," a "journalist," data submitted by her brother "Yerakhmiel Zahavi." Clicking on top of the first names of each person makes visible a few more details and the name the person who supplied the information. Slightly different family data is provided in a third source by Eran Zahavy, in a Zloczower family gene-alogy posted December 16, 2014, on the website Geni (https://www.geni.com/family-tree/index/6000000002920263005). It includes Chawa, born 1891, and Yerachmiel Zahavy (originally Zloczewer), born May 22, 1910, in Mława, Poland, died February 20, 1983, in Tel Aviv, Israel.

"Race or People" called "Hebrew": US Immigration Commission, *Dictionary of Races or Peoples* (Washington, DC: US Government Printing Office, 1911), 73–75, via Internet Archive, https://archive.org/details/dictionaryofrace00unitrich/page/n3/mode/2up.

an 1891 birth certificate: Archiwum Państwowe w Warszawie, Oddział w Mławie, Narutowicza 3, 06-500 Mława, trans. Liliana Ossowski. In this birth certificate, "Mordka Yosif Zlocower" reported in front of two witnesses on August 14, 1891, that, on June 15 (according to the Julian calendar then in use), in the afternoon, his wife, "Miriam Ruchla Migdal," gave birth to a female baby given the name "Chawa." At the bottom of the document, among the signatures, there is one by "M J Zloczewer" So despite the certificate's earlier reference to "Zlocower," he signed his last name "Zloczewer." Eve's father's casual relation to recorded birth dates is indicated by his reporting his child's birth almost two months after the event.

March 31, 1891, as her birth date: Eve listed her birthday as June 15, 1891, when a French police official wrote a receipt for money received from "Madame Eva Zloczower" on December 7, 1943; excavation book #38, 43, in French, via Mémorial de la Shoah, accessed October 12, 2020, http://ressources.memorial delashoah.org/zoom.php?code=297301&q=id:p_249347, trans. Mimi Segal

Daitz. Yet she swore at her US deportation hearing that her birth date was March 31, 1891; Eve's testimony, November 24, 1926, USDLIS #7, 2 (12 of whole file). Eve's determined self-making is evidenced by her immigrating, adopting the name Eve Adams, writing and publishing *Lesbian Love*, opening two queer-friendly tearooms—and perhaps by choosing a March 31 birth date. Why she chose that date is a mystery. One guess is that the sexual encounter she described in "How I Found Myself" occurred on March 31.

her culture's casual relation: Liliana Ossowski, born in the USSR, reports that one of her mother's sisters, who survived World War II, simply chose April 15, 1915, as her birth date. Since many births then took place at home and parents were often too busy to register a birth, they registered when they did have time or didn't register a birth at all. Liliana Ossowski, e-mail to JNK, August 29, 2019.

Tuesday, June 4, 1912: "List or Manifest of Alien Passengers," SS *Vaderland*.

first- and second-class passengers: Alison Bateman House, "Medical Examination of Immigrants on Ellis Island," *AMA Journal of Ethics* 10, no. 4 (2008): 235–241, doi: 10.1001/virtualmentor.2008.10.4.mhst1-0804.

about $600 today: CPI inflation calculator, US Bureau of Labor Statistics, accessed October 13, 2020, https://data.bls.gov/cgi-bin/cpicalc.pl.

five-foot-two-inch: Eve's height and weight are listed in an Immigration Service document dated April 11, 1927, USDLIS #7, 1–2 (11–12 of whole file). Eve also listed her height and weight in 1925, on her return to the United States. US Department of Labor, Immigration Service. List or Manifest of Alien Passengers for the United States Immigration Officer at Port of Arrival, SS *Minnekahda*, sailing from Boulogne-sur-Mer, November 28, 1925, via "Eve Zlotchever," *New York, Passenger and Crew Lists (including Castle Garden and Ellis Island), 1820–1957*, Ancestry.com.

Isidor Meegdall: Eve testified that her uncle Isidor, her mother's brother, spelled his last name Meegdall. Eve's other businessman uncle, Alexander, spelled his last name Migdall; Petition for Naturalization, dec. no. 69805.

moved in with New York City friends: Eve's testimony, April 11, 1927, USDLIS #7, 7 (17 of whole file).

anglicized the Polish version: Eve's Hebrew name, Chava (חוה), was Khave in Yiddish. Her Yiddish name was transliterated as Chawa or Chawe, the Polish equivalent of which is Ewa, from which she took the English Eve. See Alexander Beider, "Names and Naming," YIVO Encyclopedia of Jews in

Eastern Europe, accessed September 15, 2020, https://yivoencyclopedia.org
/article.aspx/Names_and_Naming.

55 West Twenty-Eighth Street: Copies of *Mother Earth* list the editors and give the
1912 address of the publication; *Mother Earth* 7 (1912–1913), via Hathi Trust
Digital Library, https://babel.hathitrust.org/cgi/pt?id=mdp.39015037030171.

The attempted assassination divided anarchists: Paul Avrich and Karen Avrich, *Sasha
and Emma: The Anarchist Odyssey of Alexander Berkman and Emma Goldman*
(Cambridge, MA: Belknap Press of Harvard University Press, 2012), 51, 89.

Goldman publicly equivocated: Emma Goldman, "The Psychology of Political Violence," in *Anarchism and Other Essays*, 3rd. rev. ed. (New York: Mother Earth
Publishing Association, 1917).

"a short, red-headed": Reitman, "Eve." Spelling corrected in quotation from Reitman. His memory of Eve is quoted and referenced by Tim Cresswell, *The
Tramp in America* (London: Reaktion Books, 2001), 102–103. It probably
dates to the early 1930s.

then common derogatory phrase: "Jew girl" appeared often in newspapers in the
early twentieth century, but by 1912 Jewish leaders were protesting the use
of the term as derogatory, saying "To speak of 'Jew boys,' 'Jew girls' or 'Jew
stores' is both objectionable and vulgar." "Gives Rules for Use of the Words
Jew and Jewish," *Davenport (IA) Democrat and Leader*, June 23, 1912, 21, via
Newspapers.com.

"You will know her": "When last seen she was in California . . ." *Good Morning*
(New York, NY), February 1, 1921, 19, and "She is now in the East . . ." *Good
Morning*, March 1–15, 1921, 18, both via Hathi Trust Digital Library, https://
babel.hathitrust.org/cgi/pt?id=inu.30000093613887.

"illustrate the ease with which": Ben Reitman, "Olga" (Eve Adams), and "Bernice" (Ruth
Olson Norlander), both in "Homosexuality (To Be Added to Part IV)," 7–8, box
3, folder 50 (Writings—"Living with Social Outcasts," 1933), Reitman Papers.

doctor who performed abortions: "Biographical Sketch," Reitman Papers over-
view, University of Illinois at Chicago, https://findingaids.library.uic.edu/sc
/MSReit71.xml. No other source refers to Eve having an abortion, but it seems
unlikely that Reitman would have invented this detail about her.

Eve's pantsuit: Edward Shanks, "The Revolution in Dress," *Saturday Review*,
August 29, 1925, via *Fascination Street* (blog), https://fascinationstreetvintage
.wordpress.com/2015/06/08/1920s-fashion-and-rebellion-article/.

passionate though conflict-laden intimacy: Goldman described her romance with
Reitman in her autobiography *Living My Life* (New York: Dover, 1970; orig.
publ. 1931). It is also detailed in two major biographies: Alice Wexler, *Emma
Goldman* (New York: Pantheon Books, 1984), and Candace Falk, *Love, Anarchy and Emma Goldman* (New York: Holt Rinehart and Winston, 1984).

His "Willie" and her "treasure box": Wexler, *Emma Goldman*, 146–148.

a "Respectable Mob" of fourteen men: Ben L. Reitman, "The Respectable Mob,"
Mother Earth 7, no. 4 (June 1912): 109–114, via Hathi Trust Digital Library,
https://babel.hathitrust.org/cgi/pt?id=mdp.39015037030171.

"who has all her life faced": Roger A. Bruns, *The Damndest Radical: The Life and
World of Ben Reitman, Chicago's Celebrated Social Reformer, Hobo King, and
Whorehouse Physician* (Urbana: University of Illinois Press, 1987), 127.

rebel women had begun to speak out: A lesbian's confident defiance of dominant
judgments was reported in Douglas C. McMurtrie, "Some Observations on
the Psychology of Sexual Inversion in Women," *Lancet-Clinic* 108, no. 18
(November 2, 1912): 488. Some English and American homosexual men also
began to speak up. In 1895, using his own name, the Englishman Edward Carpenter first published ("for private circulation only") *Homogenic Love and Its
Place in a Free Society*. Carpenter's publications in defense of "the intermediate sex" circulated in the United States. Jonathan [Ned] Katz, *Gay American
History: Lesbians and Gay Men in the U.S.A.* (New York: Thomas Y. Crowell, 1976), 363, 630n66. The 1897 edition of Havelock Ellis's *Sexual Inversion*
included an essay by Professor X (now revealed as Harvard math professor
James Mills Peirce), who defended "homosexual love" as a "natural pure and
sound passion." Katz, 374–376; Hubert Kennedy, "The Case for James Mills
Peirce," *Journal of Homosexuality* 4, no. 2 (Winter 1978): 179–184. In 1907,
the Reverend Carl Schlegel was fired from his Presbyterian church in New
Orleans for speaking for and distributing the literature of the German homosexual emancipation movement. He advocated for the equal legal status of
homosexuals, heterosexuals, bisexuals, and asexuals. Jonathan Ned Katz, "Carl
Schlegel: The First U.S. Gay Activist, 1906–1907," June 1, 2019, OutHistory.
org, http://outhistory.org/exhibits/show/schlegel/contents. In 1918 and 1922,
two pioneering autobiographies by transgender author Ralph Werther–Jennie
June urged justice for the persecuted "androgyne" communities of the time.
Earl Lind (Ralph Werther–Jennie June), *The Autobiography of an Androgyne*
(New York: Medico-Legal Press, 1918); Ralph Werther–Jennie June, *The*

Female-Impersonators (New York: Medico-Legal Journal, 1922). On December 24, 1924, the State of Illinois granted Henry Gerber, a German immigrant, the Reverend John T. Graves, an African American minister, and others a charter for the Society for Human Rights, the first homosexual emancipation organization in the United States. Katz, *Gay American History*, 385–397.

"Dr. K.": Katz, 371.

"Inverts should have the courage": Katz, 374, 631n80.

"conviction of Oscar Wilde": Katz, 376, 631n82.

"any act entered into": Lucifer, the Light Bearer, March 1901, quoted in Wexler, *Emma Goldman*, 94. In 1909, after Emma Goldman was denied a place to lecture on the modern drama, a wealthy homosexual, Alden Freeman, who "sympathized with . . . rebels," offered Goldman his East Orange, New Jersey, barn for the lecture, later supporting her work financially and corresponding with her. Terence Kissack, *Free Comrades: Anarchism and Homosexuality in the United States, 1895–1917* (Oakland, CA: AK Press, 2008), 143.

in January 1915, Goldman's lecture tours: "Emma Goldman Extended Timeline," Libcom, February 8, 2016, https://libcom.org/history/emma-goldman -extended-timeline.

"freedom in love, birth-control": Goldman, *Living My Life*, 555–556.

"She had nothing to say": Margaret Anderson, "Two Points of View," *Little Review* 1, no. 10 (March 1915): 32, quoted in Jonathan Ned Katz, *Gay/Lesbian Almanac* (New York: Harper & Row, 1983), 363–366.

"true friend of the ostracized": "Anna W.," "Emma Goldman in Washington," *Mother Earth* 11, no. 3 (May 1916): 517, via Hathi Trust Digital Library, https://babel.hathitrust.org/cgi/pt?id=mdp.39015013434926.

"heard many lectures by Emma Goldman": Katz, *Gay American History*, 272.

afterward lived as Alan L. Hart: On Hart's novels and later life, see Katz, *Gay/Lesbian Almanac*, 516–522; and for an updated understanding of Hart see Morgen Young, "Alan Hart (1890–1962)," *The Oregon Encyclopedia*, last updated October 4, 2019, https://www.oregonencyclopedia.org/articles/hart _alan_1890_1962_/. An early public assertion of lesbian love is the poetry that anarchist Elsa Gidlow published in Chicago in 1923, "obviously addressed to women." Walker Rumble, "Publishing Elsa: Will Ransom's Grey Thread," *American Printing Association*, March 21, 2016, https://printinghistory.org /gidlow-ransom/.

"prove it on me": Jonathan Ned Katz, "Ma Rainey's 'Prove It on Me Blues,' 1928," OutHistory.org, accessed September 16, 2020, http://outhistory.org /exhibits/show/rainey/rainey2; J. D. Doyle, e-mail to JNK, April 29, 2019, sending "Paramount Race Series" list of recordings from www.78discography.com.

Anderson "is crazy about you": Goldman to Reitman, October 1914, Reitman Papers, II, f. 125. quoted in Wexler, *Emma Goldman*, 308–309n35.

Sperry and Goldman: Katz, *Gay American History*, 523–530, 661n166.

a sexual intimacy developed: In one letter, responding to Goldman's invitation to visit her at the farmhouse Goldman was occupying near Ossining, New York, Sperry said, "I, too wish that I could spend a week with you in the country." Sperry to Goldman, September 19 [1912?], quoted in Clare Hemmings, *Considering Emma Goldman: Feminist Political Ambivalence and the Imaginative Archive* (Durham, NC: Duke University Press, 2017), 184. In another letter Sperry asked, "How will the 26th of August suit you for me to come to see you . . . ?" She added, "I want to touch you—I want to see whether you really have substance or whether you are merely one of my dreams." Katz, *Gay American History*, 526.

"Dearest. . . . If I had only": Falk, *Love, Anarchy*, 175.

"not to make her [Sperry] realize": Falk, 173.

"He tackled the wrong woman": Falk, 173.

"asked Hutch Hapgood": Falk, 173.

"You say you wanted Hutch": Emma Goldman to Ben Reitman, [November or December 1913], 10 PM, Reitman Papers, [no further citation in source], quoted in Wexler, *Emma Goldman*, 308–309n35.

"Yes, I have known": Emma Goldman to Ben Reitman, "10:30 Friday" [n.d.], Reitman Papers, II, f. 132, quoted in Wexler, *Emma Goldman*, 308–309n35. Whether Reitman propositioned Hapgood is not known, but Hapgood might have considered it. An astute observer of the bohemian scene, Mary Berenson, declared that Hapgood sought "God and the Absolute among thieves, anarchists, prostitutes, and pederasts"; Kissack, *Free Comrades*, 25–26. Early in Hapgood's relationship with Reitman, Hapgood liked Reitman as a hobohemian character, and both cultivated the acquaintance of the same "outcasts." Years later, in his memoir, Hapgood denounced Reitman for using "the cloak of the revolutionary movement" to practice free speech like "a vulgar and ribald salesman." Hutchins Hapgood, *A Victorian in the Modern World* (New York: Harcourt, Brace, 1939), 283.

3. 1912

Berkman was one of the first: For more on anarchist defenders of homosexuals as an oppressed group, see Kissack, *Free Comrades*.

an older prisoner, Red: Alexander Berkman, *Prison Memoirs of an Anarchist* (New York: Schocken Books, 1970; orig. publ. 1912), 167–173.

growing love for Johnny Davis: Berkman, 318–324, 343, 347–348, 350–351.

"Doctor George": Berkman, 429, 433–434, 437–440.

"Most of these experimenters": Harry Warren Zorbaugh, *The Gold Coast and the Slum: A Sociological Study of Chicago's Near North Side* (Chicago: University of Chicago Press, 1929; reprint 1976), 91.

without reference to baby-making: Christine Stansell, *American Moderns: Bohemian New York and the Creation of a New Century* (New York: Metropolitan Books, 2000); see "birth control" in the index.

Pathologizing the lesbian: Christina Simmons, "Companionate Marriage and the Lesbian Threat," *Frontiers: A Journal of Women Studies* 4, no. 3 (Autumn 1979): 54–59.

strove to realize in practice: Neith Boyce and Hutchins Hapgood, *Intimate Warriors: Portraits of a Modern Marriage, 1899–1944; Selected Works*, ed. Ellen Kay Trimberger (New York: Feminist Press, 1991).

sex o'clock in America: An article published in 1913 refers to "William Marion Reedy's memorable phrase." See "Religion and Ethics: Sex O'Clock in America." *Current Opinion* 55 (August 1913): 113–114. Reedy was the editor of the *St. Louis Mirror*, a prominent literary publication. William Marion Reedy Papers, Newberry Library, https://mms.newberry.org/xml/xml_files/Reedy .xml. The other "new" phrases were reported in newspapers and books in the United States in the early twentieth century.

textile workers in Lawrence, Massachusetts: Melvyn Dubofsky and Foster Rhea Dulles, *Labor in America: A History*, 8th ed. (Chichester, UK: Wiley-Blackwell, 2010), 195–199; Robert Forrant and Jurg Siegenthaler, eds. *The Great Lawrence Textile Strike of 1912: New Scholarship on the Bread and Roses Strike* (New York: Routledge, 2017), 105.

"not got angry": Robert Forrant and Susan Grabski, *Lawrence and the 1912 Bread and Roses Strike* (Charleston, SC: Arcadia, 2013), 71; Ross Wetzsteon, *Republic of Dreams; Greenwich Village: The American Bohemia, 1910–1960* (New York:

Simon & Schuster, 2002), 170. National publicity, much of it written or inspired by Greenwich Village radicals, helped workers win this particular strike.

Triangle Shirtwaist Factory: Doug Linder, "The Triangle Shirtwaist Factory Fire Trial," Famous American Trials, 2002, UMKC School of Law faculty website, http://www.law.umkc.edu/faculty/projects/ftrials/triangle/triangleaccount .html (page discontinued).

A first-class ticket included: Wayne Hall, "Social Class and Survival on the S.S. Titanic," *Social Science and Medicine* 6, no. 22 (1986): 687–690, via Semantic Scholar, https://www.semanticscholar.org/paper/Social-class-and-survival -on-the-S.S.-Titanic.-Hall/3b29a8a5f87e783a94566d30e6993a23a52b52e0.

"not the number but the kind": E. Dana Durand, Director of the Census, "Our Immigrants and the Future," *World's Work* 23, no. 4 (February 1912), via Gjenvick-Gjønvik Archives, https://www.gjenvick.com/Immigration /ImmigrantTypes/1912-02-OurImmigrantsAndTheFuture.html.

"There is one factor in the prevalence": Thomas Salmon, address to the Poughkeepsie Academy of Medicine, January 29, 1912, typescript, 1, Salmon Papers, American Foundation for Mental Hygiene, Payne-Whitney Clinic, New York Hospital, quoted in Richard Wightman Fox, *So Far Disordered in Mind: Insanity in California, 1870–1930* (Oakland: University of California Press, 1978), 106. For the record, Fox concludes that evidence shows the alleged link between immigrants and insanity was false.

"remarkable tendency to suicide": Thomas W. Salmon, "Immigration and the Mixture of Races in Relation to the Mental Health of the Nation," in *Modern Treatment of Nervous and Mental Diseases*, vol. 1, ed. W. A. White and S. E. Jelliffe (Philadelphia: Lea and Febiger, 1913), 258, via Hathi Trust Digital Library, https://babel.hathitrust.org/cgi/pt?id=mdp.39015022365038. Salmon is cited in Margot Canaday, *The Straight State: Sexuality and Citizenship in Twentieth-Century America* (Princeton, NJ: Princeton University Press, 2009), 31. Dr. Salmon, employed by the US Public Health Service, had first established psychiatric services for immigrants on Ellis Island. "Thomas W. Salmon Papers," Weil Cornell History of Psychiatry, http://psych-history .weill.cornell.edu/pdf/ThomasWSalmonPapers.pdf.

"In the matter of Chinese and Japanese": Woodrow Wilson continued, "Their lower standard of living as laborers will crowd out the white agriculturalist and is, in other fields, a most serious industrial menace." Masuda Hajimu, "Rumors of

War: Immigration Disputes and the Social Construction of American-Japanese Relations, 1905–1913," *Diplomatic History* 33, no. 1 (January 2009): 1–37.

Jack Johnson: Al-Tony Gilmore, "Jack Johnson and White Women: The National Impact," *Journal of Negro History* 58, no. 1, (January 1973): 18–38.

a White mob lynched four Black people: John Eligon, "Their Ancestors Were on Opposite Sides of a Lynching. Now, They're Friends," *New York Times*, May 5, 2018. See also "Jan. 22, 1912: Hamilton, Georgia Lynching," Zinn Education Project, accessed November 9, 2020, https://www.zinnedproject.org/news /tdih/hamilton-georgia-lynching/.

Sixty-two African Americans were murdered: Doug Linder, "Lynchings: By Year and Race," Famous American Trials, 2000, UMKC School of Law faculty website, http://law2.umkc.edu/faculty/projects/ftrials/shipp/lynchingyear .html.

"Prohibit any of the old time": Peter Iverson, *Carlos Montezuma and the Changing World of American Indians* (Albuquerque: University of New Mexico Press, 1982), 126–129.

US marines landed in Cuba: Hugh Thomas, *Cuba, or The Pursuit of Freedom* (Boston: Da Capo Press, 1998; orig. publ. 1971), 523.

US troops invaded Nicaragua: Lester D. Langley, *The Banana Wars: United States Intervention in the Caribbean, 1898–1934*, 2nd ed. (Lanham, MD: Rowman & Littlefield, 2001), 64.

forces intervened in China: Richard F. Grimmett, *Instances of Use of United States Armed Forces Abroad, 1798–2004*, Congressional Research Service Report RL30172, Library of Congress, 2004.

"Vast" numbers of women: "Vast Suffrage Host Is on Parade Today," *New York Times*, May 4, 1912.

"If America is ever to become": Philip S. Foner, ed., *W. E. B. Du Bois Speaks 1890–1918* (New York: Pathfinder Press, 1970), 253.

"A little band of willful women": Judith Schwarz, *Radical Feminists of Heterodoxy: Greenwich Village, 1912–1940*, rev ed. (Hereford, AZ: New Victoria, 1986); Wetzsteon, *Republic of Dreams*, 16, 176, 180.

the Lesbian Herald: "Lesbian Herald Staff," *Frederick (MD) Post*, April 19, 1912, 2, and "Lesbians of Woman's College Give Fete . . . ," *News* (Frederick, MD), May 13, 1912, 2, both via Newspapers.com.

"The prototype of the woman invert": McMurtie, "Some Observations," 487–490. McMurtrie was not a doctor but a typographer and graphic designer, and a curious, relatively nonjudgmental man who wrote a number of early articles on homosexuality published in medical journals. For McMurtrie's biography see James M. Wells, "Douglas Crawford McMurtrie," *Dictionary of American Biography*, supp. 3, 1941–1945 (New York: Scribner's, 1973), 492–493.

4. War Clouds and a Fan Letter

a multination war began: International Encyclopedia of the First World War, accessed September 21, 2020, https://encyclopedia.1914-1918-online.net.

Selective Service Act: "Selective Service Acts," Britannica.com, accessed January 28, 2021, https://www.britannica.com/event/Selective-Service-Acts.

Espionage Act: "The Espionage Act of 1917, Digital History, accessed September 21, 2020, http://www.digitalhistory.uh.edu/disp_textbook.cfm?smtid =3&psid=3904.

a fervid fan letter: Eve Zlotchever to Fania Marinoff, February 21, 1918, series 1 (Correspondence), box 175, folder 2255, Carl Van Vechten Papers (YCAL MSS 1050), Beinecke Library, Yale University.

Marinoff was the wife of Carl Van Vechten: The long, complex, and intense intimacy between Van Vechten and Marinoff is discussed in Edward White, *The Tastemaker: Carl Van Vechten and the Birth of Modern America* (New York: Farrar, Straus and Giroux, 2014).

Jacob Marinoff was the editor: "Jacob Marinoff, 94, Dead," *New York Times*, October 28, 1964. Evidence offered later documents Eve's work as a sales agent for *Der Groyser Kunder*.

she had twice seen Fania Marinoff star: Eve to Fania Marinoff, February 21, 1918. *Karen*, by Danish writer Hjalmar Bergström, appeared at the Greenwich Village Theatre from January 7, 1918, to March 1918; "Karen—Broadway Play— Original," Internet Broadway Database, accessed September 21, 2020, https:// www.ibdb.com/broadway-production/karen-8650.

"free, to be sure, and independent": "M. C. D.," "Drama: Marriage and the Playwrights," *Nation* 106, no. 273 (March 7, 1918). The reviewer commended the play as "a searching and sincere study of free love, marriage, and the relation of the sexes." Many other reviews of the play are available via Newspapers.com.

"Strumpet of a daughter": Hjalmar Bergström, Karen Borneman, and Lynggaard & Co., *Two Plays by Hjalmar Bergström*, trans. by Edwin Björkman (New York: Mitchell Kennerley, 1913), 90, via Internet Archive, https://archive.org /details/karenbornemanly00berggoog/page/n6/mode/2up.

Isadora Duncan: Duncan toured the US in 1915–1918; see photos by Arnold Genthe, New York Public Library Digital Collections, accessed September 21, 2020, https://digitalcollections.nypl.org/collections/isadora-duncan?filters [name]=Genthe%2C+Arnold+(1869-1942).

Ethel Leginska: Barbara Sicherman and Carl Hurd Green, eds. *Notable American Women: The Modern Period; A Biographical Dictionary* (Cambridge, MA: Belknap Press of Harvard University Press, 1980), 416.

"I have only one life to give": Goldman's declaration at the rally was transcribed by a shorthand reporter hired by the No-Conscription League as "I have only one life to give, and if my life is to be given for an ideal, for the liberation of the people, soldiers, help yourselves." Charles Pickler, "Meeting of No-Conscription League Including Speech by Emma Goldman," June 4, 1917, Emma Goldman Papers, https://www.lib.berkeley.edu/goldman/pdfs /Speeches-MeetingofNo-ConscriptionLeague.pdf.

Eugene O'Neill and other notable writers: Tom Miller, "The Lost Greenwich Village Theatre," *Daytonian in Manhattan* (blog), October 29, 2018, http://daytonin manhattan.blogspot.com/2018/10/the-lost-greenwich-village-theatre-7th.html.

Sholem Asch's The God of Vengeance: "The God of Vengeance—Broadway Play— Original," Internet Broadway Database, accessed September 21, 2020, https:// www.ibdb.com/broadway-production/the-god-of-vengeance-9166; Virginia Pastor, "The Greenwich Village Theatre: A Brief but Fruitful History," *Researching Greenwich Village History* (blog), November 5, 2013, https:// greenwichvillagehistory.wordpress.com/2013/11/05/the-greenwich-village -theatre-a-brief-but-fruitful-history/; Warren Hoffman, "Looking for 'Lesbians' in *God of Vengeance* and *Indecent*," July 3, 2018, HowlRound, https:// howlround.com/looking-lesbians-god-vengeance-and-indecent. Asch's play was previously staged in Russian in St. Petersburg in 1907 to much acclaim; Jeffrey Veidlinger, *Jewish Public Culture in the Late Russian Empire* (Bloomington: Indiana University Press, 2009), 174.

indicted under the same obscenity law: "'God of Vengeance' Cast Is Indicted: Grand Jury Names Fourteen in Bill Charging Play Immoral—Many Complaints Made." *New York Times*, March 7, 1923. See also: Diana McLellan, *The Girls:*

Sappho Goes to Hollywood (New York: Macmillan, 2001), 84–85; Laura Collins-Hughes, "A Kiss Forbidden No Longer," *New York Times*, May 8, 2016; Charles Isherwood, "Review: In 'God of Vengeance,' a Nice Jewish Family Lives Above a Brothel," *New York Times*, December 29, 2016.

that conviction was overturned: Mike Cummings, "Defending an 'Indecent' Play: 'The God of Vengeance' in the Yale University Library Archives," *Yale News*, October 15, 2015, https://news.yale.edu/2015/10/15/defending-indecent-play-god-vengeance-yale-university-library-archives-0.

"as good and bad as any race": Noam Sienna, ed., *A Rainbow Thread: An Anthology of Queer Jewish Texts from the First Century to 1969* (Philadelphia: Print-O-Craft, 2019), 237–240. There is now a large literature on *The God of Vengeance*; see, for example, Nanette Stahl, ed., *Sholem Asch Reconsidered* (New Haven, CT: Beinecke Library, 2004).

Marinoff's play closed in March 1918: "Karen," Internet Broadway Database, https://www.ibdb.com/broadway-production/karen-8650.

the existence of an influenza epidemic: Francesco Aimone, "The 1918 Influenza Epidemic in New York City: A Review of the Public Health Response," *Public Health Reports* 125, supp. 3 (2010): 71–79, via US National Library of Medicine, https://www.ncbi.nlm.nih.gov/pmc/articles/PMC2862336/.

5. Spied On

union leaders and members had gained ground: Dubofsky and Dulles, "Postwar Labor Upheaval," in *Labor*, 209–211.

an increasing number of "hoboettes": Dorothy Ducas, "Hobohemia Takes to the Road as Tramping Art Reaches Zenith," *New York Herald Tribune*, April 4, 1926, A5, via ProQuest Historical Newspapers.

"What a price I paid": Eve Adams to Ben Reitman, February 15, 1929, series 3, box 9, folder 151, Reitman Papers. This, Eve's first letter to Reitman, is six pages long and signed "Eve Adams" with return address WP (Mrs.) M. Zloczewer, Mława. Poland, Działdowska 19.

"Eva Adams" was in town: Warren W. Grimes and J. W. R. Chamberlin, "Eva Adams: I.W.W. Organizer," July 14 & 26, 1919, via "Eva Adams (#370872)," images 3519525, 3519529, 3519536, and 3519539, FBI Case Files, Fold3 /Ancestry.com. Fold3 requires a paid subscription to access the files, but they are also available for free via ALIC at a US National Archives facility. Case files

on "Eva Adam" or "Adams" are listed as "Bureau Section File 202600-171" and "Bureau Section File 202600-995," record group 65, Records of the Bureau of Investigation. The original records are microfilmed as publication M1085.

largely successful steps to crush: Duboksy and Dulles, *Labor*, 199–202.

Agent Grimes and agent J. W. R. Chamberlin: Agent Grimes is also cited in the Bureau's investigation of Marcus Garvey. *Guide to the Microfilm Edition of the FBI Investigation File on Marcus Garvey*, Gale, 2006, http://microformguides .gale.com/Data/Download/8306000C.pdf. Chamberlin was one of the agents surveilling Emma Goldman; he was seeking information on Ben Reitman. Candace Falk et al., eds., *Emma Goldman Papers: A Microfilm Edition*, reel 63, *Government Documents, August 1, 1919 to October 31, 1919* (Alexandria, VA: Chadwyck-Healey, 1991), 619–623, via Internet Archive, https://archive .org/details/governmentdocum9101emma_6/page/n3/mode/1up.

Anderson and her romantic and creative partner: Adrienne Monnier, *The Very Rich Hours of Adrienne Monnier* (New York: Charles Scribner's Sons, 1976), 463. Margaret Anderson's address was indeed 24 West Sixteenth Street; see *Editor* 48 (1918): 205, via Google Books, https://www.google.com/books/edition /The_Editor/mf5SAAAAYAAJ.

"Radical Division": Athan G. Theoharis, ed., *The FBI: A Comprehensive Reference Guide* (Santa Barbara, CA: Oyrx Press, 1999), 361.

could not be found in the National Archives: According to Onaona Guay, the supervisory archivist, of Archives II Textual Reference Operations at the US National Archives in College Park, MD, "We did consult Department of Justice records for Ms. Adams' name in all iterations. We found mention of her in the index Entry A1 101 Card Index to Names of Persons in General Departmental Files, 1917–1930. The index pointed to case file #202600-965. When we consulted the Straight-Numeric Files for this case file, the documents could not be located. If the documents were retained, they may be within the records of her deportation case file." Onaona Guay, e-mail to JNK, April 6, 2017. To my further inquiry Ms. Guay e-mailed, "We located two index cards in the index Entry A1 101 Card Index to Names of Persons in General Departmental Files, 1917–1930; the cards referenced each other." Guay, e-mail to JNK, April 19, 2017. I reproduce one of the cards. The other card lists "ZLOTCHEVR, EVA / Alias for Eva Adams 202600-965."

assigned "Eve Adams" to cover a peace conference: "The following press representatives have been assigned to cover the [peace] conference" called by President

Wilson in Washington, DC: "Liberator (N. Y.)—Eve Adams"; "Four Editors in Big Conference: Newspaper Men Called to Help Solve Country's Big Problems," *Fourth Estate*, October 11, 1919, 12, via Google Books, https://www.google.com/books/edition/_/XzZJAQAAMAAJ.

like many others: For more on immigrants renaming themselves, see Chad Heap, *Slumming: Sexual and Racial Encounters in American Nightlife, 1885-1940* (Chicago: University of Chicago Press, 2009), 186.

"Eve Zlotchever-Adams": *Liberator* 2, no. 11 (December 1919): 50, and *Liberator*, 4, no. 11, (November 1921): back of front cover, both via Marxists Internet Archive, https://www.marxists.org/history/usa/culture/pubs/liberator/. The hyphenated "Eve Zlotchever-Adams" suggests that Eve did not adopt "Eve Adams" as an alias to avoid identification by US officials as a noncitzen radical.

"badly beaten by the police": Robert K. Murray, *Red Scare: A Study in National Hysteria, 1919-1920* (Minneapolis: University of Minnesota Press, 1955), 196–197, 206, 207.

With them were 184 members: Kenneth D. Ackerman, *Young J. Edgar: Hoover, the Red Scare, and the Assault on Civil Liberties* (New York: Carroll & Graf, 2007), 151.

"a slender bundle": Ackerman, 155–161.

second series of Palmer Raids: Ackerman, 180–186.

"concentration camp" to hold the Reds: Murray, *Red Scare*, 205.

"Eva Adams alias Eva Zlotchevr": J. T. Suter on Eve, February 11, 1920, in E. M. Blanford, Bureau of Investigation report, November 9, 1920, 2, via "Eva Adams (#202600-171)," image 5700648, FBI Case Files, Fold3/Ancestry.com. A Bureau of Investigation agent with the name J. T. Suter is mentioned in research on the early history of the Bureau of Investigation; see Charles H. McCormick, "From Seeing Reds to Being Feds: The Pittsburgh Bureau of Investigation Field Office in Transition, 1920–1925" *Pennsylvania History: A Journal of Mid-Atlantic Studies* 69, no. 3 (Summer 2002): 367–392.

Agent Blanford informed J. Edgar Hoover: E. M[urray] Blanford, responding to "Letter signed Suter, Feby 11, 1920," "Hoover Wire 11-9-20," via "Case #202600-171" and "Case #202600-995," FBI Case Files, Fold3/Ancestry. com. See also Blandford, telegram from San Francisco to Baley, Washington, DC, November 9, 1920, re: "Letter signed Suter," dated February 11, 1920, which includes a highly garbled section; a second, corrected version of the same telegram refers to Eva Adams "alias Zlotcchevr radical" arriving "yesterday. Am covering. Any action desired"; via "Case #202600-171" and "Case #202600-995," FBI Case Files, Fold3/Ancestry.com. Information about Blanford is found in Regin Schmidt, *Red Scare: FBI and the Origins of Anti-communism in the United States, 1919–1943*, English revision by Joyce King (Denmark: Museum Tusculanum Press, 2000).

an organizer for the "Revolutionists": According to Baylis's account, Eve had claimed to represent a New York radical paper called the *Revolution*. Perhaps the informer was referring to the *Revolutionary Age*, the Marxist newspaper edited by Louis C. Fraina and published in Boston, and then in New York City, from November 1918 to August 1919. See "Periodicals" Encyclopedia of Marxism, Marxists Internet Archive, https://www.marxists.org/glossary/periodicals.htm.

about $3,300 today: CPI inflation calculator, US Bureau of Labor Statistics, accessed September 21, 2020, https://data.bls.gov/cgi-bin/cpicalc.pl.

"I for one won't stand": Jack London, *The Valley of the Moon* (New York: Review of Reviews Company, 1917; orig. publ. 1913), 170–171, via Google Books, https://www.google.com/books/edition/The_Works_of_Jack_London_The_valley_of_t/zWFBAQAAMAAJ.

"Deport the 'alien' red": *San Bernardino Sun* 48, no. 85 (November 24, 1920): 9, via California Digital Newspaper Collection, University of California, Riverside, https://cdnc.ucr.edu/?a=d&d=SBS19201124.1.9. In July 1920, Baylis gave another public lecture titled "America and the New War; or Making America Safe for Americans"; Today's Meeting, *Tribunette and Rotary* (Minneapolis, MN) 7, no. 20 (July 16, 1920), via Google Books, https://www.google.com/books/edition/_/lpgeAQAAMAAJ.

"to secret conferences with members": F. W. Kelly, Butte, MT, "Eva Adams, alias Eva Klotchevr . . . Radical Activities," November 17, 1920, via Fold3/Ancestry.com; "Continuing this investigation. Reference is made to San Francisco reports, E. M. Blanford, November 9th, and F. D. Kirk, November 13th."

a conscious decision not to bear children: Falk, *Love, Anarchy*, 30, 51.

"a complete search": E. Kosterlitzky, "Title and Character of Case: EVA ADAMS alias EVA ZLOCEVR," December 14, 1920, via "Eva Adams (#202600-171)," image 5700653, FBI Case Files, Fold3/Ancestry.com. (This is page 4 of Kosterlitzky's report, though Fold3 mistakenly lists it as page 6.) No warrant to search Eve's possessions is mentioned.

"*securing subscriptions to radical publications*": Sturgis (agent in charge, Los Angeles), January 14, 1921, quoted in Fred I. Keepers (Denver, CO), Bureau of Investigation report, February 4, 1921, via "Case #202600-171" and "Case #202600-995," FBI Case Files, Fold3/Ancestry.com.

passed on to other Bureau offices: Sturgis, quoted in Keepers, Bureau of Investigation report. Keepers adds his own comment at the end of this report.

"*information from a reliable source*": Colonel Matthew C. Smith to L. J. Baley (chief, Bureau of Investigation), January 15, 1921 (stamped January 13, 1921), via "Case #202600-171" and "Case #202600-995," FBI Case Files, Fold3/Ancestry .com. Perhaps the "reliable source" of this misinformation was the previously described anti-Jewish, antiradical lecturer Dr. Charles T. Baylis.

"*military efficiency*": "Military Intelligence Division," in *A Counterintelligence Reader*, vol. 1, *American Revolution to World War II*, ed. Frank J. Rafalko (National Counterintelligence Center, 2001), via Federation of American Scientists, https://fas.org/irp/ops/ci/docs/ci1/ch3f.htm.

"*I learned to love this country*": Eve's testimony, May 23, 1927, USDLIS #11, 4 (40 in whole file).

"*Eve Adams takes subscriptions to* GOOD MORNING": *Good Morning*, June 15–July 1, 1921, 14, via Hathi Trust Digital Library, https://babel.hathitrust.org /cgi/pt?id=inu.30000093613887. Other issues of *Good Morning* also mention the traveling Eve's selling this periodical. See *Good Morning*, July 15–August 1, 1920, 14, via Hathi Trust Digital Library, https://babel.hathitrust.org/cgi /pt?id=inu.30000093613887: "EVE ADAMS is travelling in the West securing subscriptions for GOOD MORNING. Please give her yours when she calls upon you."

"*Eve Adams, the celebrated hiker*": *Good Morning*, August 1921, 18, via Hathi Trust Digital Library, https://babel.hathitrust.org/cgi/pt?id=inu.30000093613887.

"*putting The Liberator and Good Morning and Soviet Russia and Truth into their hands*": *Soviet Russia* was the official magazine of the Russian Soviet Government Bureau. Published from 1919 until 1922, its goal was to promote the Soviet Union to American readers. John Mark Ockerbloom, "Soviet Russia," Online Books Page, accessed September 22, 2020, https://onlinebooks.library .upenn.edu/webbin/serial?id=sovrussia.

Years later, Eve fondly recalled: Eve Adams to Ben Reitman, August 15, 1934, included by Martha Reis in a set of "Transcripts" of Eve's letters in the archive of the University of Illinois at Chicago Library that Reis sent to Eran Zahavy and that Zahavy shared with me. Reis included a transcript of this letter and said it was "Typed" and that the return address was American Express, Paris. According to Reis, "Hidden Histories," 97n128 and 98n133, this letter is found in accession no. 98-36, box 2, folder 18, Reitman Papers. But researcher Marie K. Rowley was unable to find the original of this letter or two others from Eve to Reitman transcribed by Reis of Eve to Reitman in the UIC collection, and the library was unable to provide those letters' locations after the archive was reorganized sometime after Reis completed her research.

6. Chicago, the Grey Cottage, Ruth

Eve settled in Chicago: Eve's testimony, USDLIS #8, 7.

"LEARN RUSSIAN!!": *Liberator* 4, no. 4 (April 1921): 32, via Marxists Internet Archive, https://www.marxists.org/history/usa/culture/pubs/liberator/.

certainly among her language skills: Eve said in a letter to Reitman that in addition to English she spoke five "European languages." Eve Adams to Ben Reitman, September 1, 1941, series 3, box 10, folder 171, Reitman Papers.

After "primary school" in Mława: Eve's testimony, November 30, 1926, USDLIS #7, 9 (19 of whole file). For schools in Plotzk, see the section on "Education and Cultural Activities" from Yeshaya Trunk, "The History of the Jews of Plotzk from the Middle of the 17th Century until World War I," in *Plotzk; a History of an Ancient Jewish Community in Poland*, ed. E. Eisenberg (Tel Aviv: Hamenora, 1967), trans. JewishGen, https://www.jewishgen.org/yizkor /plock/plo005.html.

Yiddish for Płock: Eisenberg, *Plotzk*, https://www.jewishgen.org/yizkor/plock /Plock.html.

"Women were often permitted": Veidlinger, *Jewish Public Culture*, xv–xvi, 11–12, 79, 80, 212.

This town of 15,702: Bohdan Wasiutyński, *Ludność żydowska w Polsce w wiekach XIX i XX* (Warsaw: Wydawn. Kasy im. Mianowskiego, 1930).

General Union of Jewish Workers: Veidlinger, *Jewish Public Culture*, 3.

seething politically and culturally: Political and religious ferment in Mława was recalled by a resident, born there in 1923, thirty-two years after Eve: Baruch

G. Goldstein, *For Decades I Was Silent: A Holocaust Survivor's Journey Back to Faith* (Tuscaloosa: University of Alabama Press, 2008). On early-twentieth-century political and cultural ferment in Poland generally, see Scott Ury, *Barricades and Banners: The Revolution of 1905 and the Transformation of Warsaw Jewry* (Stanford, CA: Stanford University Press, 2012); Shmuel Levin and Wila Orbach, "Mlawa," in *Encyclopedia of Jewish Communities in Poland*, vol. 4 (Jerusalem: Yad Vashem, 1989), trans. JewishGen, https://www.jewishgen.org/yizkor/pinkas_poland/pol4_00280.html; Joshua D. Zimmerman, *Poles, Jews, and the Politics of Nationality: The Bund and the Polish Socialist Party in Late Tsarist Russia, 1892–1914* (Madison: University of Wisconsin Press, 2004); and R. Nagorski, "History of the Anarchist Movement in Poland," *Anarchist Review* 2 (1977), excerpted by Red and Black Book Project, http://freepacifica.savegrassrootsradio.org/redblack/books/polish_anarchism.htm.

Polish Revolution against Russian autocratic rule: Ury, *Barricades and Banners*.

the "woman question": Robert E. Blobaum, "The 'Woman Question' in Russian Poland, 1900–1914," *Journal of Social History* 35, no. 4 (Summer 2002): 806, 812, 813, 202.

more education than was typical: Orleck, *Common Sense*, 19–22; Trisha Franzen, *Spinsters and Lesbians: Independent Womanhood in the United States* (New York: New York University Press, 1996), 47–77.

Three of these women's labor activists: For more on Cohn's, Schneiderman's, and Newman's personal lives, see Orleck, *Common Sense*, 283, 309, and her index on their "friendships" and "relationships."

likely to have heard of Antin: Eve was particularly likely to have taken note of Antin because a printer's error in the title of Antin's first book, *From Plotzk to Boston*, mistakenly suggested that Antin came from the same Polish town in which Eve had attended secondary school. Antin was actually born in Polotzk (Polotsk or Polatsk), now in Belarus. Mary Antin, *From Plotzk to Boston* (New York: Markus Wiener Publishing, 1985; orig. publ. 1899), xii, 15.

Yiddish writer Joseph Opatoshu: Dan Opatoshu, "In New York Velder: Yosef/Joseph Opatoshu—Constructing a Multinational 20th Century, (Very) Modern Yiddish Identity," chapter 2 in *Joseph Opatoshu: A Yiddish Writer Between Europe and America*, ed. Sabine Koller, Gennady Estraikh, and Michael Krutikov (New York: Modern Humanities Research Association and Routledge Studies in Yiddish, 2013).

Opatoshu's fiction dealt frankly: Josh Lambert, "Opatoshu's Eroticism, American Obscenity," chapter 12 in *Opatoshu*, ed. Koller et al.

a lecture "before the Chicago literati": *Chicago Tribune*, April 1, 1922, 12, via Newspapers.com.

Konrad Bercovici: Michael Kraike, "Unique Jewish Persons: An Interview with Konrad Bercovici," *Canadian Jewish Chronicle*, November 27, 1931, via Google News, https://news.google.com/newspapers?id=7-ROAAAAIBAJ&sjid=10sDAAAAIBAJ&pg=2801%2C77991.

"Chicago's Greenwich Village Tea Room": *Liberator* 5, no. 5 (May 1922): 34, via Marxists Internet Archive, https://www.marxists.org/history/usa/culture/pubs/liberator/.

Chicago's Towertown, as in New York's Village: Heap, *Slumming*, 57, 61–64.

"Way down south in Greenwich Village": Clement Wood, *Bohemian Life in N.Y.'s Greenwich Village*, #1106 in Little Blue Book series, ed. E. Haldeman-Julius, 1926, quoted in Doug Skinner, "The Greenwich Village Epic," *Ullage Group* (blog), http://ullagegroup.com/2010/03/30/the-greenwich-village-epic/.

"The proprietresses were Ruth Norlander": Kenneth Rexroth, *An Autobiographical Novel* (Santa Barbara, CA: Ross-Erikson, 1982), 260. Rexroth's book is copyrighted 1964, 1966, 1978, 1982. The later part of Rexroth's life is discussed in a different book, the confusingly titled *Autobiographical Novel* edited by Linda Hamalian (New York: New Directions, 1991). In this volume Rexroth says, "Eve Adams had gone off to New York and Ruth [Olson Norlander] had opened a place at 19 West Pearson Street in an old barn," and Rexroth and his friends "all moved in"; "Rexroth Autobiography," Bureau of Public Secrets, accessed September 23, 2020, http://www.bopsecrets.org/rexroth/autobio/4.htm. A "homo" scene at 19 West Pearson Street is described in Zorbaugh, *Gold Coast*, 96.

"much the most bohemian": Rexroth, *Autobiographical Novel* (1982), 261.

the Green Mask: Kenneth Rexroth and James Laughlin, *Selected Letters*, ed. Lee Bartlett (New York: W. W. Norton, 1991), 57, citing Rexroth's interview in *The San Francisco Poets*, ed. David Meltzer (New York: Ballantine, 1971).

"where other lesbians hung out": Mabel Hampton, interview 5, Lesbian Herstory Archives, quoted in Kevin J. Mumford, *Interzones: Black/White Sex Districts in Chicago and New York in the Early Twentieth Century* (New York: Colum-

bia University Press, 1997), 79. On Hampton also see Hugh Ryan, *When Brooklyn Was Queer* (New York: St. Martin's, 2019), 111.

Richard Bruce Nugent: Mumford, *Interzones*, 79; Thomas H. Wirth, introduction to Richard Bruce Nugent, *Gay Rebel of the Harlem Renaissance* (Durham, NC: Duke University Press, 2002), 10.

Claude McKay: "The Village," Greenwich Village Bookshop Door, accessed September 23, 2020, Henry Ransom Center, University of Texas at Austin, https://norman.hrc.utexas.edu/bookshopdoor/thevillage.cfm. The same *Liberator* that advertised the Grey Cottage also offered a copy of McKay's book *Harlem Shadows* along with a one-year subscription: "McKay's passionate exhortations, even when most characteristically racial, are a stirring call to the oppressed everywhere regardless of race or color." *Liberator* 5, no. 5: 31.

"masculine women and feminine men": "Hamilton Lodge Ball an Unusual Spectacle," *New York Age*, March 6, 1926.

Wiener had "been a carnival performer": Rexroth, *Autobiographical Novel* (1982), 261–262.

Karyl Norman: Norman, born George Peduzzi in Baltimore, traveled the vaudeville circuits and was known for his fancy gowns, created mostly by his mother, who traveled with him. "George T. Teduzzi [*sic*]," 1910 US Census, via Ancestry.com; Vern L. Bullough and Bonnie Bullough, *Cross Dressing, Sex, and Gender* (Philadelphia: University of Pennsylvania Press, 1993), 236; "Karyl Norman," Ambisextrous: Gender Impersonators of Music Hall and Vaudeville, University of Saskatchewan Archives, accessed October 12, 2020, http://digital.scaa.sk.ca/gallery/genderimpersonators/karyl_norman/karylnorman_index.htm; Kissack, *Free Comrades*, 174.

"a great deal more intellectual": Rexroth, 260; spelling of "Milholland" corrected. Rexroth recalled that the Mask's customers were disorderly, and even violent, and "every night I had to kick out a savage little Mexican fairy known as Theda Bara, and her knife-toting pal, who weighed about four hundred pounds, the Slim Princess." Rexroth no doubt confronted two tough characters, but his "savage . . . Mexican" and portly princess of course traded on stereotypes. Rexroth, *Autobiographical Novel* (1982), 261–262.

pioneering defender: On Milholland and Carpenter, see Linda Lumsden, *Inez: The Life and Times of Inez Milholland* (Bloomington: Indiana University Press,

2004); and Sheila Rowbotham, *Edward Carpenter: A Life of Liberty and Love* (Brooklyn, NY: Verso, 2008).

"a fine-looking Negro": Heap, *Slumming*, 356n57.

a *"well-dressed young fellow"*: Heap, 176.

"first started to hang out": Rexroth, *Autobiographical Novel* (1982), 259–260.

"together with a few other people": Eve's testimony, November 24, 1926, USDLIS #7, 7 (17 of whole file).

"free-for-all fight": "Judge [John J. Richardson] Warns 'Grey Cottage,' Frees Proprietress and Patrons, Will Close Place Next Time," *Chicago Daily News*, November 17, 1922, 3, via GenealogyBank.com.

promised "Southern Cooking": Ad for Grey Cottage, *Chicago Tribune*, December 8, 1922, 23, via Newspapers.com.

"who foregather at the Grey Cottage": Penelope Perrill, "Society and 'Flapper' Now in Limelight: Present-Day Novelists Seem to Feel Their Themes Must Touch Along Those Lines If Offerings Meet with Public Favor," *Dayton (OH) Daily News*, 2nd news section, March 4, 1923, 3, via Newspapers.com.

"some very pleasant recollections": George H. Snyder to Ben Reitman, March 13, 1942, supp. 2, folder 80, Reitman Papers, cited in Martha Lynn Reis, "Hidden Histories: Ben Reitman and the 'Outcast' Women Behind *Sister of the Road: The Autobiography of Box-Car Bertha*," PhD dissertation, University of Minnesota, September 2000, 96n126; the cited location may no longer be accurate.

Numerous Chicago newspaper ads: "Ben Reitman 'Chairman,'" April 15, 1922, 8, "Life, A'La Boheme," May 6, 1922, 20, "Travels, Trials and Tribulations of a Literary Tramp," May 20, 1922, 20, "Vice and Virtue in the Village," June 10, 1922, 20, "Morals Versus Art," June 17, 1922, 23, "The Romance of the Road," July 15, 1922, 6, "The Penalties of Love," July 29, 1922, 20, "Sensuality in American Fiction" (by Maxwell Bodenheim), June 24, 1922, 19, "Young Chicago Poets" (talk by Samuel Putnam), May 13, 1922, 20, and additional ads for events at the Cottage, April 15, 1922, 8, May 27, 1922, 20, July 22, 1922, 20, August 5, 1922, 11, and August 19, 1922, 8, all in *Chicago Daily News*, via GenealogyBank.com.

"that refuge of thwarted intellect": "These Philistines Will Talk of Money," *Daily Northwestern*, December 6, 1922, 4, via GenealogyBank.com.

"butterfly of Chicago's bohemian quarter": "Bohemia Queen, Broken Hearted, Takes Poison," *Chicago Tribune*, April 18, 1922, 1, via GenealogyBank.com.

served as "Master of Ceremonies": Eve to Reitman, August 15, 1934.

birthday party for Reitman's son: Reitman's son Brutus, born in 1918, would have been four in 1922. Reis, "Hidden Histories," 96n124.

Reitman recalled that Eve: Gail Borden, "Ahead of the Times," *Chicago Daily Times*, November 28, 1934, 12, in supp. 2, folder 62, Reitman Papers, cited in Reis, "Hidden Histories," 96n125; the cited location may no longer be accurate.

speakers at the Pickle: "A Brief History of the Dill Pickle Club," Frontier to Heartland, accessed September 23, 2020, Newberry Library, https://publications .newberry.org/frontiertoheartland/exhibits/show/perspectives/dillpickle /briefhistory.

"Queen of the Hoboes": Ben Reitman, *Chicago Times*, August 22, 1937, quoted in St. Sukie de la Croix, *Chicago Whispers: A History of LGBT Chicago Before Stonewall* (Madison: University of Wisconsin Press, 2012), 66.

also befriended Eulalia Burke: Eulalia Burke, video interview by Communications for Change, 1970s, for "Documenting Social History: Chicago's Elderly Speak," via Media Burn Archive, https://mediaburn.org/video/eulalia-burke/.

She was born Ruth Olson: The Minnesota Territorial and State Census, June 26, 1905, via Ancestry.com, lists Ruth S. Olson, age sixteen, both parents born in Norway, as living in Minneapolis. In the 1905–1906 school years Ruth S. Olson is listed as a registered student at the Minneapolis College of Art and Design (data printed in the following year's school catalog, 1906–1907); Eva Hyvarinen (visual resource assistant, Minneapolis College of Art and Design) to JNK, June 1, 2017. The 1920 US Federal Census, via Ancestry.com, lists Ruth Norlander, age thirty, born about 1890 in Minnesota. It also lists her home in 1920 (Twenty-Sixth Street, Ward 8, Minneapolis, MN), race (white), spouse (Gideon Norlander, age thirty-three), and her ability to speak, read, and write English (yes to all).

"the zeal of our Comrades": Emma Goldman, On the Trail, *Mother Earth* 6, no. 2 (April 1911), via Anarchy Archives, http://dwardmac.pitzer.edu/Anarchist_ Archives/goldman/ME/mev6n2.html. I have corrected Goldman's mistaken spelling of Olson's last name as "Olsen."

"felt a little doubtful": Emma Goldman, "Agitation Envoyage," *Mother Earth Bulletin* 10, no. 5 (July 1915): 185. In 1914, "Ruth Olson, 1034 18th Ave. N. E." is one

of those listed for information and tickets for Alexander Berkman's talks in Minneapolis; *Mother Earth* 9, no. 10 (December 1914): 336, via Google Books, https://www.google.com/books/edition/Mother_Earth/zstCAQAAMAAJ.

"a splendid young American girl": Reitman, "Homosexuality," 7.

"teacher and friend of mine": Eve to Reitman, August 15, 1934.

Ruth's daughter Joan: The 1920 US Federal Census indicates that Ruth was living with daughter Joan Norlander, age two—meaning Joan was born about 1918.

"my beloved": Eve Zloczower to "Ruth Olsen" [*sic*], June 6 [*sic*], 1931, accession no. 42629, box group 3206, folder F-1, Beinecke Library, Yale University. Norlander apparently moved the Grey Cottage to a new Chicago location in an old barn and kept it open after Eve left for New York; Rexroth, *Autobiographical Novel* (1982), 277.

7. Greenwich Village, Eve's Place, Trouble

"to renounce forever": "Declaration of Intention," signed "Eve Zlotchever," September 11, 1923, in New York State Supreme Court, *Declarations of Intention filed in New York County, 1907–1924*, petition vol. 659, petition 45, Division of Old Records, New York County Clerk's Office. Eve also testified that she received her "first citizenship papers" in New York City on September 11, 1923; Eve's testimony, May 23, 1927, USDLIS #11, 3 (39 of whole file).

a popular little magazine: Steve Heller, "When Greenwich Village Was Bohemia," *Print*, May 1, 2012, https://www.printmag.com/post/when-greenwich-village -was-bohemia.

"Eve and Ann's": Mr. Quill's Guide, *Quill*, November 1924, cited in Chad Cottrell Heap, "'Slumming': Sexuality, Race and Urban Commercial Leisure, 1900–1940," PhD dissertation, University of Chicago, 2000, 44n23, via ProQuest, 2000.999056. Heap suggests that a listing for Eve and Ann's appeared in the *Quill* from November 1924 through February 1925, and that a listing for Eve's Hangout appeared from March through June 1925.

"Eve Adams, Director": *Quill* 15, no. 16 (December 1924): 32.

attendees at the "popular" parties: Ben L. Reitman, *Sister of the Road: The Autobiography of Box-Car Bertha* (Edinburgh: Nabat/AK Press, 2002; orig. publ. 1937), 100–102.

Eve published Lesbian Love: Eve's testimony, April 11, 1927, USDLIS #7, 8 (18 of whole file).

Eve's own "Eve's Hangout": Heap, "'Slumming,'" 44n23.

"File No. 68309": The letter from "W. W. Husband," "Commissioner General of Immigration," is quoted in Jay Fitzpatrick's sworn testimony on June 23, 1925, USDLIS #1, 1. I have not found Husband's actual letter in the files of the US Department of Labor or the US Immigration Service. The alleged date of Husband's letter, May 26, 1925, is perhaps incorrect. Husband was actually commissioner general of immigration through May 15, 1925, and then served until 1935 as assistant secretary of labor, focusing on immigration. In 1911 Husband had been the executive secretary of the US Immigration Commission, which issued a forty-three-volume report on immigration, including the aforementioned *Dictionary of Races or Peoples*; "Biography: William Walter Husband," American Catholic History Classroom, accessed September 24, 2020, https://cuomeka.wrlc.org/exhibits/show/immigration/documents/bio-husband. Harry E. Hull took over as commissioner general of immigration on May 16, 1925, serving until April 26, 1933; "Harry E. Hull," US Citizenship and Immigration Services, accessed September 24, 2020, https://www.uscis.gov/history-and-genealogy/our-history/commissioners-and-directors/harry-e-hull.

return permit 74702: On September 25, 1925, the US Immigration Service in Washington, DC, issued "Eve Zlotchever" a visa that included a "return permit." Certificate of Admission of Alien, April 11, 1927, USDLIS #7, 20 (30 of whole file).

Her traveling out of the United States: Since Eve was already a US immigrant, the new quota restrictions limiting the numbers of citizens from particular nations, imposed by the Immigration Act of 1924, did not apply to her. The 1924 act preserved the provisions of the 1917 immigration law, and added quota restrictions for people from different nations; Immigration Act of 1924 (HR 7995), 68th Cong. (May 26, 1924), via Library of Congress, https://www.loc.gov/law/help/statutes-at-large/68th-congress/session-1/c68s1ch190.pdf.

"or other crime or misdemeanor": Immigration Act of 1917 (HR 10385), 64th Cong. (February 5, 1917), via Library of Congress, https://www.loc.gov/law/help/statutes-at-large/64th-congress/session-2/c64s2ch29.pdf.

set quotas on immigrants: "The Immigration Act of 1924," Office of the Historian, US Department of State, accessed September 24, 2020, history.state.gov/milestones/1921-1936/immigration-act.

eugenics, the junk racial science: Douglas C. Baynton, *Defectives in the Land: Disability and Immigration in the Age of Eugenics* (Chicago: University of Chicago Press, 2016), 18, 40, 44, 147.

brought a letter of introduction: Fitzpatrick, "Sworn Statement," June 23, 1925.

James C. Thomas: New York State Black, Puerto Rican, Hispanic and Asian Legislative Caucus, *1917–2014: A Look at the History of Legislators of Color*, 2014, https://nyassembly.gov/comm/BlackPR/20140213/index.pdf, 38.

"A gentleman came to my table": USDLIS #12, 22.

Fitzpatrick was unmarried: The 1940 Federal Census, which surveyed Fitzpatrick on April 8, 1940, in the Bronx, recorded him as "widowed," and if this is not his lie or the enumerator's mistake, he married unusually late in life, between ages forty-seven and fifty-six. In records from 1930 and earlier, Fitzpatrick was always listed as single, and in the 1931 city directory there is no one else by the name of Fitzpatrick listed at his MacDougal Street address. This suggests that Fitzpatrick married, if he did, sometime between 1931 and 1940, and that his wife died by 1940. If Fitzpatrick was born in 1884, as his birth data indicates, he was forty-seven in 1931 and fifty-six in 1940. However, the 1940 Census lists his age as "67" ("70" is crossed out). The same 1940 Census asked whether Fitzpatrick "Attended School or College" and the answer was "No." That information was followed by "Highest Grade Completed" followed by "College, 3rd year." Fitzpatrick's lies or enumerator mistakes about college and age suggests that "widowed" may also be a lie or mistake. Census and other documents via Ancestry.com.

Fitzpatrick would move into an artist's studio: "Jay Fitzpatrick," *Greenwich Village: A Local Review*, April–May 1929, [no. 1—in pencil 7; pages not numbered], Local History Division, New York Public Library. The *Greenwich Village* is an early version of the paper later called the *Greenwich Village Weekly News*. The 1930 US Census (via Ancestry.com) documents James Gaylord "Jay" Fitzpatrick as living at 129 MacDougal Street.

as an appraiser and real estate broker: Fitzpatrick was first listed as an "appraiser" in a 1915 New York City directory, and as a "real estate broker" in the 1920 Federal Census; both via Ancestry.com.

a prominent married couple: The house at 129 MacDougal was owned by Harold Gilmore Calhoun and his wife, Dorothy Donnell Calhoun. Did Eve's landlords hear, in 1925, about Eve's *Lesbian Love* and/or Eve's tearoom's reputation as hangout for radicals, bohemians, lesbians, and gay men? Were they worried about their property's reputation and dollar value? The questions are many, the clues suggestive. The Calhouns bought 127 and 129 MacDougal Street in 1920, and 131 MacDougal in 1940, so they were investing in Greenwich Village real estate; Jay Shockley, "131 MacDougal Street House Designation Report," New York City Landmarks Preservation Commission, June 8, 2004, https://a860-gpp.nyc.gov/concern/nyc_government_publications /rn301252q, 1, 5. The assessed value of Village properties increased 75 percent between 1920 and 1930 (compared with 69.5 percent in the whole of Manhattan); Ware, *Greenwich Village*, 442.

"matron of social prominence": Mary Sullivan, *My Double Life: The Story of a New York Policewoman* (New York: Farrar & Rinehart, 1938), 207.

friends in the US government: Harold Gilmore Calhoun was a graduate of Columbia University Law School and the Sorbonne, from which he held a PhD in political science. His ties to Washington, DC, officials are suggested by his later job as assistant to the US attorney general from 1936 to 1945. Obituary for Harold Gilmore Calhoun, *New York Times*, May 14, 1953. (See also obituary for Dorothy Donnell Calhoun, *New York Times*, December 3, 1963.) Dorothy Calhoun also later worked for the US government. In 1938, the Calhouns together coauthored radio scripts for educational purposes, published by the US government; Harold Gilmore Calhoun and Dorothy Calhoun, *Let Freedom Ring!: 13 Scripts*, Bulletin 1937, no. 2, (Washington, DC: US Department of the Interior, 1938), via Google Books, https://www.google.com/books/edition/_/mpB2F_lseoMC. From 1939 to 1942 Dorothy Calhoun was employed by the second assistant secretary of labor, who was also commissioner of the Immigration and Naturalization Bureau (then part of the US Labor Department). In November 1940, she was supervisor of citizenship programs for the Immigration and Naturalization Service (by then part of the Justice Department). In August 1941, her new job was as the service's director of citizenship programming. One of her tasks was to administer a "New Citizens" program, helping those who had fled European fascism to secure US citizenship—ironic in view of Eve's history. A New Deal Democrat, she was wary of Communists reputed to be working in government jobs. She maintained a close working relationship with Richard Krebs, who, under the pseudonym Jan Valtin, authored a bestselling anti-Communist autobiography, heavily fictionalized for dramatic effect. So if Dorothy Calhoun knew of Eve's ties to radical leftist deportees, as well as lesbians, she would probably have disapproved. Dorothy

Donnell Calhoun folders, box 5, Marshall Dimock Papers, Franklin D. Roosevelt Presidential Library; the folders include over two hundred pages of career and personal correspondence, memoranda, scripts, and other writings. See also series 130 (News Items, 1934–1945), box 922, Eleanor Roosevelt Papers, Franklin D. Roosevelt Presidential Library, which includes a letter from Dorothy Donnell Calhoun to Roosevelt in 1940 and seven scripts from the *I Am an American!* program that Calhoun helped to produce. Biographical information about Donnell Calhoun was obtained through Smith College's online archival collection. Dorothy Donnell correspondence is also located in the Frances Perkins Papers, Columbia University Library. As for Dorothy Calhoun's friend Richard Krebs, he was an unsavory character who served three years in San Quentin for attempted murder, and whose wife, in divorcing him, charged him with violence. See John V. Fleming, *The Anti-Communist Manifestos: Four Books That Shaped the Cold War* (New York: W. W. Norton, 2009), 116; and Bonnie L. Petry and Michael Burgess, eds., *San Quentin: The Evolution of a California State Prison* (San Bernardino, CA: Borgo Press, 2005). On Dorothy Donnell Calhoun's support of and close collaboration with Krebs and his anti-Communist manifesto *Out of the Night* see Fleming, *Anti-Communist Manifestos*. 144, 158, 160–161, 174.

"a clean-up campaign": Ware, *Greenwich Village*, 96–97; George Chauncey, *Gay New York: Gender, Culture, and the Making of the Gay Male World* (New York: Basic Books, 1994), 237–243. Chauncey's book contains two pages on Eve Adams, and citations to documents.

police drive had closed "Greenwich Village 'joints'": "Village 'Joints' Out or Tame: Another Police Drive About Closes All," *Variety*, May 6, 1926, 19, via Internet Archive, https://archive.org/details/variety78-1925-05/page/n8/mode/2up.

period slang for homosexuals: "Over in New York . . . clubs and bars where homosexual people could meet would often advertise in the newspapers using the coded phrase 'we cater to the Temperamental Set'"; Max Décharné, *Vulgar Tongues: An Alternative History of English Slang* (New York: Pegasus Books, 2017), 136. See also Ann-Marie Cusac, "Meet Pioneer of Gay Rights, Harry Hay," *Progressive*, August 9, 2016, https://progressive.org/magazine/meet-pioneer-gay-rights-harry-hay/.

"boasted at least 20": "Village 'Joints' Out or Tame," *Variety*, 19.

Greenwich Village Too Costly: *Christian Science Monitor*, August 29, 1927, cited in Ware, *Greenwich Village*, 21.

"artist, sportsman, and big game hunter": "Jay Fitzpatrick," *Greenwich Village*. A search of Ancestry.com for all passport applications up to 1925 reveals no passport for Fitzpatrick.

hosted a testimonial dinner: "Dinner for Philip Elting: Notables Join Fitzpatrick in Tributes to Collector," *New York Times*, February 2, 1933. As the *Times* put it, "Among the guests" were "Police Commissioner and Mrs. Edward Mulrooney, Walter W. [H]usband, Assistant Secretary of Labor; Solicitor General and Mrs. Maurice Dupre of Ottawa, Commissioner [of Motor Vehicles] and Mrs. Charles A. Hartnett, H. R. Landis, Assistant Commissioner General of Immigration; United States Commissioner Garret W. Cotter, Mayor and Mrs. Edward T. Buckingham of Bridgeport, Conn., Thomas W. Whittle, Surveyor of Customs; Charles S. Hand, Herbert C. Henstler of the Department of State, Phelps Phelps, United States Marshal Damon Lewis, Mr. and Mrs. Thoms V. Underhill, Judge Richard P. Lydon, Judge and Mrs. William E. Slevin, Judge Gerald Nolan, John J. Curtin, Colonel Charles J. O'Brien, Major and Mrs. George W. Drake, C. W. Roberts, Major and Mrs. Louis B. Joyce, Thomas S. Burke, Mrs. Anna Jane Phillips and Police Lieutenant Patric McDonald." It would be interesting to know more about the backgrounds and careers of these guests and how and if they might have influenced Eve Adams's life.

an associate of Elting's: "10th Anniversary of Elting's Death," *Kingston (NY) Daily Freeman*, July 20, 1951.

boarded the steamship Minnekahda: List or Manifest of Alien Passengers, SS *Minnekahda*, sailing from Boulogne-sur-Mer, November 28, 1925. On the steamship *Minnekahda* (or *Minnehaha*) on the Atlantic Transport Line, see "SS Minnehaha Ephemera Collection," Gjenvick-Gjønvik Archives, accessed September 24, 2020, https://www.gjenvick.com/OceanTravel/ImmigrantShips/Minnehaha.html.

Jews were second-class citizens in Poland: Eve to Reitman, February 15, 1929, 1–2. For more on Jews in Poland, see "Poland in the 20th Century," Britannica.com, accessed September 24, 2020, https://www.britannica.com/place/Poland/Poland-in-the-20th-century.

"ever incurred the enmity": USDLIS #7, 16 (26 of whole file).

between June 1921 and June 1926: "The Greenwich Village Quill," Hathi Trust Digital Library, accessed September 24, 2020, https://catalog.hathitrust.org/Record/000542037. Edwards may have also contributed to the *Masses*,

Broadway Brevities, and other periodicals. The most detailed research on Edwards I have found is Doug Skinner, "Bobby Edwards, the Troubadour of Greenwich Village," parts 1–14, *Ullage Group* (blog), January 5–18, 2011, http://ullagegroup.com/2011/01/05/bobby-edwards-the-troubadour-of-greenwich -village-1/. Edwards advertised his multi-services, including making "Restaurants Famous," in many issues of the *Quill*; Doug Skinner, e-mail to JNK, January 22 & 27, 2017.

"the great craving for ideas": Robert Edwards, Bobby Edwards' Column, *Quill* 5, no. 1 [published as vol. 4, no. 8] (June 1919): 23.

"Men: A Hate Song": Dorothy Parker, "Men: A Hate Song," *Vanity Fair*, February 1917, https://www.vanityfair.com/news/1917/02/dorothy-parker-hate -song-men. Parker makes fun of four kinds of men: I, "Serious Thinkers"; II, "Cave Men"; III, "Sensitive Souls" (male homosexuals, apparently); and IV, those "Steeped in Crime."

"I hate women": Robert Edwards, "I Hate 'Em," *Quill* 10, no 4 (April 1922): 9, via Google Books, https://www.google.com/books/edition/_/QuRFAQAAMAAJ. The poem is signed "R. E.," and Edwards was at the time the *Quill's* editor.

"hangout of dainty elves": *Quill*, April 1925, 33, quoted in Chauncey, *Gay New York*, 240.

moved out of the Village: Chauncey, *Gay New York*, 239–240.

"Eve's Hangout": *Quill* 18, no. 6 (June 1926): 28. At the same address as Eve's old tearoom, 129 MacDougal, the *Quill* lists "Ann" as "Open evenings. Fireplace, Books, Batik, Art, etc. Poetry Reading." A map of Greenwich Village, drawn by Robert Edwards and published in the *Quill* in July 1925, places "Anne" a few spaces down from the Provincetown Playhouse; Sheryl Woodruff, "My Favorite Things: Greenwich Village To Day," Greenwich Village Society for Historic Preservation, January 6, 2014, https://gvshp.org/blog/2014/01/06 /my-favorite-things-greenwich-village-to-day/.

"'Eve's Place,' a lesbian hangout": Kin, *Women Without Men*, 101. A condensed version of Plotkin's book was published as a paperback under the byline Noel O'Hara and titled *The Last Virgin and Other Stories of Lesbian Love in Greenwich Village* (Chariot Books, 1959). It does not contain the reference to Eve's cafe.

John Rose Gildea: Gildea's status as he-man interested in women is indicated in Wetzsteon, *Republic of Dreams*, 329–330, which also discusses the he-men Maxwell Bodenheim and Eli Siegel.

"Who'll put the first penny": Henry Harrison, Local Color, *Greenwich Village Quill* 19, no. 1 (July 1926): 45. The masthead of this July issue of the *Quill* indicates the start of Henry Harrison's editorship, as well as the expansion of the publication's title from the *Quill* to the *Greenwich Village Quill*.

account of this raucous event: Harrison, Local Color, 46.

Mr. Beltrome: "Mr. Beltrome," "Mr. Zam," and "Dave Rosenberg" have not been identified.

Eve was arrested in her tearoom: USDLIS #7, 5 (15 of whole file).

fullest description of Eve's arrest: Mrs. Mary Sullivan (director of policewomen, New York City), "The Tea Room Case," *IAWP Bulletin*, October 1926, 5–6, via NYPL Periodicals & Microforms, call no. *ZAN-10352; Evens, "Plainclothes Policewomen."

what was then called a "personality club": Chauncey, *Gay New York*, 238, 239.

For two or three nights previous: "Sapphic Sisters Scram," *Broadway Brevities* 3, no. 3 (November 16, 1931): 10.

in a chapter on "Strange People": Sullivan, *My Double Life*, 199–210.

"Eve's Tea Room' Boss": "'Eve's Tea Room' Boss Ran into Policewoman," *Variety*, June 23, 1926, 35, via Internet Archive, https://archive.org/details /variety83-1926-06/page/n259/mode/2up.

about $37,000 today: CPI inflation calculator, US Bureau of Labor Statistics, accessed September 24, 2020, https://data.bls.gov/cgi-bin/cpicalc.pl.

Eve's first trial: People of the State of New York v. Evelyn Addams, July 2, 1926, USDLIS #3, 5. The other two judges in the case were Henry W. Herbert and Joseph D. Kelly.

her supporters would have had to pay: Kenneth R. Cobb (assistant commissioner, New York City Municipal Archives), e-mail to JNK, March 29, 2017.

"sells, lends, gives away or shows": Article 106 ("Indecency"), section 1141 ("Obscene Prints and Articles"), in James C. Cahill, ed., *Cahill's Consolidated Laws of New York*, 2nd ed. (Chicago: Callaghan, 1930), 1664–1666; copy of Section 1141 in USDLIS #8, 32.

"to deprave and corrupt": Chabon, "'Ulysses' on Trial," 4–8.

did not consider her book "immoral": "Sentenced for Giving Book: Tea Room Owner Gets Indeterminate Term for Distributing Work," *New York Times*, July 3,

1926. Calling Eve "Evelyn Addams," the *Times* referred to Eve's "conviction last week" for distributing an objectionable book. Eve's first trial had actually taken place the previous day, on July 2. The *Times* also mistakenly listed Eve's Polish last name as "Czlotcheber," and claimed incorrectly that "she attended Washington Irving High School."

A second story in Variety: "Evelyn Addams, 1 Yr and Deportation: Boss of Eve's in Village Sold 'Dirty' Book—Man-Hater Besides," *Variety*, July 7, 1926, 33, via Internet Archive, https://archive.org/details/variety83-1926-07.

Nolan found her guilty: USDLIS #3, 5.

"take up the matter of deporting": Thomas R. Minnick to Benjamin M. Day, October 4, 1926, USDLIS #12, 42, attached to Thomas J. Conry, "Migrant Inspector," June 3, 1927, USDLIS #12, 41.

deserved the maximum one year: The October 1926 letter from Thomas Minnick to Commissioner Day concluded that she would serve one year in prison on the charge of possessing and publishing an indecent book; Minnick to Day, October 4, 1926.

"a stiff sentence": Jay A. Gertzman, *Bookleggers and Smuthounds: The Trade in Erotica, 1920–1940* (Philadelphia: University of Pennsylvania Press,1999), 33.

selling Frank Harris's memoir: Susanne G. Frayser and Thomas J. Whitby, *Studies in Human Sexuality: A Selected Guide*, 2nd ed. (Santa Barbara, CA: Libraries Unlimited, 1995), 67. Other books that ran afoul of obscenity law prosecutors in the 1920s included *Madeleine: An Autobiography* (a prostitute's story); James Branch Cabell's *Jurgen: A Comedy of Justice* (a fantasy); Théophile Gautier's *Mademoiselle de Maupin* (a translated French novel about a woman who disguises herself as Theodore and finds herself the object of a woman's love interest); Arthur Schnitzler's *Casanova's Homecoming* (the famous lover, old and tired, finds women no longer attracted to him); and Giovanni Boccaccio's *The Decameron*, an Italian prose classic dating to the fourteenth century.

"Few types of books are considered": Anonymous, "The Enforcement of Laws Against Obscenity in New York," *Columbia Law Review* 28, no. 7 (November 1928): 950.

sentenced to "one year or more": Immigration Act of 1917, https://www.loc.gov/law/help/statutes-at-large/64th-congress/session-2/c64s2ch29.pdf.

who conspired against her: In his own letter to Commissioner Day, Thomas Minnick of the Parole Commission noted that Eve had been found guilty of authoring an "indecent book" and that he had requested his office to contact the Immigration Service "with the view of deporting her." Minnick to Day, October 4, 1926.

prisoner 684: Minnick to Day, October 4, 1926.

disorderly conduct law: Cahill, ed., *Cahill's Consolidated Laws*, 1638–1639. The crime of keeping "disorderly houses," or a "house of ill-fame or assignation" did not actually fall under the disorderly conduct law but under the separate "indecency" law covering "obscenity," under which Eve was later tried.

Eve's second trial: Eve's third hearing, February 10, 1927, USDLIS #7, 11–19 (21–29 of whole file).

Eve was to serve six months: "City Magistrate's Court, 1st Manhattan District: Eve Adams . . . Charged with: Disorderly Conduct. Officer: Margaret Leonard, 13th Division. Disposition, Workhouse, 6 months. Date, July 7, 1926. Magistrate, [Andrew] Macrery," October 7, 1926, USDLIS #3, 3, 6.

went on to a long career: Other notable events in her career include the following. On July 3, 1926, shortly after the raid on Eve's, Leonard and another policewoman, "dressed and acting as if they were visiting flappers seeking a thrill," provided evidence leading to prohibition agents' raid on Texas Guinan's New York nightclub. "Many Notables in Raided Night Club," *Arkansas Gazette* (Little Rock, AR), July 4, 1926, 5, via Genealogybank.com. In 1927, Leonard was fined for an infraction of police department rules—seemingly, drinking on the job. "Drinkers Expelled from Police Force," *New York Times*, November 20, 1927. Later that year, Leonard, "out to make a pinch," arrested a man who pinched her knee. "'Pincher Gets Pinched . . . ,'" *Dubuque (IA) Telegraph Herald and Times Journal*, December 16, 1927, via NewspaperArchive.com. In 1928 Leonard arrested a woman for fortune telling. "Spooks Won't Bet; Fined $10," *Standard Union* (Brooklyn, NY), September 6. 1928, 3, and "Occult Powers Fail in Court," *Nassau Daily Review* (Long Island, NY), September 6, 1928, front page, both via FultonHistory.com.

Leonard arrested a man who offered: "Salesman Held as Fake Doctor," *Daily News* (New York, NY), September 18, 1934, 12, via Newspapers.com.

the first woman appointed to the narcotics squad: In 1939 Leonard was officially transferred from "uniform duty with the women's bureau to plainclothes work" with the Manhattan detective bureau. "Astoria Policewoman Is Transferred," *Long Island Star-Journal* (Long Island City, NY), February 17,1939, 5, and "Two Promoted to Detectives," *Long Island Daily Press*, February 17,

1939, 5, both via FultonHistory.com. In 1949, Leonard "played the drab role of a cleaning woman," helping to trap criminals engaged in distributing drugs worth, at the time, almost $2 million (about $20 million today). "'Maid' Helps Trap 3 in Narcotics Ring: Policewoman Locates Gang's Cache," *New York Times*, March 21, 1949; "Cocaine Trail Leads to $3,000,000 Cache," *Daily News* (New York, NY), March 23, 1949, 27, and "Woman Sleuth Nabs 2 in Narcotics Ring Hunt," *Brooklyn Eagle*, April 3, 1942, both via Newspapers.com. That same year, Leonard was also involved in a drug bust in which another detective was shot. "Detective Is Shot as Drug Suspects Flee from Trap," *Brooklyn Daily Eagle*, June 9, 1949, 1, via Newspapers.com. In the 1950s, until Leonard retired in 1954, she was still helping to catch drug rings. "$1.8 Millions Dope Seized," *Daily News* (New York, NY), February 9, 1950, 40, via Newspapers.com.

received awards in 1941, 1949, and 1951: "The 8 Million," *Daily News* (New York, NY), August 8, 1954, 2, via Newspapers.com. The article's summary of Leonard's career is accompanied by a photo of her in uniform.

transition to "fulltime housewife": "Granny Quits the Force: Warred on Dope 19 Yrs.," *Daily News* (New York, NY), September 5, 1954, 80, via Newspapers.com.

Decoy: "*Decoy*: Full Cast & Crew," Internet Movie Database, accessed November 9, 2020, https://www.imdb.com/title/tt0050010/fullcredits.

verdict for acting "insultingly": "Six Months More for Woman," *New York Times*, July 9, 1926.

the "proprietress of Eve's tearoom": "Greenwich Village Eve Gets 6 Months More," *Journal* (Milwaukee, WI), July 8, 1926, via GenealogyBank.com.

convictions for "selling an obscene book": "Seller of Obscene Books [*sic*] Given 6 Months," *Tablet* (Brooklyn, NY), July 17, 1926, 1, via GenealogyBank.com.

"Eve's Tea Room has had a cop": "Cop Detailed in Vil 'Joints' Ruin Business," *Variety*, July 21, 1926, 46, via Internet Archive, https://archive.org/details /variety83-1926-07/page/n31/mode/2up.

Eve *"was being financed"*: "Addams' Ring of Rich Cultists: Investigation into Surrounding Circumstances and Companions in Village," *Variety*, July 28, 1926, 37, via Internet Archive, https://archive.org/details/variety83-1926-07/page /n205/mode/2up.

Blackwell's had been renamed: "What Was Blackwell's Island?," New-York Historical Society, accessed September 25, 2020, https://www.nyhistory.org /community/blackwells-island.

Radclyffe Hall and The Well of Loneliness: Katz, *Gay American History*, 397–405; William N. Eskridge Jr., "Law and the Construction of the Closet: American Regulation of Same-Sex Intimacy, 1880–1946," *Iowa Law Review* 82 (1996–1997): 1072–1073.

his "ideal of the Village": Robert Edwards, What I Think of Greenwich Village, *Greenwich Village Quill* 18, no. 7 (July 1926): 8. The "more the Village was abused" by radicals, Edwards added, "The more the [male] rotters came down here and the more sordid and exhibitionist were the jades [females] who appeared for their gratification." Edwards had thought many times of leaving the Village but hoped for change. "Now it looks as if we were going to have a real Village again. Behaviorism, the opposite of Misbehaviorism (i. e. Psychoanalysis) . . . is taking hold."

Benito Mussolini: Gaetano Salvenini, "The Grand Council of Fascism," *Foreign Affairs*, January 1929; https://www.foreignaffairs.com/articles/italy/1929-01-01/grand-council-fascism.

Girolamo Savonarola: "Bologna," *New York Times*, April 6, 1921; "Near Dictatorship," *New York Times*, November 26, 1922.

"crusade against lesbians": "Sapphic Sisters Scram!," *Broadway Brevities* 3, no. 3 (November 16, 1931): 10.

"no romance in the Village": George Bogner, What I Think of Greenwich Village, *Greenwich Village Quill*, 19, no. 1 (July 1926): 11–12.

imagined "none but the emasculate": "A Letter from Robert Edwards," *Greenwich Village Quill* 19, no. 2 (August 1926): 43.

"Eve's place is gone": Peter Pater, Village News and Local Color, *Greenwich Village Quill*, September 1926, 57.

"The Greatest Need Now": Heap, *Slumming*, 158.

"The Quill will be excellent": Peter Pater, Local Color, *Greenwich Village Quill*, May 1927, 25.

"They led her a hell of a life": May English to Ben L. Reitman, January 7, 1928, 9–11, University of Illinois at Chicago Library. May English also told Reitman that she "met a girl who knew Eve Adams in Chicago" who said that Eve, perhaps referring to her jail term, "had but very few friends, and they were what we would call the 'scum.'" It's hard to judge the words of this eccentric witness.

8. Eve Adams's *Lesbian Love*

whose name she refused to reveal: Eve's testimony, April 11, 1927, USDLIS #7, 8 (18 of whole file).

Jewish writers in the late Russian Empire: Veidlinger, *Jewish Public Culture*, 6.

welcoming spaces to meet and greet: Proprietors of tearooms often opened them with the goal of welcoming favored groups—in contrast to proprietors of cabarets and speakeasies, who usually opened such businesses with the goal of making money. Ware, *Greenwich Village*, 53.

Little Jimmie: Adams, *Lesbian Love*, 37–43 (182 in appendix).

belongs to the associated union: For various "waistmakers" unions, see the papers of the International Ladies' Garment Workers Union; "ILGWU, Local 22 Records," Cornell University Library, https://rmc.library.cornell.edu/EAD /htmldocs/KCL05780-015.html.

probably Unity House: "Unity House Historical Marker," ExplorePAhistory .com, accessed September 25, 2020, https://explorepahistory.com/hmarker .php?markerId=1-A-366; Alice Kessler-Harris, *Gendering Labor History* (Urbana: University of Illinois Press, 2007), 47.

a repeated, poignant theme: Katz, *Gay American History*, 262, 263.

a *number of bed-sharing intimacies*: For stories of romantic friendships between women leading to sexual encounters, see Lillian Faderman, *Odd Girls and Twilight Lovers: A History of Lesbian Life in 20th Century America* (New York: Columbia University Press, 1991); and Rachel Hope Cleves, *Charity and Sylvia: A Same-Sex Marriage in Early America* (Oxford: Oxford University Press, 2014).

Miki, a "wanderer": Adams, *Lesbian Love*, 53–58 (192 in appendix).

"a blue silk windsor tie": In the United Kingdom, a "Windsor tie" is a wide silk necktie, tied in a loose double knot; "Windsor Tie," Lexico, accessed September 25, 2020, https://www.lexico.com/definition/windsor_tie.

Dr. Marie Equi: Michael Helquist, *Marie Equi: Radical Politics and Outlaw Passions* (Corvallis: Oregon State University Press, 2015), 242–244.

photographed with a "white turn-over collar": Photograph of Marie Equi, 1910s, Wikimedia Commons, https://commons.wikimedia.org/wiki/File:Marie _Equi_(1872-1952).jpg.

Jonnie is rich: Adams, *Lesbian Love*, 9 (172 in appendix).

Ann comes from the West Coast: Adams, 9 (172 in appendix).

Sara, "a slip of a girl": Adams, 10 (172 in appendix). However restrained, Eve's text certainly affirmed women's sexual acts with women.

another male friend brings dinner: Adams, 25 (178 in appendix).

Willie, is about eighteen: Adams, 17–19 (175–176 in appendix).

Sulamith (called Sol): Adams, 11–12 (173 in appendix).

Eve's palling around with militant atheists: Emma Goldman, for example, published an essay concluding, "Atheism in its negation of gods is at the same time the strongest affirmation of man, and through man, the eternal yea to life, purpose, and beauty." Emma Goldman, "The Philosophy of Atheism," *Mother Earth*, February 1916, via Marxists Internet Archive, https://www.marxists .org/reference/archive/goldman/works/1916/atheism.htm.

Dawn, a "little Jewish girl": Adams, *Lesbian Love*, 12–13 (174 in appendix).

Juliet (called Julius) and Ottilia (called Otto): Adams, 23–29 (177–180 in appendix). Eve titled Otto and Julius's story "Just a Snatch," undoubtedly meaning "Just a Brief Encounter." Although *The Oxford English Dictionary* (2020) lists 1904 as the earliest use of *snatch* as slang for the "female pudenda," the serious Eve, I'm convinced, would never have deployed the term if she had known of its derogatory double meaning.

Sammie and Dottie: Adams, *Lesbian Love*, 33 (181 in appendix).

"the mythic, mannish lesbian": Esther Newton, "The Mythic Manish Lesbian: Radclyffe Hall and the New Woman," *Signs* 9, no. 3 (1984), reprinted in revised form in *Margaret Mead Made Me Gay: Personal Essays, Public Ideas* (Durham, NC: Duke University Press, 2000), 176–188.

the new idea of a "female homosexual": George Chauncey Jr., "From Sexual Inversion to Homosexuality: Medicine and the Changing Conceptualization of Female Deviance," *Salmagundi* 58/59 (Fall 1982–Winter 1983): 114–146.

gendered costume played this role: See Shari Benstock on "Costume as Mataphor" and "Stein's Iconography of Costume," in *Women of the Left Bank, Paris, 1900–1940* (Austin: University of Texas Press, 1986), 177–184.

the Flower Pot: Chauncey, *Gay New York*, 237, 238–239.

the Green Mask: This establishment's basement location is described in De la Croix, *Chicago Whispers*, 61.

actress and retired burlesque queen: Rexroth, *Autobiographical Novel* (1982), 161–171.

Diana Thornton: Adams, *Lesbian Love*, 63–64 (194–195 in appendix).

Sorine meets a romantic partner, Irene: Adams, *Lesbian Love*, 44–50 (186–188 in appendix).

Sorine is Ruth Norlander: The 1940 US Census enumeration of Minnewaska Township, MN, via Ancestry.com, lists Ruth Norlander, age forty-four, "widowed," "working on own account" as a "Boat Line Landscape Painter" in the "Fishing Precast" industry. It reports that Norlander was living with Jean Cambpell, thirty-three, single, a "wage or salary worker in Government," working as a "Clerk & Typist."

gave birth to a daughter, Joan: Since the 1920 US Census gives Ruth's age as thirty and daughter Joan's as two, she would have been about twenty-eight when her daughter was born.

"Arabian Nights Ball": Such balls were popular events circa 1920–1930; see various articles archived at Newspapers.com.

"negro dancing": John Perpener, *African American Concert Dance: The Harlem Renaissance and Beyond* (Urbana: University of Illinois Press, 2005), quoted in Saidiya Hartman, *Wayward Lives, Beautiful Experiments: Intimate Histories of Social Upheaval* (New York: W. W. Norton, 2019), 414n302.

liberals supported eugenics: John D'Emilio and Estelle Freedman, *Intimate Matters: A History of Sexuality in America*, 3rd ed. (Chicago: University of Chicago Press, 2012), 165–166, 245, 368–369.

Members of the Polish "race": US Immigration Commission, *Dictionary of Races or Peoples*, 104–105, via Internet Archive, https://archive.org/details/dictionaryofrace00unitrich/page/n3/mode/2up.

"twenty-three and boyish": Per the age given in the 1940 US Census, Jean Cambpell would have been about twenty-three in 1930, a *discontinuity* between Cambpell and the character of Irene. Cambpell was at least five years younger than the character who seems based on her.

"far away in the North-West": Minnewaska Township, MN, where Ruth Norlander and Jean Cambpell were reportedly living at the time of the 1940 US Census, is on Lake Minnewaska.

Eve later complained: Zloczower to "Olsen," June 6, 1931.

"How I Found Myself": Adams, *Lesbian Love*, 69–72 (196–198 in appendix).

those few early immigrants: See Katz, *Gay American History*, 688; and Katz, *Gay/Lesbian Almanac*, 739.

"*Lesbians kissing across their smitten / Lutes*": "Sapphics" appears in Swinburne's
   Poems and Ballads (London: Saville and Edwards, 1866). Apparently 1866 was
   a big year for lesbians and lutes: a reference to a "story passed into a strain of
   music / Set for sweet singers, and to Lesbian lutes" appeared in Edward Bul-
   wer Lyon, *The Lost Tales of Miletus* (New York: Harper and Brothers, 1866),
   reviewed in the *Buffalo (NY) Courier*, May 19, 1866, 8, via Newspapers.com.

The community study: Claude Hartland, *The Story of a Life: For the Consideration of
   the Medical Fraternity* (St. Louis, MO: Lewis S. Matthews, 1901), the earliest
   known autobiography of a US homosexual, presented not only its author's
   extreme alienation but also a sense of the developing homosexual community
   life in St. Louis. See the discussion of Hartland and his book in Jonathan Ned
   Katz, *Love Stories: Sex Between Men Before Homosexuality* (Chicago: University of Chicago Press, 2003). Edward Irenaeus Prime-Stevenson discussed
   communities of male and female homosexuals ("Uranians" and "Uraniads")
   emerging into view in cities around the world; Xavier Mayne (pseudonym
   of Edward Irenaeus Prime-Stevenson), *The Intersexes: A History of Simili-
   sexualism as a Problem in Society Life* (privately printed, [1908]), via Internet
   Archive, https://archive.org/details/mdptemp/page/n17/mode/2up. Djuna
   Barnes's *Ladies Almanack*, in 1936, employed modernist literary techniques
   to satirize and celebrate the amours of a lesbian group headed in Paris by
   Natalie Clifford Barney; see Benstock, *Women of the Left Bank*, 235. Barnes's
   experimental *Nightwood*, also published in 1936, mixed autobiography and
   fiction to survey the unhappy, conflicted romances of a small community of
   women; see Debra L. Niven, "Fictive Elements Within the Autobiographic
   Project: Necessary Conflation of Genres in *Nightwood* by Djuna Barnes," MA
   thesis, University of North Carolina Wilmington, 2007. Allen Bernstein's
   1940 work "Millions of Queers (Our Homo America)," unpublished in his
   lifetime, was also a community study; the 149-page manuscript was first published via OutHistory.org, 2014, http://outhistory.org/exhibits/show/1940
   -defense/millions-of-queers. Another such study was sociologist Edward
   Sagarin's *The Homosexual in America: A Subjective Approach* (New York:
   Greenberg, 1951), published under the pseudonym Donald Webster Cory.
   Esther Newton's pioneering thesis "The 'Drag Queens': A Study in Urban
   Anthropology" (PhD dissertation, University of Chicago, 1968), published
   as *Mother Camp: Female Impersonators in America* (Englewood Cliffs, NJ:
   Prentice-Hall, 1972; Chicago: University of Chicago Press, 1979), focused on
   the social interactions of a community of men (mostly gay) who performed as

women. Newton's *Cherry Grove, Fire Island: Sixty Years in America's First Gay and Lesbian Town* (Boston: Beacon Press,1993) used interviews to document the history of the long-standing community on Long Island, New York. And *Boots of Leather, Slippers of Gold: The History of a Lesbian Community* by Elizabeth Lapovsky Kennedy and Madeline D. Davis (New York: Routledge, 1993) focused on a group in Buffalo, New York.

A lesbian, Mildred Berryman: Berryman's manuscript is discussed in Vern Bullough and Bonnie Bullough, "Lesbianism in the 1920s and 1930s: A Newfound Study," *Signs: Journal of Women in Culture and Society* 2 (Summer 1977): 895–904. See also "Finding Aid for the Mildred Berryman Papers," Online Archive of California, https://oac.cdlib.org/findaid/ark:/13030/c87s7qx2/.

The Stone Wall: Mary Casal (pseudonym of Ruth Fuller Field), *The Stone Wall* (Chicago: Eyncourt Press, 1930), via Internet Archive, https://archive.org/details/stonewallautobio00casa/page/6/mode/2up. For more information about Field see "Mary Casal, Pseudonym of Ruth Fuller Field: The Autobiography of an American Lesbian (1930)," OutHistory.org, accessed September 25, 2020, http://outhistory.org/exhibits/show/casal.

"the honorific title": Veidlinger, *Jewish Public Culture*, xvi, 259, 334 n102.

using the same vocabulary: On the contradictions of romantic love discourse, see Julie Abraham, *Are Girls Necessary: Lesbian Writing and Modern Histories* (Minneapolis: University of Minnesota Press, 1996), 11–13 especially; Laura Kipnis, *Against Love: A Polemic* (New York: Vintage Books/Random House, 2003).

"reverse discourse": Michel Foucault, *The History of Sexuality*, vol. 1 (New York, Vintage, 1980), 101.

describing as "Lesbian love": Dr. P. M. Wise, M.D., "A Case of Sexual Perversion," *Alienist and Neurologist* 4, no. 1, (January 1883): 87–96.

the "Lesbian Love and Murder": "Lesbian Love and Murder," *New York Medical Record* 42 (July 23, 1892): 104.

"a chronic masturbator": William Lee Howard, M.D., "Sexual Perversion," *Alienist and Neurologist* 17, no. 1 (January 1896): 1–6 (quote p. 4). Howard's paper was read at the summer meeting of the Medico-Legal Society, NYC, September 4–6, 1885.

pioneering lesbian bibliographers: Jeannette Howard Foster, *Sex Variant Women in Literature* (New York: Vantage Press, 1956); Barbara Grier, "The Lesbian in Literature, 1967–1981," OutHistory.org, http://outhistory.org/exhibits/show/lesbian-in-literature.

"finds herself falling into Lesbian love": "Latest Novel by Colette Treats Unnatural Theme," *Lexington (KY) Leader*, May 5, 1935.

"frank and unashamed": Rowena Wilson Tobias, review of *We Too Are Drifting* by Gale Wilhelm, Books and People, *Evening Post* (Charleston, SC), September 7, 1935, 3, via GenealogyBank.com.

she declared "writer": New York State Census, 1925, for Eve Zloczewer (misspelled as "Zloczewes"), via Ancestry.com.

9. The Bureaucrats Attack

the case for her deportation was outlined: L. V[incent] F. Jankovski, to Commissioner of Immigration [Henry H. Curran], October 7, 1926, USDLIS #3, 3–4. That Jankovski was himself an immigrant makes his advocating for Eve's deportation especially ironic.

Harry E. Hull: "Harry E. Hull," US Citizenship and Immigration Services, https://www.uscis.gov/history-and-genealogy/our-history/commissioners-and-directors/harry-e-hull.

Jankovski recommended that officials: Jankovski to Curran, October 7, 1926, USDLIS #3, 3–4.

a Jewish émigré from Lithuania: See Vincent F. Jankovski in the 1920 US Federal Census, via Ancestry.com.

second call for deportation hearings: W. W. Brown, call for hearings, October 11, 1926, USDLIS #4, 7.

The document actually initiating: Husband, call for hearings, October 16, 1926, USDLIS #5.

Eve's first deportation hearing: Eve's first hearing, November 24, 1926, USDLIS #7, 1–2 (11–12 of whole file).

right to be represented by counsel: USDLIS #7, 2 (12 of whole file).

Eve's second hearing: USDLIS, #7, 3–10 (13–20 of whole file).

Turk & Eilperin: It would be interesting to know more about the partners of the firm representing Eve, Harold L. Turk and George Eilperin. The Jewish Telegraphic Agency reported on November 2, 1926, "George Eilperin, formerly Acting Collector and Chief Field Deputy of Internal Revenue, left the Treasury Department after many years of service, to enter the practice of law. He . . . will be associated with Harold L. Turk, Republican leader of the Eighth Assembly District, Brooklyn, N.Y., in the firm of Turk and Eilperin"; "Max Reinhardt Honored by European Dramatic and Stage Celebrities," Jewish Telegraphic Agency, November 2, 1926, https://www.jta.org/1926/11/02 /archive/max-reinhardt-honored-by-european-dramatic-and-stage-celebrities. For more on Eilperin's career, see "New G.O.P, Law Post Won't Faze Mr. Eilperin," *Brooklyn Daily Eagle* (Brooklyn, NY), March 31, 1946, 13, via Newspapers.com. As for Harold Turk, one case in which he participated was in 1931, in defense of a client accused of breaking the "National Prohibition Law"; United States v. Pulver, 54 F.2d 261 (2d Cir. 1931).

Rosenblum was twenty-three: The *US Social Security Death Index, 1935–2014* and other documents on Ancestry.com indicate that Manuel Rosenblum was born on June 8, 1903, and so was twenty-three in November 1926 when he represented Eve. Manuel Rosenblum, "became a lawyer June 3, 1926"; "3 Boro Lawyers Suspended on Bar Complaints," *Brooklyn Daily Eagle*, June 23, 1943, 15, via Newspapers.com.

he was suspended: "Trio of Attorneys Suspended 3 Years," *Daily News* (New York, NY), June 23, 1943, Brooklyn section, B3, via Newspapers.com; "3 Boro Lawyers Suspended," *Brooklyn Daily Eagle*.

"Dweller": Harvey W. Zorbaugh, "The Dweller in Furnished Rooms: An Urban Type," in *Papers and Proceedings of the American Sociological Society*, vol. 20 (Chicago: University of Chicago Press, 1926), 83–96.

"If the court had read": Eve's testimony, November 30, 1926, USDLIS #7, 8 (18 of whole file).

"the tragedy of a young woman": J. Brooks Atkinson, The Play, *New York Times*, September 30, 1926. See also "The Captive—Broadway Play—Original," Internet Broadway Database, accessed October 7, 2020, https://www.ibdb .com/broadway-production/the-captive-10133.

the play's "Lesbian motif": George Jean Nathan, George Jean Nathan Looks on the Drama, *Hartford (CT) Courant*, October 10, 1926, part 5, 45, via News papers.com.

play was shut down: Laura Horak, "Lesbians Take Center Stage: The Captive (1926–1928)," in *Girls Will Be Boys: Cross-Dressed Women, Lesbians, and American Cinema, 1908–1934* (New Brunswick, NJ: Rutgers University Press, 2016).

"Obscene, indecent, immoral": "Immoral Plays and Exhibition and the Use and Leasing of Real Property Therefor," section 1140-a in *The Penal Law and Code of Criminal Procedure of the State of New York* (Albany, NY: Matthew Bender, 1917), 308, via Hathi Trust Digital Library, https://babel.hathitrust.org/cgi/pt?id=umn.31951d0242768oo.

"sex degeneracy, or sex perversion": "The Enforcement of Laws Against Obscenity in New York," *Columbia Law Review* 28, no. 7 (November 1928): 957.

"Lesbian Show . . . off the Boards": Morris L. Ernst and William Seagle, *To the Pure: A Study of Obscenity and the Censor* (New York: Viking Press, 1928), 12.

"Drama courses in young ladies' finishing schools": Upton Sinclair, "What the Public Wants," *Daily Worker*, October 26, 1927.

March Hares: "March Hares—Broadway Play—Original," Internet Broadway Database, accessed October 7, 2020, https://www.ibdb.com/broadway-production/march-hares-12601. See also Alan Sinfield, *Out on Stage: Lesbian and Gay Theatre in the Twentieth Century* (New Haven, CT: Yale University Press, 1999), 91.

printed edition of the play: Harry Wagstaff Gribble, *March Hares (The Temperamentalists): A Fantastic Satire in Three Acts* (Cincinnati, OH: Stewart Kidd, 1921).

Cigarette companies had convinced: Allan M. Brandt, *The Cigarette Century: The Rise, Fall, and Deadly Persistence of the Product That Defined America* (New York: Basic Books, 2007), 70–73. Ware, *Greenwich Village* also discusses smoking.

A Hartford, Connecticut, businessman: Per *Geer's Hartford City Directory*, 1923, via "Alexander Migdall," *U.S. City Directories, 1822–1995*, Ancestry.com, Eve's uncle lived at 52 South Street, Hartford, CT, in 1923.

"surely did not believe": USDLIS #7, 9–10 (19–20 of whole file).

nearly $15,000 today: CPI inflation calculator, US Bureau of Labor Statistics, accessed October 7, 2020, https://data.bls.gov/cgi-bin/cpicalc.pl.

At Eve's third deportation hearing: USDLIS #7, 11–12 (21–22 of whole file).

All other evidence: USDLIS #7, 12 (22 of whole file).

"degenerates of male and female type": Leonard's testimony, USDLIS #7, 22, 25 (32, 35 of whole file).

recommended "the alien's deportation": Thomas J. Conry, "Summary," February 11, 1927, USDLIS #7, 20–21 (30–31 of whole file).

"High Deportable": Byron Uhl (first assistant commissioner, Immigration Service), memo, April 12, 1927, USDLIS, #8, 32.

recommended that Eve's case be reopened: George J. Harris to commissioner of immigration, Ellis Island, April 25, 1927, USDLIS #10. Harris cited Smith v. Hays, 10 F.2d 145 (8th Cir. December 31, 1925). Howard Allen, acting chairman of the Immigration Service's Board of Review, asked that Eve's hearings be reopened, that the record clarify the crimes for which she had been convicted and include the length of Eve's sentence as fixed by the Parole Commission, and that Eve and her lawyer should be permitted to inspect the updated record. USDLIS #9, 35.

Eve's last hearing: USDLIS #11, 1–4 (37–40 of whole file).

Conry later claimed: T. J. Conry to commissioner of immigration, Ellis Island, June 3, 1927, UDLIS #12, 41.

Judge Nolan's Catholicism: The judge's Catholicism is evident in his obituary; "Thomas J. Nolan, Jurist, Dies at 64," *New York Times*, January 24, 1937.

titled, provocatively, Sex: "Sex—Broadway Play—Original," Internet Broadway Database, accessed October 7, 2020, https://www.ibdb.com/broadway -production/sex-10051. For insightful scholarly comment on *Sex*, see June Sochen, *Mae West: She Who Laughs, Lasts* (Wheeling, IL: Harlan Davidson, 1992).

Daily Mirror called it "Offensive": For critics' responses to *Sex*, see Marybeth Hamilton, "Mae West Live: SEX, The Drag, and 1920s Broadway," TDR 36, no. 4 (Winter 1982): 85.

West was sentenced to ten days: "Mae West Begins Nine Days in Jail," *Evening Star* (Washington, DC), April 20, 1927.

She served her time: Simon Louvish, *Mae West: It Ain't No Sin* (New York: Macmillan, 2006), 136.

published an account of her time: Mae West, "Ten Days and Five Hundred Dollars: The Experiences of a Broadway Star in Jail," *Liberty*, August 20, 1927, 53–56.

"However," Conry added: USDLIS #12, 41. On June 7, Byron Uhl sent the record of Eve's last hearing to the commissioner general of immigration in Washington, DC; USDLIS #13, 43.

"probation for a year": Harold L. Turk to commissioner general of immigration, Washington, DC, June 13, 1927, USDLIS #16, 47.

"are not supported": USDLIS #14, 45.

"very carefully considered": USDLIS #16, 48.

"No adequate grounds": USDLIS #17, 49.

stay of deportation was denied: Harold E. Hull to Turk & Eilperin, December 7, 1927: USDLIS #19. 52.

answered Congressman Thomas H. Cullen: Harold E. Hull to Thomas H. Cullen, December 7, 1927, USDLIS #20, 54–55.

None of these drawings: Dr. Clifford Scheiner, the historian of erotica, advises me that the four illustrations "were considered 'galant' in the 1920s and 1930s," meaning something like "brave," "noble," "courtly," and "amorous," and "sexy-erotic" but "not offensive or illegal." Dr. Clifford Scheiner, e-mails to JNK, October 20, 2019.

"can be exhibited in any place": USDLIS #7, 8 (18 of whole file).

"the envelope attached": USDLIS #21, 57.

"The book in question": USDLIS #21, 56.

Ellis Island clerk executed: "Warrant for Deportation of Zlotczewer, Chawa Eva, Alias Adams Evelyn, Port of New York, Executed December 7, 1927, SS *Polonia*," USDLIS #22, 58. A few days later, a final document in Eve's file affirmed that Eve had been deported; Byron W. Uhl to the commissioner general of immigration in Washington, DC, December 12, 1927, USDLIS #23, 59.

Kenny that day published: Jack Kenny, "Modern Eve Adams Driven from Eden, *Daily News* (New York, NY), December 7, 1927, main ("Pink") ed., 4, via Newspapers.com. A slightly smaller, slightly different version of this story appears as ibid., other ("Extra") ed., 16, via Newspapers.com.

"Smooth-tongued": See also the reference to "supple tongued sirens" in chapter 11.

"The morals of this 35-year-old": "Eve Adams Uses One-Way Ticket," *Daily News* (New York, NY), December 8, 1927, 16, via Newspapers.com. The report adds that Eve had spent "one year in the workhouse." Eve was actually jailed for a year and a half.

"must have been heartbroken": English to Reitman, January 7, 1928, 9–11.

10. Eve in Exile

"cold and hunger": Eve to Reitman, February 15, 1929, 1.

Eve listed for Reitman: Eve to Reitman, August 15, 1934.

Violet Dixon: Violet H. Dixon, an artist, born in Illinois in about 1879, was married to Canadian-born Frank M. Dixon, also an artist. See the US Census for 1910, 1920, and 1930 at Ancestry.com. According to an online database of artists, Dixon's artworks are rare; "Violet H Dixon," askART, accessed October 7, 2020, https://www.askart.com/artist/Violet_H_Dixon/11224258/Violet_H _Dixon.aspx. Many years after Eve's Chicago days, Ben Reitman wrote to Eve, "I saw Violet Dixon the other day and she looks as charming and as young as ever, although she has grown grandsons. She is still painting pictures and living by herself and blessing all those whom she meets." Ben Reitman to Eve Adams, August 27, 1933 [*sic*, actually 1934], "Eva Adams" file, Reitman Papers. I concur with the careful researcher Martha Reis, who points out that Reitman misdated the year of this letter and that it was actually written in 1934 (Reis, "Hidden Histories," 97n131). Reitman's reference to Eve's "delightful long letter of the fifteenth" must refer to her 1934 missive, which is the only one she sent to him dated August 15. In Reitman's letter he also says that "I understand that Emma's going to get another vise [visa] and will come to America soon for 3 months. She is still in Toronto, Canada." Emma Goldman was indeed in Toronto waiting on a visa in August 1934. Candace Falk et al., eds., "Chronology (1920–1940)," Emma Goldman: A Guide to Her Life and Documentary Sources, Emma Goldman Papers, accessed October 9, 2020, https://www.lib.berkeley.edu/goldman/pdfs/EG-AGuideToHerLife _Chronology1920-1940.pdf, 28–30. See also "Emma Goldman Extended Timeline," Libcom, https://libcom.org/history/emma-goldman-extended-timeline.

"Have faith, have faith": Eve slightly misquoted lines from Tennyson's "Sea Dreams: An Idyll," in which a husband tells his wife how he has been defrauded by a supposed friend who urged, "Have faith, have faith! . . . And all things work together for the good . . ." etc. John Batchelor, *Tennyson: To Strive, to Seek, to Find* (New York: Open Road Media, 2013).

"The present is the vassal": Here Eve slightly misquoted lines from Tennyson's "The Lover's Tale": "The Present is the vassal of the Past: / So that, in that I *have* lived, do I live." Alfred Tennyson, *The Lover's Tale* (London: C. Kegan Paul, 1879), 14.

a "dramatization of 'Lesbian Love'": "Queer Show Quits Before Cops Cop It," *Variety*, February 6, 1929, 1, via Internet Archive, https://archive.org/details /variety94-1929-02/mode/2up. *Variety* reminded its readers that "Jane Adams," the author of *Lesbian Love*, had been convicted as a "disseminator of obscene literature" and had been deported after serving a term on Welfare Island two years earlier. I've discovered no additional information about the intriguing play *Modernity* or the "Scientific Players" who apparently put it on; the New York Public Library's Theatre Division contains no references to either.

Pleasure Man: "Pleasure Man—Broadway Play—Original," Internet Broadway Database, accessed October 7, 2020. https://www.ibdb.com/broadway-production/pleasure-man-10730. For more on both *The Drag* and *Pleasure Man*, see Jordan Schildcrout, *Murder Most Queer: The Homicidal Homosexual in the American Theater* (Ann Arbor: University of Michigan Press, 2014).

11. The Crash

"a new sex play": "Police Prevent Play," *Daily Times* (Chicago, IL), September 21, 1929, 20, via GenealogyBank.com. In 1930 *Variety* reported that the Play Mart Players were vacating the Play Mart, which was "being demolished and replaced with [a] modern apartment house." The company was planning to move its productions to MacDougal Alley, and open in July with *The Clothes Line Revue*; "Open-Air Backyard Drama in the Village," *Variety*, June 11, 1930, 1, via Internet Archive, https://archive.org/details/variety99-1930-06/mode/2up. As with *Modernity* in the previous chapter, I uncovered no further information, at the NYPL's Theatre Division or elsewhere, on the Play Mart Players, the Play Mart venue on Christopher Street, or *Modernity*'s producer Harold Paine. Future research might look for more information about Paine and a possible link between the aforementioned Scientific Players and Eve's actor friend Watson White, referenced later.

"a long time": Eve Adams to Ben Reitman, December 12, 1930, scan and typed copy included by Martha Reis in the set of "Transcripts" of Eve's letters in the archive of the University of Illinois at Chicago Library that Reis sent to Eran Zahavy and that Zahavy shared with me. Though the transcript lists the original letter as in the Reitman Papers, my researcher Marie K. Rowley was unable to find it there. Reis, "Hidden Histories" also lists this as in the Reitman Papers, box 9, folder 151, but this locator is now invalid after a library reorganization. Whether Reitman helped pay for Eve's ticket out of Warsaw is unknown.

"Sam Putnam, for his magazine": Putnam's *New Review* favored realist writing opposed to the formalist, experimental features preferred by his rival Eugene Jolas, editor of the modernist *transition* magazine (with a small *t*), also published in Paris. Samuel Putnam, *Paris Was Our Mistress: Memoirs of a*

Lost & Found Generation (Carbondale: Southern Illinois University Press, 1970; orig. publ. Viking Press, 1947), 225–229.

listed as forthcoming: Brianna Cregle (Rare Books and Special Collections, Firestone Library, Princeton University), e-mail to JNK, January 19, 2017.

Eve's story did not appear: I have found no reference to Eve or her manuscripts in Samuel Putnam's papers; Cregle, e-mail to JNK, January 19, 2017. The Southern Illinois University library also holds a collection of Samuel Putnam's Papers, but it likewise reports no reference to Eve Adams or her prison stories. She is not mentioned in Putnam's correspondence 1929–1931; Aaron M. Lisec (research specialist, Special Collections Research Center, Morris Library, Southern Illinois University), e-mail to JNK, January 24, 2017.

rebelling against Putnam: Samuel Putnam, Henry Miller, and Alfred Perles all published conflicting accounts of Miller and Perles's attempted coup at the *New Review*. All three accounts are included in Robert Cross, *Henry Miller: The Paris Years* (Big Sur, CA: PeerAmid Press, 1991), 25–28.

other prison stories to Max Eastman: I discovered no reference to Eve or her manuscripts in Max Eastman's archive at Indiana University Bloomington; Rachel Makarowski (reference assistant, Lilly Library, Indiana University Bloomington), e-mail to JNK, January 27, 2017. The finding aid for Eastman's Papers at the New York Public Library (http://archives.nypl.org/the/21313) does not refer to Eve Adams or any variation on her name.

"A weird little land": Putnam, *Paris Was Our Mistress*, 116.

small cottage in Saint-Tropez: Cottage in Saint-Tropez: Falk, *Love, Anarchy*, 343; "Emma Goldman Extended Timeline," Libcom, https://libcom.org/history /emma-goldman-extended-timeline.

"surrounded by a group of lesbians": Putnam, *Paris Was Our Mistress*, 86.

"Not far away": Zloczower to "Olsen," June 6, 1931.

Norlander dropped by Barnes's house: Norlander wrote at least four notes to Barnes, in 1926, 1932, 1937, and 1947, scans via Amanda McKnight (associate archivist and librarian, Barnes Foundation), e-mails to JNK, June 13, 2017.

The writer was Peter Neagoe: Emma Goldman's archive includes correspondence with Peter Neagoe in Mirmande, France, in 1931 and 1934, which enabled me to identify Neagoe and his wife as the unnamed writer and painter mentioned by Eve; "Emma Goldman Papers," International Institute of Social History, accessed October 8, 2020, https://search.iisg.amsterdam/Record

/ARCH00520/ArchiveContentList. Of particular interest, Peter Neagoe edited *Americans Abroad: An Anthology, with Autographed Photographs and Biographic Sketches of the Authors* (The Hague: Servire Press, 1932). This collection contains entries by many American writer-tourists of the time. Neagoe also published many works of fiction and some nonfiction. The Peter Neagoe Papers at Syracuse University contain "Correspondence, diaries, drawings, manuscripts, photographs, sketches, memorabilia, and material relating to Neagoe's wife, painter and muralist, Anna Neagoe"; "Peter Neagoe Papers 1918–1974," WorldCat, accessed October 8, 2020, https://www.worldcat .org/title/peter-neagoe-papers-1918-1974/oclc/902672679. In addition, the Archives of American Art in Washington, DC, has an Anna and Peter Neagoe Papers collection; "Anna and Peter Neagoe Papers, 1911–1980," accessed October 8, 2020, https://www.aaa.si.edu/collections/anna-and-peter-neagoe -papers-8076. Neither of these archives mentions Eve Adams in their finding aids. My examination of five paintings of women by Peter Neagoe in the collection of the Syracuse University Art Galleries do not look like Eve; scans via Laura J. Wellner (registrar, Syracuse University Art Galleries), e-mails to JNK, November 26, 2018.

"my little piece of Transylvanian sassafras": Emily Holmes Coleman, *Rough Draft: The Modernist Diaries of Emily Holmes Coleman, 1929–1937* (Newark: University of Delaware Press, 2012), 290: Djuna Barnes "gets inspired when she talks about Neagoe. 'My little piece of Transylvanian sassafras, spitting in the prune keg.' I was laughing." See also Elizabeth Podnieks and Sandra Chait, eds., *Hayford Hall: Hangovers, Erotics, and Modernist Aesthetics* (Carbondale: Southern Illinois University Press, 2005). On Peter's nickname "Muffin," see G. C. Guirl-Stearley, introduction to "The Letters of Djuna Barnes and Emily Holmes Coleman (1935–1936)," *Missouri Review* 22, no. 3 (1999): 105–146.

with his "young wife": Berkman and Eckstein were not in fact married, but she was thirty years his junior; Falk, *Love, Anarchy*, 378.

a "No-Jury Exhibit" in 1922: "The Art Exhibit at Field's," *Svenska Tribunen-Nyheter*, October 11, 1922, trans. Foreign Language Press Survey, via Newberry Library, https://flps.newberry.org/article/5423404_2_1192. Norlander's name and address are listed in the show's catalog as 10 E. Chestnut Street, the address of the Grey Cottage. *First Annual Exhibition of the Chicago No-Jury Society of Artists* (Chicago: No-Jury Society of Artists, 1922), cat. no. 253, 254; Joel Dryer (director, Illinois Historical Art Project), e-mail to JNK, May 4, 2020.

No-Jury Society of Artists: Herbert R. Hartel Jr., *Raymond Jonson and the Spiritual in Modernist and Abstract Painting* (New York: Routledge, 2018).

about sixty dollars today: CPI inflation calculator, US Bureau of Labor Statistics, accessed October 8, 2020, https://data.bls.gov/cgi-bin/cpicalc.pl.

"little Joan": Norlander's daughter Joan was about thirteen in 1931.

Norlander's stand-in "Sorine": Adams, *Lesbian Love*, 47 (186 in appendix).

"one of the most delightful": Billy Scully, "Village on Parade," *Greenwich Village Weekly News*, October 10, 1931, cited in Chauncey, *Gay New York*, 242, I have not located my own copy of the original document.

SAPPHIC SISTERS SCRAM!: "Sapphic Sisters Scram! Depression Drives Ladies of Lesbos to Normalcy Deserting Boat Boys for Jobs and Feminine Frills; Village and Beeway Camps Left Lonely as Rich Dames Vanish, Only Old Guard Carries On," *Broadway Brevities* 3, no. 3 (November 16, 1931): 1, 10, via New York Public Library.

"the boy in the boat": Eric Partridge, *The New Partridge Dictionary of Slang and Unconventional English*, vol. 2, J–Z (London: Routledge, 2005), 1218, identifies terms for the clitoris, dating to 1896, in the United Kingdom: "little man in a boat," "man in the boat," and "boy in the boat." The dictionary explains, "The 'little man' or 'boy' represent the clitoris as a small penis, and the vulva is imaged to be boat-shaped." A 1930 song by the homosexual George Hannah titled "The Boy in the Boat" alludes to the clitoris and oral sex; "Obscure Queer Blues," *Queer Music Heritage*, November 2014, https://www.queermusicheritage.com/nov2014.html.

"And when they came to the ash": Susan Sniader Lanser, "Speaking in Tongues: 'Ladies Almanack' and the Language of Celebration," *Frontiers: A Journal of Women's Studies* 4, no. 3 (Autumn 1979): 44. Lanser, a lesbian feminist literary critic, says of Barnes's text, "The glorification of the tongue as the ultimate sexual instrument must surely have provided an antidote to the ethos of phallic supremacy and clitoral insufficiency of a newly Freudian age."

12. Fascism

greater control of the state: "1933: Key Dates," Holocaust Encyclopedia, US Holocaust Memorial Museum, accessed October 8, 2020, https://encyclopedia.ushmm.org/content/en/article/1933-key-dates.

arson attack on the German parliament: "The Reichstag Fire," US Holocaust Encyclopedia, US Holocaust Memorial Museum, accessed October 8, 2020, https:// encyclopedia.ushmm.org/content/en/article/the-reichstag-fire.

In Dachau, near Munich: "Dachau," US Holocaust Encyclopedia, US Holocaust Memorial Museum, accessed October 8, 2020, https://encyclopedia.ushmm .org/content/en/article/dachau.

many lesbians suffered: The multiple, intersecting reasons that a lesbian might fall victim to the Nazis is discussed in a thoughtful essay: Laurie Marhoefer, "Lesbianism, Transvestitism, and the Nazi State: A Microhistory of a Gestapo Investigation, 1939–1943," *American Historical Review* 121, no. 4 (October 2016): 1167–1195. The literature on lesbians under the German Nazi regime is analyzed in Willam J. Spurlin, "The Politics of Gender Difference: Lesbian Existence Under the Third Reich," in *Lost Intimacies: Rethinking Homosexuality Under National Socialism* (New York: Peter Lang, 2008), 45–63.

parliament abolished democracy: William L. Hosch, "The Reichstag Fire and the Enabling Act of March 23, 1935"; *Britannica Blog*, March 23, 2007, http:// blogs.britannica.com/2007/03/the-reichstag-fire-and-the-enabling-act/.

nationwide action against German Jews: "Boycott of Jewish Businesses," Holocaust Encyclopedia, US Holocaust Memorial Museum, accessed October 8, 2020, https://encyclopedia.ushmm.org/content/en/article/boycott -of-jewish-businesses.

attacked the Institute for Sexual Science: Robert Beachy, *Gay Berlin: Birthplace of a Modern Identity* (New York: Alfred A. Knopf, 2014), 241–242.

French antifascist groups formed: Joel Colton, "Politics and Economics in the 1930s," in *From the Ancien Regime to the Popular Front*, ed. Charles K. Warner (New York: Columbia University Press, 1969), 183.

passport, signed July 2, 1934: Eve's polish passport is in the Daniel Olstein Collection.

"All that has such a great memory": Eve to Reitman, August 15, 1934.

"the most infamously obscene book": Chabon, "'Ulysses' on Trial," 4.

featured on college freshman reading lists: Ben W. Heineman Jr., "Rereading 'Ulysses' by James Joyce: The Best Novel Since 1900," *Atlantic*, November 29, 2010, https://www.theatlantic.com/entertainment/archive/2010/11/rereading -ulysses-by-james-joyce-the-best-novel-since-1900/67092/.

"the active girl with bobbed": Wambly Bald, La Vie de Bohème (As Lived on the Left Bank), *Chicago Tribune and the Daily News, New York* (Paris), January 3, 1933, 4, via Gallica, https://gallica.bnf.fr/ark:/12148/bpt6k4777547q/f4.item. For the history of the *Chicago Tribune*'s Paris edition, see Nissa Ren Cannon, "The American Colonies: Paris's *Tribune* and Paris-American Identity," *Journal of Modern Periodical Studies* 8, no. 1 (2017): 34–55.

red tie: In 1915, a "well-informed American correspondent" of Havelock Ellis had related that few of his medical school classmates "ever had the courage to wear a red tie." Havelock Ellis, *Studies in the Psychology of Sex*, vol. 2, *Sexual Inversion*, 3rd. ed. (New York: Random House, 1936; orig. publ. 1915), 350–351, cited in Katz, *Gay American History*, 52–53.

"the famous Grey Cottage": I silently corrected Bald's inaccurate "Gray Cottage."

an affectionate caricature of Eve: The drawing of Eve was possibly by Brassaï, the Hungarian French artist and photographer who illustrated and signed very similar portraits illustrating other Wambly Bald columns. But other artists signed similar drawings.

a set of sexy postcards: Miller biographer Robert Ferguson claims that during a 1928 trip to Paris with his wife, June, Miller "had discovered Eve Adams' pornographic bookshop in Montparnasse and purchased a copy of Fanny Hill and a set of dirty postcards"; Robert Ferguson, *Henry Miller: A Life* (New York: W. W. Norton, 1991), 177. However, Ferguson provides no source for these claims, and no other source says that Eve ran a bookshop, pornographic or otherwise.

Lovely Lesbians: Miller's novel was finally published in 1991 as *Crazy Cock*. In this autobiographical fiction, Miller's wife, June (called Hildred), begins a lesbian affair with Vanya (the Millers' roommate Jean Kronski). Since *Lovely Lesbians* wasn't published during Eve's lifetime, she may not have known of its anti-Jewish and anti-homosexual content. See Mary V. Dearborn, introduction to *Crazy Cock* by Henry Miller (New York: Grove Press, 1991), xix–xxi, xxv. According to Ferguson, 133, roommate Jean Kronski's real name was Mara or Martha Andrews.

"I'm going to put on a red necktie": Miller. *Crazy Cock*, 110–111.

"called something like 'Eve's Adam'": *Greenwich Village Weekly News*, November 21, 1931, cited in Chauncey, *Gay New York*, 242.

The Young and Evil: Chauncey, 242. See also Sam See, "Making Modernism New: Queer Mythology in *The Young and Evil*," *English Literary History* 76, no. 4

(Winter 2009): 1075, 1083; and Charles Ford and Parker Tyler, *The Young and Evil* (Paris: Obelisk Press, 1933), 11.

"pornographic books and highbrow magazines": Alfred Perles, *My Friend Henry Miller* (New York: John Day, 1956) 32–34, 122.

"That naughty old Sappho of Greece": Norman Douglas, *Some Limericks* (1928), excerpted in "Norman Douglas Limericks," https://www.blueridgejournal. com/poems/lim-ten.htm.

"ostensibly to give them away": Perles, *My Friend Henry Miller*, 32–34, 122. Perles says that Eve, successful at selling *Tropic of Cancer*, also found customers for the *New Review*, the same periodical that had been slated to publish her prison stories in 1931 before Perles and Miller took over from Samuel Putnam; Perles, *My Friend Henry Miller*, 27.

"the habit of buggering": Henry Miller, *Henry Miller's Book of Friends: A Trilogy* (Santa Barbara, CA: Capra Press, 1987), 43.

"Zink bar": Many Paris bars then boasted zinc countertops, but Eve's particular "Zink bar" has not been identified.

"many of American art's advance guard": Charles Estcourt Jr. "Intelligentsia Desert Paris and Flock Back to New York," *Los Angeles Times*, December 30, 1934, 35, via Newspapers.com. Estcourt's column was syndicated to multiple newspapers, and his article mentioning Eve also appeared, for instance, in the *Dayton (OH) Daily News*, the *Indianola (MS) Enterprise*, and the *Atlanta (GA) Constitution* (per Newspapers.com).

American writer James T. Farrell: Edgar Marquess Branch, *A Paris Year: Dorothy and James T. Farrell, 1931–1932* (Athens: Ohio University Press, 1998), 32–33, 120, 165n15–16, 185n10.

Eve would not have been welcome: Shari Benstock, "Paris Lesbianism and the Politics of Reaction, 1900–1940," in *Hidden from History: Reclaiming the Gay and Lesbian Past*, ed. Martin Duberman, Martha Vicinus, and George Chauncey Jr. (New York: Meridian, 1990), 332–346.

silent pact between "respectable" lesbians and their societies: Elizabeth Lapovsky Kennedy, "'But We Would Never Talk About It': The Structure of Lesbian Discretion in South Dakota, 1928–1933," in *Inventing Lesbian Cultures in America*, ed. Ellen Lewin (Boston: Beacon Press, 1996), 15–39, 198–200.

by heterosexual men: Three of the known reports from Paris about Eve and *Lesbian Love* are by Alfred Perles, James Farrell, and Wambly Bald, all discussed previously.

none by lesbians: Among the American lesbians in Paris, Eve would have been most likely to befriend Margaret Anderson, who also greatly admired and visited Emma Goldman, but I've discovered no documentation of Eve and Anderson interacting in Paris. The finding aids of the Margaret C. Anderson Papers at the University of Wisconsin and at the Elizabeth Jenks Clark Collection at Beinecke Library, Yale University, do not mention Eve Adams, Zloczewer, Zlocsewer, or Zloczower.

"adopted child, a grown woman of 28": Eve did not explicitly say that she was referring to Hella. But Hella Olstein, born on March 5, 1905, was twenty-nine when Eve wrote Reitman on August 15, 1934. "Hella Soldner," Central Database of Shoah Victims' Names, Yad Vashem: The World Holocaust Remembrance Center, Jerusalem, https://yvng.yadvashem.org /nameDetails.html?itemId=1682354. This "page of testimony" under her later married name of Hella Olstein Soldner, was submitted by her brother Georges Olstein on November 26, 1998, lists her birth date as March 5, 1905, identifies her as a *sängerin* (singer), and gives a probable death date of August 1944.

"presents and affection": Reitman, "Eve."

adopting the nurturing role: Eve's grandnephew recalls that he heard his grandfather Yerachmiel, Eve's brother, describe "Eve as the oldest child of multiple brothers and sisters," and as "the right hand of her mom until she left home"; Eran Zahavy, e-mail to JNK, June 9, 2020.

born into a Jewish family: Information and documentation on Hella Olstein's family background was supplied by Daniel Olstein, whose father was Hella's brother André Olstein. Daniel Olstein, e-mail to JNK, May 12, 2020.

singing in French cabarets: A search in 2020 of historical French newspapers for "Nora Waren" and "Norah Waren" revealed numerous advertisements for her appearances as singer.

photo she sent to her brother: "Hella Soldner," Central Database of Shoah Victims' Names, https://yvng.yadvashem.org/nameDetails.html?itemId=1682354.

two snapshots of herself: A search of the Reitman Papers did not reveal the two photos of Eve.

Eve's "delightful long letter": Reitman to Eve, August 27, 1933 [*sic*, actually 1934].

"None of them were honest": The books disparaged by Reitman were Margaret C. Anderson, *My Thirty Years' War* (New York: Covici, Friede, 1930); Gold-

man, *Living My Life* (New York: A. A. Knopf, 1931); and Gertrude Stein, *The Autobiography of Alice B. Toklas* (New York: Harcourt, Brace, 1933.)

"powerful and most fascinating": Zloczower to "Olsen," June 6, 1931.

Ben Reitman "wasn't so bad": Anderson, *My Thirty Years' War*, 70, cited in Paul Avrich and Karen Avrich, *Sasha and Emma*, 434n21. Reitman quotes Anderson's comment about him in a letter to Goldman on August 23, 1930; Falk, *Love, Anarchy*, 392, 562n21.

the club he'd established: "A Brief History of the Dill Pickle Club," Frontier to Heartland, https://publications.newberry.org/frontiertoheartland/exhibits/show/perspectives/dillpickle/briefhistory.

hoping for a US visa: As early as 1927, in Canada, Goldman had asked friends to help her secure a US visa. Falk, *Love, Anarchy*, 363. On December 15, 1933, Goldman arrived in Canada and, in Toronto, applied for a US visa. Thanks to the help of prominent civil libertarians and well-known writers, Goldman received permission for a three-month tour starting on February 2, 1934. But she was not allowed to speak publicly about politics, only literature. Paul Avrich and Karen Avrich, *Sasha and Emma*, 365–368. Back in Toronto in the summer of that year, she hoped to obtain a new US visa with the assistance of Roger Baldwin in Washington, DC. Candace Falk et al., eds., "Chronology (1920–1940)," https://www.lib.berkeley.edu/goldman/pdfs/EG-AGuideToHerLife_Chronology1920-1940.pdf, 28–30.

"a very fine glimpse": Ben Reitman to Ena Douglas, August 25, 1934, series 3, box 23, folder 274, Reitman Papers.

"a splendid article": Ben Reitman to Emma Goldman, December 21, 1934, Emma Goldman Archive, cited in Reis, "Hidden Histories," 96n122. In the published version of Reitman's *Sister of the Road*, the only mention of Paris is in relation to a woman born there named "Yvonne the Tzigane." Reitman, *Sister of the Road*, 47–48. The finding aid for the Reitman Papers does not reveal any other writing specifically about women hobos.

the profound guilt he felt: Bruns, *The Damndest*, 15–16, 212–213; Falk, *Love, Anarchy*, 507.

calling herself Jan Gay: Helen Reitman and her partner Eleanor Byrnes both changed their last names to Gay, with Byrnes becoming Zhenya Gay; Dale Sheldon, "Helen Reitman," Gay History Wiki, accessed October 9, 2020, http://gayhistory.wikidot.com/helen-reitman. Jan Gay founded the Committee for the Study of

Sex Variants and initiated the study conducted and published under the name of
Dr. George W. Henry. Information about the fascinating Jan Gay is available in
Jennifer Terry, *An American Obsession: Science, Medicine, and Homosexuality in
Modern Society* (Chicago: University of Chicago Press, 1999); Henry L. Minton,
*Departing from Deviance: A History of Homosexual Rights and Emancipatory
Science in America* (Chicago: University of Chicago Press, 2001); Reis, "Hidden
Histories"; and Mecca Reitman Carpenter, *No Regrets: Dr. Ben Reitman and the
Women Who Loved Him* (Council Bluffs, IA: SouthSide Press, 1999).

deserted by his father: Reitman was one year old and his brother three when the boys'
father abandoned them and his wife, and Reitman's parents later divorced;
Carpenter, *No Regrets*, 11.

"bumming around the battery": Reitman, "Homosexuality," 3. On Reitman and
the "sailor," see also Jim Elledge, *The Boys of Fairy Town: Sodomites, Female
Impersonators, Third-Sexers, Pansies, Queers, and Sex Morons in Chicago's
First Century* (Chicago: Chicago Review Press, 2018), 231, 269. On Reitman
and homosexual behavior among hobos, see also Todd DePastino, "Homosexuality," in *Citizen Hobo: How a Century of Homelessness Shaped America*
(Chicago: University of Chicago Press, 2010), 85–91.

"fell prey to the sexual will": Reitman, "Following the Monkey" (unpublished manuscript), n.d., 80–82, folder 11, Reitman Papers, cited in Elledge, *The Boys of
Fairy Town*, 231, and DePastino, *Citizen Hobo*, 89, 186n117. The world of
men jockers and boy punks certainly included predatory relationships. In
contrast, the heterosexual sociologist of hobo life Nels Anderson noted several
"attachments between men and between men and boys 'that surpass the love
of woman.'" He added, "Many of these are not more than a few days' duration,
but while they last they are very intense and sentimental." One eighteen-year-
old migrant, interviewed by Anderson, was first "disgusted with himself" for
having participated in a homosexual encounter. But the youth later sought out
partners for homosexual liaisons, desire succeeding disgust. Nels Anderson,
"The Juvenile and the Tramp," *Journal of Criminology and Criminal Law* 14
(August 1922): 306, cited in DePastino, *Citizen Hobo*, 87, 286n110. See also
Josiah Flynt, "Homosexuality Among Tramps," appendix A in Ellis, *Sexual
Inversion*, 360–367.

youths who "experiment": Reitman, "Homosexuality," 6.

"and all of them were suspicious": Reitman, 4.

Taunted as "Sheeny Ben": Bruns, *The Damndest*, 5.

adamantly rejected the Christian Poland: Eve to Reitman, February 15, 1929.

Reitman identified with society's outcasts: Bruns, *The Damndest*, 215–220.

by promoting birth control: Bruns, 170, 175–177.

"vagrancy": Bruns, 35.

"disorderly conduct": Bruns, 55–56.

first book was on pimps and their networks: Ben Lewis Reitman, *The Second Oldest Profession: A Study of the Prostitute's Business Manager* (New York: Vanguard Press,1931).

America "has no patience": Bruns, *The Damndest*, 179.

13. War

Hitler declared himself Führer: "1934: Key Dates," Holocaust Encyclopedia, US Holocaust Memorial Museum, accessed October 9, 2020, https://encyclopedia .ushmm.org/content/en/article/1934-key-dates.

a short postcard in Yiddish: Eve Adams, postcard to Yerachmiel Zahavy, August 24, 1934, Eran Zahavy Collection, trans. Naomi Cohen.

changed his last name: Eran Zahavy, "Yerachmiel Zahavy" and Zloczower family tree, Geni, accessed October 9, 2020, https://www.geni.com/people /Yerachmiel-Zahavy/6000000003018412504, https://www.geni.com /family-tree/canvas/6000000002920263005.

strict terms for tourists: Andrew McFadyean, "Immigration and Labor in Palestine," *Foreign Affairs* 12, no. 4 (July 1934): 685.

"Khavetshe": Alexander Beider's *A Dictionary of Ashkenazic Given Names* (Bergenfield, NJ: Avotaynu, 2001) lists "Khave" as the Ashkenazi spelling of the Polish "Chawa." The diminutives "Chawcia" and "Khavtshe" are derived forms attested in twentieth-century Poland. The spelling "Khavetshe" is based on Eve's spelling "חוהטשע": three Hebrew letters for "Khave" as it is found in the Torah, plus "-tshe."

"Eve Adams is neglecting": Butch Anderson, "Through Montparnasse with Gun and Camera," *Paris Tribune: Europe's American Weekly*, December 1, 1934, via Gallica, https://gallica.bnf.fr/ark:/12148/bpt6k4773362g/f4 .item.

262   Notes, pp. 133–136

Eve in Paris, September 1934: "Chava Zloczewer, a Jewish Woman from Mława" (photograph), France, September 1934, via Ghetto Fighters' House Archive, https://www.infocenters.co.il/gfh/notebook_ext.asp?book=91378. This photo was sent to the Ghetto Fighters' House in 1972 by Eve's brother Yerachmiel Zahavy in Tel Aviv.

German legislators passed laws: "The Nuremberg Race Laws," Holocaust Encyclopedia, US Holocaust Memorial Museum, accessed October 9, 2020, https://encyclopedia.ushmm.org/content/en/article/the-nuremberg-race-laws.

"were very happy to hear from you": Eve Adams to Ben Reitman, February 20, 1936, series 3, box 10, folder 274, Reitman Papers. The three-page letter was written on Le Dôme stationery with a return address of 6 Place Bienvenue, Paris 15ᵉ.

probably visiting Emma Goldman: Emma Goldman was in Saint-Tropez during the summer of 1935; "Emma Goldman Extended Timeline," Libcom, https://libcom.org/history/emma-goldman-extended-timeline.

Nazi troops invaded the Rhineland: "The Holocaust and World War II: Key Dates," Holocaust Encyclopedia, US Holocaust Memorial Museum, accessed October 9, 2020, https://encyclopedia.ushmm.org/content/en/article/the-holocaust-and-world-war-ii-key-dates.

countries met in Evian, France: "The Evian Conference," Holocaust Encyclopedia, US Holocaust Memorial Museum, accessed October 9, 2020, https://encyclopedia.ushmm.org/content/en/article/the-evian-conference.

meeting in Munich: "Agreement Reached at Munich Conference," Holocaust Encyclopedia, US Holocaust Memorial Museum, accessed October 9, 2020, https://encyclopedia.ushmm.org/content/en/film/agreement-reached-at-munich-conference.

"Eve Adams is just beginning": Ian S. MacNiven, ed., *The Durrell-Miller Letters: 1935–1980* (New York: New Directions Publishing, 1988), 107.

50 francs each: Jay Martin, *Always Merry and Bright: The Life of Henry Miller; An Unauthorized Biography* (Santa Barbara, CA: Capra Press, 1978), 319, 531.

about $1.45 in 1938: "Historical Currency Converter," Portal for Historical Statistics, accessed October 12, 2020, http://www.historicalstatistics.org/Currencyconverter.html.

$27 today: CPI inflation calculator, US Bureau of Labor Statistics, accessed October 12, 2020, https://data.bls.gov/cgi-bin/cpicalc.pl.

Georges Olstein: Information from Georges's nephew, Daniel Olstein, who inherited Henry Miller's painting and showed it to me during a Zoom meeting on May 5, 2020.

good terms with Hella's family: A large collection of letters Hella Olstein wrote to her family, with notes by Eve, are in the Daniel Olstein Collection.

Nazi troops seized parts of Czechoslovakia: "Czechoslovakia," Holocaust Encyclopedia, US Holocaust Memorial Museum, accessed October 9, 2020, https://encyclopedia.ushmm.org/content/en/article/czechoslovakia.

"Eve Adams saw me riding by": Anaïs Nin, *Nearer the Moon from "A Journal of Love": The Unexpurgated Diary of Anaïs Nin, 1937–1939*, vol. 4 (New York: Harcourt, 1996), 345. For continuity reasons I have excluded the following section from Nin's description of this meeting with Eve and Hella: "At a table in front of us sat three people. One of the women looked intently at me. She asked Eve Adams: 'Is this Anaïs Nin?' As she asked I recognized her: Mary, the girl of my orgy with Donald Friede. Mary, beautiful, fatter, married to an editor of an American magazine. Mary talked to me and introduced me to her friends. Just then Gonzalo passed by, never looking at me, mouth compressed. I felt the storm brewing and I left my friends. I went home. Gonzalo had agreed to wait there for me. Instead he had come to the port to watch me. As I came back to the port I met him, dark and furious. I could not see what he was jealous of, so I was gentle. He burst into a speech about my sitting at cafés with corrupt Montparnassians. They were drug addicts. And worse, he had met them at a partouze [orgy]. At this I jumped, and said it was ironic that he should get angry at me for meeting in full daylight, in a café, with friends he had slept with."

Nin fled to New York: Deirdre Bair, *Anaïs Nin: A Biography* (New York: Putnam, 1995), 253.

Nazis occupied Mława: Baruch G. Goldstein, *For Decades I Was Silent: A Holocaust Survivor's Journey Back to Faith* (Tuscaloosa: University of Alabama Press, 2008), 4, 27; "Mława," in Guy Miron and Shlomit Shulhani, eds., *The Yad Vashem Encyclopedia of the Ghettos During the Holocaust*, vol. 1, (Jerusalem: Yad Vashem, 2009), 487–489. A more detailed history is Levin and Orbach, "Mlawa," https://www.jewishgen.org/yizkor/pinkas_poland/pol4_00280.html.

Nazis had occupied Paris: Julian Jackson, *France: The Dark Years, 1940–1944* (Oxford: Oxford University Press, 2001), 119.

train carried the first prisoners: "Auschwitz Calendar: 1940," Auschwitz-Birkenau State Museum, accessed October 9, 2020, http://www.auschwitz.org/en /history/auschwitz-calendar/year-1940.

"I would like very much": Eve Adams, postcard to Yerachmiel Zahavy, June 15, 1940, Eran Zahavy Collection.

stay in France, out of sight, and hope: Hanna Diamond, *Fleeing Hitler: France 1940* (Oxford: Oxford University Press, 2007), 125.

Pétain's officials signed an armistice: Emanuele Sica, *Mussolini's Army in the French Riviera: Italy's Occupation of France* (Champaign: University of Illinois Press, 2016), xi; Susan Zuccotti, *The Holocaust, The French, and the Jews* (New York: Basic Books, 1993), 37. Article 19 of the German-French armistice allowed the Nazis to send all foreign Jews in France back to their countries of birth. Jackson, *France: The Dark Years*, 127, 128; Diamond, *Fleeing Hitler*, 125.

"packed like sardines": Hella Olstein Soldner and Eve Adams to André Olstein, July 21, 1940, Daniel Olstein Collection. The letter was sent from 58 rue de France, Nice, France.

thanking him for the "help": Eve adds a note to Hella Olstein, postcard to André Olstein, September 13, 1940, Daniel Olstein Collection.

their first law excluding Jewish citizens: Jackson, *France: The Dark Years*, 150, 355.

immediate arrest of foreign Jews: Jackson, 151, 356, 362.

a "very worried" Eve: Eve Adams, postcard to André Olstein, August 4, 1941, Daniel Olstein Collection. In this missive, sent from 58 rue de France, Nice, France, Eve wrote that she left Hella Olstein a week before in Haute-Savoie, and had received no word from her in eight days.

Nine days later: Eve Adams, postcard to André Olstein, August 13, 1941.

a camp in Drancy: Jackson, *France: The Dark Years*, 634; Richard Vinen, *The Unfree French: Life Under the Occupation* (New Haven: Yale University Press, 2006), 142–143.

"I need not tell you": Adams to Reitman, September 1, 1941. This four-page letter was sent from 58 rue de France, Nice, France.

"sculptor, writer, millionaire": Watson White, born January 3, 1888, in Cambridge, MA, is nowhere identified as a sculptor, as Eve claimed. He was the author of a detailed historical guidebook, *The Paris That Is Paris* (New York: Charles Scribner's Sons, 1930).

"Harvard man": White wrote about himself for a Harvard class report: "On gradu-
ation [in 1910] I went abroad. I returned November 1910; was a reporter on
the *New York Sun*, 1910–1911; 1911 to 1912 I attended Harvard Law School;
went abroad in the summer of 1912; studied at the University of Grenoble;
returned to the Harvard Law School, 1912 to 1913; 1913 to 1915, at the American Academy of Dramatic Arts; in the summer of 1915 I played in a stock
company at Ottawa, Canada. Member: The Players, New York [the old private
social club founded by the actor Edwin Booth]. *Harvard College Class of 1910:
Secretary's Third Report* (Cambridge, MA: Crimson Printing, 1917), 314, via
Internet Archive, https://archive.org/details/1910report03harvuoft/page/n7
/mode/2up.

a lifelong bachelor: Per Ancestry.com, Watson White died in New York City in
January 1968, having never married.

then pursued an acting career: For a list of theatrical productions in which White
appeared between 1916 and 1950, see "Watson White," Internet Broadway
Database, https://www.ibdb.com/broadway-cast-staff/watson-white-64784. It
would be interesting to know if the actor had any link to the Scientific Players,
mentioned earlier.

he played the defense attorney: "Verdict from Space," season 1, episode 1 of *Tales
of Tomorrow*, first aired August 3, 1951.

had died in 1935: "Alexander Migdall," Find a Grave, accessed November 10, 2020,
https://www.findagrave.com/memorial/78044071/alexander-migdall.

a man named Gaston Soldner: "Hella Soldner," Central Database of Shoah Victims'
Names, https://yvng.yadvashem.org/nameDetails.html?itemId=1682354. The
first documented reference to Hella Olstein using the name Soldner is in an
August 1940 letter she wrote her brother André, a month before Eve wrote to
Reitman; "H. Soldner" to André Olstein, August 1, 1940, Daniel Olstein Col-
lection. The letter was sent from 58 rue de France, Nice, France, and signed
"Helly."

Eve's father had actually died: Eran Zahavy reports that Eve's father died just before
Rosh Hashanah in 1933, based on a letter from the family in Yiddish; Eran
Zahavy to JNK, April 21, 2020.

the Zloczewer family living in Mława: Central Database of Shoah Victims' Names,
https://yvng.yadvashem.org/index.html.

she "writes me pathetic letters": Reitman, "Homosexuality," 7.

"Had a letter from Eve Adams": Ben Reitman to Harry Kelly, September 18, 1941, series 3, box 10, folder 171, Reitman Papers.

Swiss immigration officials denied: Bureau Suisse de Passeports, Annemasse, to Hella Olstein, September 30, 1941, Daniel Olstein Collection. The missive transmitted immigration officials' letter of the previous day, saying Olstein was denied entry to Switzerland. Just over a month later, Hella sent word to her family in Switzerland, reporting that she had been denied permission to join them; Hella Olstein to her family, November 3, 1941, Daniel Olstein Collection.

Auschwitz-Birkenau: "Auschwitz," Holocaust Encyclopedia, US Holocaust Memorial Museum, accessed October 12, 2020, https://encyclopedia.ushmm.org/content/en/article/auschwitz.

"But let us hope dear Ben": Eve Adams, postcard to Ben Lewis Reitman, October 31, 1941, series 3, box 10, folder 172, Reitman Papers. The postcard was again sent from 58 rue de France, Nice, France.

framed photo of Emma Goldman: Letters between Dolly Stamm and Emma Goldman are in "Emma Goldman Papers," International Institute of Social History, https://search.iisg.amsterdam/Record/ARCH00520/ArchiveContentList. I have not located the Goldman photo by Stamm.

"Final Solution of the Jewish Question": "Wannsee Conference and the 'Final Solution,'" Holocaust Encyclopedia, US Holocaust Memorial Museum, accessed October 12, 2020, https://encyclopedia.ushmm.org/content/en/article/wannsee-conference-and-the-final-solution.

March 27, 1942: Jackson, *France: The Dark Years*, 217.

"Honorable Mr. André": Eve Adams to André Olstein, May 26, 1942 [sent May 27], Daniel Olstein Collection.

Rumors began to spread: Jackson, *France: The Dark Years*, 218

June 5, 1942: Jackson, 217.

pillaged the city's synagogue: Sica, *Mussolini's Army*, xiii.

June 22, 1942: Jackson, *France: The Dark Years*, 217.

French police arrested 12,884: Jackson, 218; Vinen, *The Unfree French*, 143.

Five hundred Jews, arrested in Nice: Sica, *Mussolini's Army*, xiii.

Roundups in the French zone: Jackson, *France: The Dark Years*, 218.

warned that gas was being used: Jackson, 369.

the reimbursement of twenty-nine francs: The report referenced an invoice dated May 29, 1942, to "MM ZLOCZOWER et WEISS"; Board of Directors of the General Union of Israelites of France in the South Zone, report, October 15, 1942, 16, via Centre de Documentation, Mémorial de la Shoah, administrative document CDX-9, http://bdi.memorialdelashoah.org/internet/jsp/core /MmsRedirector.jsp?id=1264031&type=NOTICE.

secret, illegal rescue work: Zuccotti, *The Holocaust*, 64; Richard I. Cohen, *The Burden of Conscience: French Jewry's Response to the Holocaust* (Bloomington: Indiana University Press, 1987), 165.

played some part in the resistance: Daniel Olstein heard the rumor of Hella's involvement as a boy from his father, André, and uncle Georges, Hella's brothers; Daniel Olstein, Zoom meeting with JNK, May 5, 2020.

Nazi troops invaded the area of France: Zuccotti, *The Holocaust*, 37; Jackson, *France: The Dark Years*, 223; Vinen, *The Unfree French*, 101.

a postcard to her father, Jacques: Hella Olstein Soldner, postcard to Jacques Olstein, February 8, 1943, Daniel Olstein Collection.

Hella wrote from Nice: Hella Olstein Soldner to André Olstein, February 22, 1943, Daniel Olstein Collection.

réaliste singer: Regina M. Sweeney, *Singing Our Way to Victory: French Cultural Politics and Music During the Great War* (Middletown, CT: Wesleyan University Press, 2001), 23.

antifascists shot three Italian Fascist officers: Sica, *Mussolini's Army*, xiv.

antifascists bombed Italian Fascist soldiers; Sica, xiv.

Italian Fascists arrested civilians: Sica, xiv.

Theodor Wolff: "Theodor Wolff," Holocaust Encyclopedia, US Holocaust Memorial Museum, accessed November 10, 2020, https://encyclopedia.ushmm.org /content/en/article/theodor-wolff.

anti-Jewish incidents were frequent: The Germans pressured the Italians to turn over Jews in the Italian-occupied area of France. On July 15, 1943, Renzo Chierici, chief of police in the Italian area, agreed to the Germans' demand to turn over all German Jews who had fled to France. Davide Rodogno, *Fascism's European Empire: Italian Occupation During the Second World War* (Cambridge: Cambridge University Press, 2006), 399.

occupy the Italian island of Sicily: Rick Atkinson, *The Liberation Trilogy*, vol. 2, *The Day of Battle: The War in Sicily and Italy, 1943–1944* (New York: Henry Holt, 2007), 272.

no confidence in Prime Minister Benito Mussolini: Zuccotti, *The Holocaust*, 180.

Hella Soldner wrote again from Nice: Hella Soldner to Jacques Olstein, August 10, 1943, in French, trans. Hannah Leffingwell, Daniel Olstein Collection.

armistice between Italian Fascists and antifascist Allies: "End of the Regime" in "Italy," Britannica.com, accessed November 10, 2020, https://www.britannica .com/place/Italy/End-of-the-regime.

"violently sadistic" Alois Brunner: Jackson, *France: The Dark Years*, 361.

arrived in Nice with a highly trained team: Zuccotti, *The Holocaust*, 181.

"Confidential" memo from Heinz Röthke: Leon Poliakov and Jacques Sabille, *Jews Under the Italian Occupation* (New York: Howard Fertig, 1983).

Serge Klarsfeld: Zuccotti, *The Holocaust*, 182.

Samuel Straussman: Researcher Keava McMillan searched 10 rue Alphonse Karr, one of Eve's addresses in Nice, via "Searching the Memorial to the Jews Deported from France in One Step," https://stevemorse.org/france/. McMillan discovered Straussman and Hella Olstein Soldner at that address. McMillan then found that the Central Database of Shoah Victims' Names at Yad Vashem: The World Holocaust Remembrance Center, https://yvng.yadvashem.org/index .html, also includes data about Straussman from Serge Klarsfeld's *Memorial to the Jews Deported from France, 1942–1944* (New York: Beate Klarsfeld Foundation, 1983), as well as a form indicating that Straussman was born October 26, 1904, in Michałowice, Poland. It says that he was deported from France on convoy 61 on October 28, 1943. Additional data about Straussman are listed under his name at Mémorial de la Shoah, http://www.memorial delashoah.org.

On Tuesday, December 7, 1943: Excavation book, 43, http://ressources.memorial delashoah.org/zoom.php?code=297301&q=id:p_249347. There is no direct evidence that Hella Olstein Soldner was arrested with Eve, but solid evidence cited in other notes shows that Soldner was living at the same address as Eve.

Hella "was not in hiding": Lillian [no last name listed] to André Olstein, [date uncertain], in German, trans. Keanu Heydari, Daniel Olstein Collection. The letter is now in an envelope from the Geneva Red Cross dated December 6, 1944, but André Olstein may not have returned it to its original envelope.

"official black Citroëns cruised the streets": Jackson, *France: The Dark Years*, 361.

a receipt for cash confiscated: The "Reçu" for "Eva Zloczower, 10 rue Alphonse Karr, Nice," dated December 7, 1943, is signed by a French police official whose name is unclear; excavation book, 43, http://ressources.memorialdelashoah .org/zoom.php?code=297301&q=id:p_249347.

about $7.82 in 1943: "Historical Currency Converter," Portal for Historical Statistics, accessed October 12, 2020, http://www.historicalstatistics.org /Currencyconverter.html.

about $117 today: CPI inflation calculator, US Bureau of Labor Statistics, accessed October 12, 2020, https://data.bls.gov/cgi-bin/cpicalc.pl.

Rumors were circulating: Zuccotti, *The Holocaust*, 177

Eve arrived five days after her arrest: "Eva Zloczower," of 10 rue Alphonse Karr, Nice, was interned in Drancy under the registration number 9765. She arrived on December 7, 1943, and received #43 in excavation book #38. Excavation book, 43, http:// ressources.memorialdelashoah.org/zoom.php?code=297301&q=id:p_249347.

Hella Soldner was also sent: "Hella SOLDNER," Mémorial de la Shoah, accessed October 12, 2020, http://ressources.memorialdelashoah.org/notice.php?q =identifiant_origine:(FRMEMSH0408707132539).

that made Drancy notorious: "Drancy," Holocaust Encyclopedia, US Holocaust Memorial Museum, accessed October 12, 2020, https://encyclopedia.ushmm .org/content/en/article/drancy. Drancy, founded by the Germans in August 1941 as an internment camp for foreign Jews in France, was first staffed by French police under German supervision. It then became the main transit camp for the deportation of Jews from France. On July 1, 1943, the Germans took direct control of the camp's operation, and the anti-Jewish fanatic SS officer Alois Brunner became its commander. For more on Brunner see Jackson, *France: The Dark Years*, 361; James M. Markham, "In Syria, A Long-Hunted Nazi Talks," *New York Times*, October 29, 1985; and "Alois Brunner," Jewish Virtual Library, accessed October 12, 2020, https://www.jewishvirtual library.org/alois-brunner.

deport 850 Jews: "Convoy 63, December 17, 1943" in Serge Klarsfeld, *Memorial to the Jews Deported from France, 1942–1944: Documentation of the Deportation of the Victims of the Final Solution in France* (New York: Beate

Klarsfeld Foundation, 1983), 484; "Transport 63 from Drancy, Camp, France to Auschwitz Birkenau, Extermination Camp, Poland on 17/12/1943," Deportations Database, Yad Vashem: The World Holocaust Remembrance Center, accessed October 12, 2020, https://deportation.yadvashem.org/index .html?itemId=5092635.

Eve was number 847: A neatly typed, yellowing list of convoy 63 deportees in German includes the name "ZLOCZOWER Eva," born June 15, 1891, internment number 9765, deported from Drancy, number 847 on convoy 63. "Eva ZLOCZOWER," Mémorial de la Shoah, http://ressources.memorialdelashoah.org/notice .php?q=identifiant_origine:(FRMEMSH0408707144358). See also Klarsfeld, *Memorial to the Jews*, 484.

Soldner was number 715: Hella Soldner's deportation is documented on another page of the German list of persons on convoy 63. Her date of birth is incorrectly listed as November 14, 1915—either a clerical mistake or she declared herself ten years younger than her actual birth date. "Hella SOLDNER," Mémorial de la Shoah, http://ressources.memorialdelashoah.org/notice .php?q=identifiant_origine:(FRMEMSH0408707132539).

asked that "high-grade" food; Brunner, "Der Befehlshaber der Sicherheitspolizei und des SD," December 14, 1943, XLIX-61, via Diane Afoumado (Holocaust and Victims Reseource Center, International Tracing Service, US Holocaust Memorial Museum), e-mail to JNK, December 21, 2017, trans. James Steakley.

about 930 miles: Google Maps, accessed October 12, 2020, https://www.google.com /maps.

"The operation began": Camille Touboul, *Le plus long des chemins: De Marseille à Auschwitz* [The longest road: From Marseille to Auschwitz], 2nd ed. (Nice, France: Losange, 1998), 39–40, trans. Laurence Senlick.

When transport 63 departed: "Transport 63," Deportations Database, https:// deportation.yadvashem.org/index.html?itemId=5092635.

"all the other occupants of the car": Smulevic's testimony in French is quoted in English translation in "Transport 63," https://deportation.yadvashem.org /index.html?itemId=5092635. Though I have edited that English translation for clarity, nothing of substance has been changed.

"From time to time": Arditti's testimony is likewise quoted in "Transport 63," https://deportation.yadvashem.org/index.html?itemId=5092635. See also

Léon Arditti, oral history, June 22, 1995, Shoah Foundation Institute Visual History Archive, University of Southern California, via US Holocaust Memorial Museum, https://collections.ushmm.org/search/catalog/vha3443; Klarsfeld, *Memorial to the Jews*, 485.

"We were too many in each car": Touboul, *Le plus long des chemins*, 41–42.

requested a "quick answer": Yerachmiel Zahavy to HICEM, February 14, 1944, Eran Zahavy Collection. The acronym HICEM named the Jewish relief organization formed by the merger of three earlier organizations. "HICEM," Yad Vashem: The World Holocaust Remembrance Center, accessed October 12, 2020, https://www.yadvashem.org/odot_pdf/Microsoft%20Word%20-%20 6368.pdf. When Zahavy wrote the letters he recalled that Eve had last written him from Biarritz, but she had actually written him from Cannes.

Zahavy's letters were returned: Yerachmiel Zahavy's two letters were marked "Returned to Sender By The Censor For Reasons Explained In Memorandum Enclosed In This Cover."

the British Mandate for Palestine: The League of Nations established the British colonial occupation of Palestine from 1920 to 1948.

wrote to several organizations: André Olstein to Comité International de la Croix-Rouge, Geneva, August 23 & November 27, 1944 (re: Hella), République française, Commissariat aux Prisonniers, Déportés et Réfugiés, Geneva, October 16, 1944, and July 28, 1945 (re: both Hella and Eve), and Jüdische Zentralkartothek, Geneva, July 28, 1945 (re: both Hella and Eve), Daniel Olstein Collection.

about 233 men and 112 women: Klarsfeld, *Memorial to the Jews*, 484. See also "Transport 63," Deportations Database, https://deportation.yadvashem.org /index.html?itemId=5092635.

6 were women: The six women on transport 63 who survived Auschwitz were Geneviève Gonse, Fanny Ickovic, Chaja Lederman, Denise Rudowicz, Camille Touboul, and Sarah Vigderhaus. My source for those names is Serge Klarsfeld's research in 1977 and 2016 in the World War II archive of the French Ministry of War. Serge Klarsfeld, e-mails to JNK, September 6, 2018.

Epilogue: Eve Then, Us Now

"I have no doubt we shall win": Jeffrey Weeks, *Coming Out: Homosexual Politics in Britain, from the Nineteenth Century to the Present* (London: Quartet Books, 1977), 115.

"a little help" immigrating: A typed copy of Zecharia Zloczewer's undated letter in Yiddish, addressed to Jacob Alter, is included with a typed letter from Alter to Yerachmiel Zahavy, in Hebrew, dated December 24, 1972, from Tel Aviv, on the stationery of the Mława Emigrants Organization; Eran Zahavy Collection, trans. Naomi Cohen. Alter was on the editorial board of *Jewish Mlawa: Its History, Development, Destruction*, ed. David Shtockfish (Tel Aviv: Mlawa Societies in Israel and in the Diaspora, 1984). An, affectionate, fictionalized version of Zacky Zloczewer appears in a short story by his son: Don Zacharia, "My Legacy," *Kenyon Review* 7 (new series), no. 1 (Winter 1985): 97–110; Don Zacharia, phone call with JNK, August 13, 2020.

other groups marked by the Nazis: "Classification System in Nazi Concentration Camps," Holocaust Encyclopedia, US Holocaust Memorial Museum, accessed November 11, 2020, https://encyclopedia.ushmm.org/content/en/article /classification-system-in-nazi-concentration-camps.

Herbert J. Freudenberger: M. B. Canter and L. Freudenberger, "Obituary: Herbert J. Freudenberger (1926–1999)," *American Psychologist* 56, no. 12 (2001): 1171; Douglas Martin, "Freudenberger, 73, Coiner of 'Burnout,' Is Dead," *New York Times*, December 5, 1999. A passenger manifest accessed via "Herbert Freudenberger," *New York, Passenger and Crew Lists*, Ancestry.com indicates that Freudenberger arrived in the United States on March 14, 1940, on the ship *Rex*, and gives his age as sixteen—not twelve, the age at which the Canter and Freudenberger obituary reports he came to America. The 1940 Census (also per Ancestry.com) likewise gives his age as sixteen, placing the year of his birth around 1924.

he did sit for an interview: Herbert Freudenberger, oral history, April 27, 1998, Shoah Foundation Institute Visual History Archive, University of Southern California, via US Holocaust Memorial Museum, https://collections.ushmm .org/search/catalog/vha43679.

among the victims of a notorious, illegal CIA project: "Mail Intercept Program," CIA, January 21, 1975, https://www.cia.gov/library/readingroom/document /0001420864; "CIA Expands Secret and Illegal Mail Opening Program,"

Today in Civil Liberties History, accessed October 12, 2020, http://todayinclh .com/?event=cia-to-expand-mail-opening-program.

Watson White: *US Social Security Death Index, 1935–2014*, Ancestry.com.

Kenneth Rexroth: "Rexroth, Kenneth, 1905–1982," Libcom, February 18, 2006, http://libcom.org/history/rexroth-kenneth-1905-1982.

Index

Los Angeles, California, 40–41
Love 'Em and Leave 'Em, 5
Lovely Lesbians (Miller), 120
l'Union générale des Israélites de
    France (UGIF-South), 145, 151
lynch mobs, 27

Macrery, Andrew, 71
March Hares (Gribble), 93
Marchesini, Mrs. A., 3
Marie, Romany, 56
Marinoff, Fania, 29–32, *29*
Marinoff, Jacob, 29, 33
marriage, 80–81
Martin, Anne, 76
McKay, Claude, 48
McMurtrie, Douglas C., 27
Meegdall, Isidor, 10, 141
men, 25, 48–49, 62–64, 71, 73–74,
    80, 85
"Men: A Hate Song" (Parker), 62
Migdall, Alexander, 9, 94, 100–102,
    142
Milholland, Inez, 49
Military Intelligence Division, US
    Department of War, 40
Miller, Henry, 111, 119–122,
    136–137
Miller, June, 120
Milwaukee, Wisconsin, 73
Minneapolis, Minnesota, 51–52
Minnekahda, 60
Minnick, Thomas R., 70–71
Mirmande, France, 112–113
misogyny, 62
Mitchell, Alice, 87
Mława, Poland, 9–10, 43–44, 46, 138

Modernity, 108–110
Montparnasse, Paris, 111, 119–122.
    See also Paris, France
Moore, John, 27
Moré, Gonzalo, 137–138
Moscow, Russia, 125
Mother Earth, 11–12, 16, 20, 51
Mueller, Robert, 158
Museum of Jewish Heritage, 161
Mussolini, Benito, 75, 147
My Life and Loves (Harris), 70

Nagasaki, Japan, 160
Nathan, George Jean, 92
National Woman Suffrage
    Association, 27
Native Americans, 27
Nazis, 83, 117–118, 136–138, 142–
    145, 148–149, 155–160
Neagoe, Anna (a.k.a. Anna
    Frankeul), 112
Neagoe, Peter, 112–113, 119
New Review, 110–111, 121
New York City, 9–11, 54
New York Medical Record, 87
New York Society for the
    Suppression of Vice, 69
New York State Parole Commission,
    70–71
New York Times, 69–70, 72
New York University, 67
Newman, Pauline, 45
Newton, Esther, 81
Nice, France, 139–140, 145–148
Nin, Anaïs, 119, 137–138
No-Jury Society of Artists, 113
Nolan, Thomas J., 69–71, 99